Aug.

Dear Eleanor,

I hope you enjoy "ADRIFT." It intends to be a wake up call to complacency.

The solution is "We the People" engaging and refusing to accept mediocrity. Forget the Rs+ Ds — let's become real citizens and ensure a future.

Love,
Cousin Bill

"Today's national security threats are fast, flexible, and technologically adept. Staying ahead of these adversaries requires strategic management, wise investment, and public-private partnerships that involve a mosaic of disciplines. *Adrift* is an astute, well-reasoned look at how America went off course and provides the thoughtful, keen road map the national security establishment needs to ensure the nation's safety and prosperity."

—Cody Monk, professor of strategic intelligence and cyber affairs, National Defense Intelligence College

"Harris and Beschloss provide a readable and comprehensive overview of the political and economic threats to US competitiveness along with a menu of policy prescriptions. Their examples of what's worked and what hasn't give a clear sense of what's at stake and what might be done about it."

—David Goldston, former chief of staff, US House Committee on Science

"*Adrift*'s immigration chapter should be required reading for all the Democrats and Republicans in Congress who think that preventing the world's smartest people from coming to America is somehow a good idea."

—Neil Patel, former chief policy advisor to Vice President Dick Cheney and publisher and cofounder of the *Daily Caller*

ADRIFT

FOREWORD BY
GOVERNOR BILL RICHARDSON OF NEW MEXICO

ADRIFT

CHARTING OUR COURSE BACK TO A GREAT NATION

WILLIAM C. HARRIS
AND STEVEN C. BESCHLOSS

 Prometheus Books

59 John Glenn Drive
Amherst, New York 14228–2119

Published 2011 by Prometheus Books

Cover image of water © 2011 PhotoDisc, Inc.
Cover image of United States © 2011 Media Bakery, Inc.
Cover design by Grace M. Conti-Zilsberger

Inquiries should be addressed to
Prometheus Books
59 John Glenn Drive
Amherst, New York 14228–2119
VOICE: 716–691–0133
FAX: 716–691–0137
WWW.PROMETHEUSBOOKS.COM

15 14 13 12 11   5 4 3 2 1

Library of Congress Cataloging-in-Publication Data

Harris, William C.
    Adrift : charting our course back to a great nation / by William C. Harris and Steven C. Beschloss.
        p.   cm.
    Includes bibliographical references and index.
    ISBN 978–1–61614–403–6 (cloth : alk. paper)
    ISBN 978–1–61614–404–3 (e-book)
    1. United States—Economic conditions—21st century. 2. Education—United States—Forecasting. 3. United States—Politics and government—21st century. 4. United States—Economic policy—21st century. I. Beschloss, Steven C., 1958– II. Title.

HC106.83.H367 2011
320.60973—dc22

                                                                            2011009826

Printed in the United States of America on acid-free paper

Contents

6 CONTENTS

Foreword

by Governor Bill Richardson
of New Mexico

Our country is facing hard times, and we have to ask a hard question: Are our best days ahead of us or are they past? Many of our nation's schools are struggling with teaching our children. Cities and states are struggling with painful choices caused by budget deficits. The national debt is growing while we work to recover from the recession. National politicians seem to be locked in partisan wars while the public is becoming more pessimistic about the economy. We have arrived at a moment, a crossroads, that calls us to decide what kind of country we are going to be.

This should be the time for the best of us to emerge. Yet rather than roll up our sleeves and engage in the hard work and sacrifice required to fix our problems, we seem to be letting our differences divide us and allowing our common purpose to be forgotten or ignored. While the global competition for excellence and preeminence intensifies, our country drifts, hampered by this destructive stalemate.

I don't believe this troubled path is inevitable, an unstoppable reality that requires us all to merely accept a future of lowered expectations. Quite the contrary. I believe we are capable of taking a hard look at what ails us, figuring out how it happened, engaging in an adult conversation about what we should do about it, and then getting down to business reestablishing our national greatness.

That's why I was pleased to be asked by Bill Harris and Steven C. Beschloss to write a foreword for their book. They have engaged in serious reflection, gathered together many of the central threads that explain our current challenges, and created a compelling and inspiring narrative that should be at the center of a national conversation about our nation's future. The publication of *Adrift* can help reset our course. It couldn't be more important or more timely.

As a governor, I am glad they have tackled many of the key questions so close to my heart in my ongoing effort to make New Mexico an example of excellence. Their insights ring true because they are drawn from experience: Harris, as the director of science foundations in both Arizona and Ireland, has been devoted to spurring innovative, world-class science and research; he understands that it requires strategic leadership and public commitment to quality education from the earliest years straight through the universities. Beschloss, an award-winning writer and widely traveled journalist, has always sought out the human dimension in complicated economic, political, and global issues. That's evident throughout the book and so important in helping readers feel connected and involved.

As *Adrift* notes, economic development depends on nurturing talent and building partnerships to create a global, twenty-first-century future for our cities, states, and nation—it's what we have aggressively pursued in New Mexico. The book's discussion of the disaster of Detroit, the revival of Pittsburgh, and the creative dynamism of Austin is especially eye opening. They also remind us how a dedicated and diverse population, along with highly motivated immigrants, is so important to a city's or the nation's future.

At a time when many of our public figures seem reluctant to speak out about the role that government can and must play in strengthening our increasingly global economy, Harris and Beschloss are unabashed in singing the praises of good government. As they assert, such government requires building greater trust and cooperation between our citizens and their elected officials and a willingness to face hard problems together.

The authors are smart enough to point out simple things: facing our challenges requires not only cooperation and collaboration, but a heightened sense of urgency and a renewed commitment to honesty, decency, hard work, and common purpose. These are old-fashioned values that must be refashioned for our times.

Harris and Beschloss remind us that in some of our nation's darker moments, we recognized and reasserted our shared beliefs. We dreamed boldly and acted bravely, overcoming threats to our way of life during World War II and the Sputnik era, launching a man to the moon, and inspiring innovations that transformed our modern world. Why not think this big and act this energetically once again? *Adrift* is a much-needed wake-up call.

Preface

Why We've Written This Book

Let's be clear from the beginning: America is at a precipice. Sitting still is not an option. Our problems, while not hopeless, are urgent. And they require rediscovering something fundamental that we have lost: our shared sense of purpose.

Before twelve million of our soldiers began returning from the battlefields of Europe and the Pacific in 1945, America passed the GI Bill to open the doors to college education and homeownership. As the Cold War took root and the United States recognized the need to expand the frontiers of knowledge, the National Science Foundation was created in 1950 to support basic research in science and engineering. After the Soviets launched Sputnik in 1957, America set its sights on sending a man to the moon—and marshaled the brains and resources to make it happen. These were meaningful and long-reaching decisions inspired by national purpose, a public will to action, and, yes, an awareness that our survival was at stake. They ushered in an extraordinary period of prosperity and innovation.

But that was then.

How do we nourish potential and inspire the best among us?

11

What will it take to unleash the creativity pent up by structures that are too rigid and outmoded? What kind of strategic partnerships can spur innovation? How do we build an ecosystem that supports risk taking and experimentation? How do we direct our resources to improve the quality of life? How do we reinvigorate our nation to secure its status as a model to the world and driver of prosperity? Isn't it better to risk failure than suffer complacency? These are the kinds of questions that have driven my work in science, education, and government.

My name is Bill Harris. I am a scientist by education. It's my job to look at the world with clarity and a cool head. That's not easy these days; the country I love is in trouble. On so many fronts, the United States seems determined to sit idly by while other nations—even some of the least developed economically— are applying their minds and limited resources to educating their young. At a time when the United States seems increasingly unable or unwilling to see how slow moving and vulnerable it has become, China, India, and a growing number of other countries are boldly positioning themselves for global success. Nations that once longed to catch up with us are now passing us by in everything from educational achievement to technological mastery.

The risks of ignorance and inaction are enormous. Twenty-five years ago, a seminal report on US education described a nation at risk.[1] That's still true, except that the problems are now worse. *A Nation at Risk* gave hope that the urgency of its call could be and would be answered. Yet today the United States is a nation adrift, and it's not certain that we Americans have the will to turn course. It's my belief that our survival will depend on rediscovering our shared values and common purpose to make the necessary changes. This book will explain why.

Where do we find good ideas? There's no single rule, of course. But throughout my career, I've tried to create the conditions for scientists and engineers to make connections across disciplines— for a physicist to feel free to pursue a lead into biology, say, or a chemist to follow an idea into the realm of physics. It may seem obvious, but financing that research required creating a structure that enabled scientists to expand their focus; the system had grown too rigid and restricted. As the assistant director of the Mathematical and Physical Sciences (MPS) at the National Science Foundation (NSF), I asked my colleagues how we could create more flexibility and give scientists and engineers more options. I wanted to see what ideas were out there. The result was the creation of the Office of Multidisciplinary Activities.

In the first year, we drew about $5 million from each division within the MPS directorate, totaling about $30 million. Some program directors didn't like this: They thought I was taking away their money. But I believed that it was taxpayers' money—money intended to keep America on the cutting edge of research. After all, the US Congress had to approve the budget plan. If I didn't think the money would make a difference, I didn't spend it.

One of the scientists supported by that program was Ahmed Zewail, an extraordinary chemist who was thinking about leaving the United States and heading to the Max Planck Institute in Germany for research exploring the links between chemistry and physics. The good news? He was able to stay, his work using lasers to capture images of chemical reactions earned him a Nobel Prize, and he's Caltech's long-standing Linus Pauling Professor of Chemistry and Physics.

While I began my career as a working scientist and teacher (I was a professor of chemistry at Furman University in South Carolina), I soon realized that I could help other scientists achieve their full potential. I went to the NSF after taking a one-year leave of absence and stayed twenty years. To put it simply, I felt my job was to try to figure out how to make things better: to provide strategic management, build partnerships, and create opportunities that would help other people succeed. I believed that science, including basic research, matters most when meaningfully connected to the world that surrounds it.

So I worked to build partnerships that not only crossed academic disciplines but also linked universities, industry, and government—and that meant getting scientists, educators, business leaders, and government officials to talk to each other and recognize their shared interests. No small task, then or now.

In 1987, after President Reagan reversed his plan to eliminate the NSF and announced in the State of the Union that he would double NSF's budget and initiate funding for new science and technology centers, I was charged by NSF director Erich Bloch to kick-start this program. Within a few years, we launched twenty-five new research centers, awarding expansive multi-year grants to support them rather than individual scientists. That meant combining the resources of universities, industry, and government to advance key technologies. And it required collaboration to solve problems, even when it was hard to work together, even when it meant a competing university, corporation, or elected official would get a bigger share of the funding or credit. The result was extraordinary undertakings like the Center for Molecular Biology, led by Leroy Hood, a gifted scientist and educator who developed the first automated gene sequencer, which revolutionized genomics and played a crucial role in the rapid pace of the Human Genome Project.

So often such successes depend on making hard choices. In my first weeks leading the NSF's mathematical and physical sciences directorate and managing federal grants totaling $750 million, I was confronted simultaneously with several enormously complicated projects that were in trouble. One involved complex construction work by Caltech and MIT to build LIGO (Laser Interferometer Gravitational-Wave Observatory), then the largest physics project ever undertaken by NSF, with a price tag of $230 million. Its goal was to detect gravity waves envisioned by Einstein's theory of relativity and, in the process, profoundly expand our understanding of the origins of the universe.

LIGO was over budget, off track, and rife with infighting—a clear path to failure. So I froze the funding for a year, conducted a cost review, and ultimately replaced the leadership team. While nearly everyone expected LIGO would die, its advocates believed deeply in its significance and fought to turn things around. The effort worked. Having earned the unanimous support of the National Science Board, two gravitational wave observatories were constructed on time and on budget in Louisiana and Washington State. Today, some six hundred individuals at roughly forty institutions—part of this joint Caltech-MIT project—continue to analyze data to detect activity of spiraling neutron stars, black holes, and the cores of collapsing stars. Albert Einstein's brain lives on.

If I had to summarize my approach in the simplest possible terms, I would put it this way: Connect science to the world that surrounds it. Pursue bold projects committed to innovation. Build partnerships that cut across fields. If you want to make things better, solve problems that need fixing—don't avoid them.

That's why I was drawn to Biosphere 2. Columbia University made a brave decision in 1996 to take responsibility for this unusual facility. Built near Tucson, Arizona, nearly twenty-five hundred miles away from Columbia's New York campus, the glass-and-metal dome attracted headlines and mockery for both its originality and its trouble in creating a self-contained artificial environment that could support life, much like a space colony. (It didn't help that oxygen levels fell and fresh O_2 had to be pumped in—or that the eight "biospherians" who entered in blue jumpsuits were reported to be at each other's throats.) But the university's leaders saw an opportunity, before many others did, to research climate change by modeling the impact of CO_2 on oceans, trees, and other ecosystems in this controlled environment. They knew it would be risky to manage, but they also understood that there was nothing else like it, and they wanted to be at the forefront of global climate-change research. The project intrigued me, not only for the important science driven by Professor Wally Broecker, a highly prized scientist and one of the most respected researchers of earth systems and climate change, but also for the chance to enhance some challenging partnerships.

It was the hardest job I've ever had—an entrepreneurial enterprise (supported by Texas billionaire Ed Bass) that was an experimental earth sciences lab that combined modeling planetary conditions with a school, business, and tourist attraction. I was responsible for creating a research campus and a semester-long program for about 150 students from thirty universities and colleges, managing the project's hotel and conference center, even overseeing its restaurant. I worked to make the project a tool for Arizona teachers and tried to draw in state universities and legislators who were reluctant to invest in it. It was a little like taking the Edsel and putting it back on the road. But Biosphere 2 taught me that there's no reason to limit our vision for the kinds of partnerships that can inspire innovation.

I left the desert landscapes of Arizona in 2000 and headed a year later to Dublin, Ireland. I was invited to be the founding director general of Science Foundation Ireland, an agency within the Irish government working to attract world-class scientists and innovative researchers to support and sustain the long-term growth of the Irish knowledge economy. This required forming close partnerships between the universities (which are typically detached from other spheres) and their counterparts in government and industry. Backed by nearly $1 billion over five years, SFI resulted from a year of thoughtful study by national leaders. With their trust, I took an active role in shaping the national legislation that established a framework for novel public-private research partnerships.

My five years in Ireland were, in a word, stunning. Working closely with government, university, and business leaders, I saw firsthand how a small nation, fueled by a sense of urgency and common purpose, energetically pursued growth. I admired the proximity of ordinary citizens to their politicians—they knew their leaders' names, and they demanded responsiveness, competence, and clearly articulated goals. And I was deeply impressed by policies that understood the critical link between investments in education and economic growth. Yet I struggled with the judgment of the deputy prime minister and her economic team, already in 2001, that the United States may have peaked and that

Ireland needed to expand its business partnerships with China and India to maintain momentum. In response, I traveled frequently to China and India on behalf of the Irish government and learned how energetically those countries were working to compete on a global scale. They were looking for models to emulate and partnerships to pursue, and I was invited in January 2005 to a state dinner in the Great Hall of the People in Beijing after signing a research and development agreement between Ireland and China. I came to see more clearly, with the distance and separation that an ocean provides, what was failing in America.

I returned to the United States in 2006 with a hunger to achieve in Arizona what I saw happening then in Ireland and other European countries. Rather than focus my attention on national efforts, I felt that innovative state and city initiatives can and must play a central role in shaping America's global future. Supported by then governor Janet Napolitano and working with business, university, and other political leaders, I helped launch Science Foundation Arizona to create a competitive advantage and a stronger, more diversified economy for Arizona. This public-private partnership has funded strategic research on the edge of discovery and startup companies positioned to release new products. In the first two years, Science Foundation Arizona helped launch a dozen new technology companies and numerous research labs, including one focused on producing commercially viable jet fuel from algae and another that's researching early detection of skin cancer using satellite remote sensing technology now used by the military.

While the focus on solar energy and biofuels takes advantage of Arizona's natural resources, these inventive state-centric projects offer models that can benefit the nation. (The skin cancer work involves the unusual pairing of a cancer research center and a defense contractor.) Arizona is not alone: I have worked with leaders of other states and cities that are demonstrating the creativity that can reap results well beyond their own borders. But the work ahead will not be easy. At a time when nearly every state is searching desperately for ways to slash its budget, I have struggled with state legislators who do not grasp that education and research funding are two of the most critical routes to improving their state's economic fortunes—and that, in an increasingly competitive global landscape, building a knowledge economy is not a luxury.

Is there still a will to succeed in America? Of course. Do parents want the best education for their children, and do our citizens want government to be proactive and long-range in its thinking? I believe most do. Are Americans still capable of pursuing a common purpose? For our ultimate survival, the answer must be yes. But it will require a clearheaded view of what's failing —indeed, brutal honesty—and a strong-minded commitment to identifying and making fixes.

I don't think Americans are ready to accept a position as a second-rate nation, dwarfed in size *and* ambition by China, India, and other emerging countries. We don't want to be dragged down by declining educational levels, a preference for entertainment and consumption over hard work, a failure to reconfigure our educational and political institutions, an unwillingness to demand honesty and straight talk from our leaders, a tolerance of virulent partisanship and fact-free rhetoric, and a lack of creativity in forming partnerships that can spur innovation and reignite global advantage. If the 1940s' GI Bill, the 1950s' commitment to scientific development, and the 1960s' mission to the moon created modern America, a fresh focus on national purpose—fueled by strategic thinking and genuine bipartisan policy making—can help create a reinvigorated America for the twenty-first century.

It's the reason for writing this book.

To bring this book into reality, I turned to Steven C. Beschloss, whose combination of literary skill, wide-ranging international experience, and journalistic acumen have helped shape the book's insights and content. He has written stories from the United States and overseas for the *New York Times*, the

New Republic, Newsday, the *Chicago Tribune,* the *San Francisco Chronicle,* the *Village Voice, Parade* magazine, and many others. In addition to earning a master's degree from Northwestern University's Medill School of Journalism, he studied economic and social history in the graduate school of the London School of Economics. His award-winning work has frequently examined urban and national affairs—economically, culturally, and politically—in such diverse settings as Helsinki, Moscow, London, New York, and Los Angeles. As both a journalist and filmmaker, he covered the collapse of the Soviet Union and the emergence of a post-Soviet Russia. He and I first met in Dublin. And he, like me, is a strong believer in the notion that our nation's solutions depend on creative thinking across disciplines and the willingness to rediscover our shared values as Americans.

In the following chapter, we look at several moments of bold action in our recent history and explore whether we have lost the ability to act with common purpose. After that, we will turn to the historical debate about America's decline and the shift away from hard work and excellence as the path to success. In the succeeding chapters, we will explore the diminishing faith in government, the decrease in civic education and engagement with the democratic process, the need for educational reform, the importance of foreign-born graduates to achieve global advantage, the centrality of innovation, and the urgency of strategic policy making and moderate decision making at the national, state, and city levels to reinvigorate our economic standing and body politic.

Finally, we envision an informed electorate that demands political leaders who are not narrowly partisan, not rigidly ideological, and not risk averse—leaders who are devoted to excellence, comfortable with complexity, global in outlook, capable of inspiring civil discourse and civic responsibility, aware of the urgencies that require attention, willing to speak honestly, and focused on solving problems. Is that too much to ask? We don't think so.

Chapter 1

Are Americans Still Capable of Bold Action and Common Purpose?

I t was a tiny speck in the black night sky, 560 miles from Earth and traveling at a speed of 18,000 miles an hour. *Sputnik 1*, a shiny aluminum sphere about twice the size of a basketball and weighing just 184 pounds, rocketed into space on October 4, 1957.[1] Launched by the Soviets, the silver satellite with four radio antennae ushered in the Space Age with a simple message: *beep, beep, beep.*

That radio transmission was a sound heard round the world, triggering a combination of admiration, confusion, and fear from Americans. Circling the globe every ninety-six minutes, Sputnik provided a vivid symbol of the Soviet Union's capacity for scientific and technological superiority. Millions of Americans, dazzled by this stunning human achievement, gathered at night to try and catch a glimpse of Sputnik traveling overhead. Many, beset by darker concerns about the Soviets' intentions, worried that this was more than a satellite to study space—this was a Cold War demonstration of an intercontinental missile capable of transporting atomic bombs, the ultimate weapon of mass destruction.

The startling success of *Sputnik 1*, followed by the launch of *Sputnik 2* a month later with the dog Laika on board, was a serious blow to American prestige and morale. It was a wake-up call for Americans who had grown complacent in their presumption of dominance. It was a shock to the system, representing a kind of "technological Pearl Harbor," as David Halberstam put it, and a worldwide boon to Soviet propaganda hailing communism as the more advanced system.[2] Yet even though Sputnik wrought havoc with American pride, it also presented the United States with a rare gift, a singular moment for reflection and action—to focus its collective mind, question what it had accomplished and where it was failing, and think boldly about the future. With the calm leadership of President Dwight D. Eisenhower, Sputnik spurred a fresh emphasis on basic research and the importance of science and math education to the nation's success, even its very survival.

At first this was more about action than reflection. In its terrible haste to respond, the United States prepped the Vanguard rocket for a December 6 launch at Cape Canaveral in Florida. Yet seven seconds after its engines were ignited that Friday morning, the rocket exploded in flames. A fantastic failure that further shook the nation's confidence, Vanguard was dubbed in the media "Kaputnik" and "Stayputnik" and "Flopnik."[3] Lyndon Johnson, then the Senate Majority Leader, described his reaction to this new blow to American morale: "I shrink a little inside of me when the United States announces a great event—and it blows up in our face. Why don't they perfect the satellite and announce it after it is in the sky?"[4]

Less than two months later, though, the United States celebrated the achievement of German rocket scientist Wernher von Braun, by then a US citizen and working for the US Army. On January 31, 1958, his *Explorer 1* lifted off from Cape Canaveral and became the first US rocket to orbit Earth. The space race with the Russians was officially on.

In the following months, President Eisenhower responded to

the growing fear of Soviet domination and the fresh doubt about the quality and focus of American schooling. He named James R. Killian, the president of MIT, as his first special assistant for science and technology.[5] He stressed the importance of education to the nation's security by proposing the creation of the National Defense Education Act to encourage students to pursue degrees in science and technology; Congressional backing of the program led to dramatically increased funding for scientific research and the teaching of science, math, and foreign languages. The civilian-led National Aeronautics and Space Agency (NASA) was formed in July 1958. And the National Science Foundation substantially expanded its funding for new curricula and textbooks as well as scholarships for potential scientists, engineers, and mathematicians.[6]

Suddenly, science education was not only cutting edge—it was at the center of American life. The existential threat posed by the Soviets had focused the nation's collective mind. As we have learned all too well in the post-9/11 world, fear is a powerful motivator.

Yet as deeply felt as the Cold War fears were in the late 1950s, early 1960s, and even decades later, the Sputnik era elicits a remarkable sense of nostalgia, above and beyond the typical gaze at bygone times. It's easy to see why: The children of Sputnik benefited from a strong sense of common purpose and community. They had a clearly defined enemy and an obvious reason for pulling together to achieve shared goals. At their most acute, Americans felt that the nation's existence was at stake. But so too was its pride and identity as a world leader. America's technological prestige and self-confidence had been seriously dented by the Soviets' success; Americans had something to prove.

Something to prove. How far the nation has drifted from that mind-set.

In the coming pages, we will explore the dangerous rise of complacency, the decline of ambition, the growing alienation from government, the failure to educate our children, the deepening pessimism over public solutions, the shrinking confidence of our global peers, the mind-numbing partisanship that is stifling constructive action—and why a turnaround is so urgent. Much of this discussion will spotlight what's broken: how it happened and why we need to fix it. But it's energized by the optimistic belief that we are capable of regaining a sense of purpose and unity.

To be clear, we need a sense of urgency. We need incentives that inspire excellence. We need to compete globally, we need to cooperate locally, and we need to work harder to make change. Yes, our schools are struggling, our economic underpinnings are shaky, our political culture is filled with rancor and cynicism, and our popular culture is fixated on celebrity and easy pleasures. Yet success in the 21st century depends on brains and speed, innovation and new partnerships. It requires long-range thinking and a reinvigorated commitment to hard work, excellence, and purposeful action.

And we need this now. Before it's too late. Because we have something to prove.

Let's recall how a sense of urgency has influenced modern America. Not many years before Sputnik pierced the sky, American leadership demonstrated the ability to take action in a way that could dramatically move the nation. The landmark GI Bill, officially the Servicemen's Readjustment Act of 1944, passed by unanimous votes in both the House and the Senate, making it possible for millions of returning US veterans to go to school or college and buy homes. By 1951, more than eight million vets, nearly one out of seven in the labor force of fifty-nine million, had benefited from these government subsidies for education, at a cost of $14 billion—including financial assistance for half a million engineers, 250,000 teachers, 200,000 men with medical training, and 117,000 metal workers.[7] The visionary bill opened the door for a generation to expand their skills and their ambitions. It was an extraordinary national investment that not only smoothed the postwar transition but also spurred a generation of workers to gear up for a changing world and participate in the expansion of American prosperity. This was a far different outcome than many returning vets had feared: one survey found that the majority expected to face an economic depression when they got back.[8]

College students who had not served in the military were often startled by the level of seriousness of these returning vets, their new classmates. "All they care about is their school work," complained one Lehigh College senior to a writer from the *New York Times* who visited the leafy Pennsylvania campus in 1946. "They're grinds, every one of them. It's books, books all the time with them. They study so hard, we have to slave to keep up with them." From the veterans, there was no apology, even if they showed little interest in the frivolities of college life. "We didn't come to college to play games," explained one new Lehigh student. "We've lost several years out of our lives, and we have to make up for it. . . . We've come to study."[9]

Like Sputnik, the GI Bill inspired a shared will. Veterans returning from the battlefronts of Europe and Asia acted out of self-interest, but they were determined to put their lives back together and give meaning to the years of sacrifice on foreign soil. The GI Bill recognized this by creating a financial infrastructure that would reinvest them on American soil. Just as Americans would later feel the need for action because of Sputnik, Americans understood that fourteen million returning vets required a clear plan of action. "Think of what the after-effects would have been had there been no G.I. Bill," noted the administrator of Veterans Affairs, Carl Grey Jr., in 1951. "These young men would have returned home hoping to assume their rightful places in their communities and eager to become the leaders of tomorrow —but entirely unprepared for the task."[10] That sense of urgency created the conditions for the nation to showcase its best self.

Nearly a decade later, doubts persisted whether America's best was good enough. On April 12, 1961, the Soviets beat the United States again when cosmonaut Yuri Gagarin shot into space, the first human to do so. Gagarin, aboard the spacecraft *Vostok*, orbited the globe for eighty-nine minutes before returning safely. Only twenty-three days later, on May 5, astronaut Alan B. Shepard became the second human and the first American to travel in space. His fifteen-minute, suborbital flight, inside the Redstone rocket named *Freedom VII*, ended with a splashdown in the Atlantic.[11] (Shepard's reported thoughts while awaiting liftoff: "The fact that every part of this ship was built by the low bidder."[12])

Shepard's heroic feat only intensified the hunger to surpass the Russians. This was dramatically symbolized by the announcement three weeks later from the new American president, John F. Kennedy, that the United States should commit itself to landing a man on the moon and returning him safely to Earth by the end of the decade. The May 25 speech, before a joint session of Congress, was titled "Urgent National Needs." Kennedy opened by addressing what he believed was at stake: "to win the battle that is now going on around the world between freedom and tyranny," he said, adding that the adventures in space were influencing "the minds of men everywhere, who are attempting to make a determination of which road they should take."[13]

The costs of a mission to the moon would run into the billions, Kennedy acknowledged, and the burdens of achieving success would be heavy; they would require diverting resources and technical manpower from other important projects. And why hadn't this commitment already happened? The United States had "never made the national decisions or marshaled the national resources required for such leadership," Kennedy told Congress. "We have never specified long-range goals on an urgent time schedule, or managed our resources and our time so as to insure their fulfillment."

Then he summoned a call to action, a goal that he admitted would be difficult and expensive to achieve, an effort that would require a shared commitment: "In a very real sense, it will not be one man going to the Moon—if we make this judgment affirmatively, it will be an entire nation. For all of us must work to put him there."[14]

The speech stunned Robert Gilruth, the director of NASA's Manned Spacecraft Center in Houston. "I could hardly believe my ears," he recalled years later. "I was literally aghast at the size of the project. . . . It was a tremendous act of faith by the President." Gilruth heard Kennedy's address on a radio while flying on a DC-3 with James E. Webb, NASA's top administrator. "I knew how much work was required before an American, or any other spacemen, could set foot on the moon's hostile surface," said Gilruth.[15]

By every measure, this was a major commitment, rooted in a combination of American confidence and competitive fear, as well as a new president struggling with the aftermath of the failed Bay of Pigs invasion in Cuba. It was by no means certain that the mission would be successful: In contrast to the Soviets, the United States had not yet succeeded at sending an astronaut into orbit. (While astronaut Gus Grissom successfully replicated Alan Shepard's suborbital flight several months after Kennedy's bold decision, Grissom narrowly escaped drowning after splashdown when his capsule hatch opened prematurely and sank to the bottom of the Atlantic.[16]) The first manned orbit by a US astronaut was nearly a year later, in February 1962, when John Glenn circled Earth three times in four hours and fifty-six minutes.[17]

It took public opinion a while to catch up with the president's initiative. Before Kennedy's 1961 speech, a Gallup poll found that only a third of Americans supported spending the money to send a man to the moon. By 1963, more than two-thirds believed that the United States should maintain or increase the speed of the lunar effort. The majority's wish was granted. Within three years of Kennedy's commitment, NASA's budget rose more than 500 percent to $5.3 billion in 1965, and the lunar landing program involved more than 34,000 NASA workers and 375,000 employees of university and industrial contractors at its peak. By one estimate, the manned moon mission's total cost exceeded $20 billion (more than $130 billion in 2007 dollars).[18] Kennedy was not reluctant to argue on behalf of the expenditure: Speaking in 1962 at Rice University in Houston, he promised benefits in science and education, industry and medicine. The billions spent that year, he noted, were less than Americans were spending on cigarettes and cigars.[19]

The investment paid off. On July 20, 1969, eight years and two months after Kennedy launched the program, *Apollo 11* landed on the moon and American Neil Armstrong set foot on the lunar surface. It was a remarkable technical achievement; the success was a testament to America's capacity to respond to a perceived threat, grasp the potential of change, marshal the nation's resources, and act with great urgency.

One small step for man, indeed.

Fast forward to July 1979, exactly one decade after Armstrong planted the American flag on the moon and two decades after Sputnik. The contrast between Kennedy's initiative and President Jimmy Carter's effort for energy reform is like looking in a funhouse mirror: One was robust and energizing, the other was fallow and ultimately dispiriting. It was not what Carter intended when he sat before the hot television lights and a skeptical nation to deliver his fateful "crisis of confidence" speech.

Clad in his modest wool cardigan, Carter called his six-point plan to reduce oil consumption by 4.5 million barrels a day by 1990 "the most massive peacetime commitment of funds and resources in our nation's history." Its purpose: to develop alternative energy sources and reduce the nation's dependence on foreign oil. Sober and determined, Carter's speech came amid the second oil crisis of the 1970s, as the Iranian revolution had cut off oil production and the United States faced gas shortages. It followed a much-publicized ten-day delay during which he gathered views from a diverse collection of Americans, "people from almost every segment of our society," he said, "business and labor, teachers and preachers, governors, mayors, and private citizens."[20]

Yet as strongly as the president aimed to describe the urgency of the moment, he faced a much altered world. He sought to inspire action by describing the conditions gripping the nation, yet his words failed to resonate in the way he had hoped. Typically known as his "malaise" speech, it may well have sunk his chances for reelection the following year against the sunnier Ronald Reagan.

But let's inspect the contents of that speech. While it failed to push the nation toward energy independence, it offered an impressive detailing of the conditions responsible for the nation's increasing disconnection from shared purpose. Influenced by social theorists like Christopher Lasch, who wrote the bestselling book *The Culture of Narcissism*,[21] Carter described a crisis in confidence and a decline of belief in government, political solutions, and democracy itself. The country had been harmed by the tragic murders of John F. Kennedy, Robert Kennedy, and Martin Luther King Jr., he said. America had not yet escaped "the agony of Viet Nam" and the "shock of Watergate," and Washington had become "an island" separated from the people and their concerns.

> It is a crisis that strikes at the very heart and soul and spirit of our national will. We can see this crisis in the growing doubt about the meaning of our own lives and in the loss of a unity of purpose for our nation. . . . In a nation that was proud of hard work, strong families, close-knit communities . . . too many of us now tend to worship self-indulgence and consumption. Human identity is no longer defined by what one does, but by what one owns. But we've discovered that owning things and consuming things does not satisfy our longing for meaning. We've learned that piling up material goods cannot fill the emptiness of lives which have no confidence or purpose. . . . As you know, there is a growing disrespect for government . . . and for schools, the news media, and other institutions. This is not a message of happiness or reassurance, but it is the truth and it is a warning.[22]

The president's message rang clear. The nation had drifted from its core values and a shared sense of purpose. Yet as a wake-up call to underscore the need for energy independence and motivate full-blooded action, the speech was clearly a failure. Thirty years later, the United States is significantly more dependent on foreign oil than it was then. In contrast to the space race with its clearly defined enemy, Carter struggled to define the threat in a way that would ensure public support. In 1977, he had already described the energy shortages as "the moral equivalent of war."[23] In this speech, he tried again, his voice rising: "The energy crisis is real. It is worldwide. It is a clear and present danger to our nation. These are facts and we have to face them."

But the public was not having it—not rallying around the president in the midst of an oil crisis, not following his call for renewed respect for government and schools and a new foundation for shared purpose. While the speech garnered an initial uptick in the polls, criticisms gradually mounted that the real crisis of confidence was Jimmy Carter's own. His failure to inspire action caused the words to ring hollow, raised new doubts about his abilities, and set the stage for Ronald Reagan's ascendancy. His mass dismissal of cabinet members days later didn't help; that became the focus of the media.[24]

Carter's speech followed a remarkable period of soul searching within his administration about the direction of the country, indeed, the sense of being adrift. His pollster Pat Caddell identified a rising national mood of pessimism and cynicism. As much as Carter aimed to remind Americans of their core values, he faced an increasingly fragmented country, a government rife with special interests, and a growing resistance to common solutions. Lasch's *Culture of Narcissism* resonated because it described a people increasingly immersed in material consumption, drawn to self-awareness over political involvement, and separated from a sense of belonging to the past and future—instead choosing to live for the moment.

Is it any wonder that Carter's calls for conservation and sacrifice fell flat? Or that President Reagan's antigovernment stance, combined with a deregulation fervor and a focus on getting rich, captured the nation's attention and votes? Or that greed and short-term thinking—two flip sides of an alienated and cynical populace—profoundly undermined American security and prosperity?

In the week after Carter's speech, *New York Times* correspondent John Herbers questioned its impact: "What Mr. Carter seemed to be trying Sunday night, through his philosophical and moral tone, was to echo the great debate over 'national purpose' prompted in the 1950s by Sputnik. It is too early to tell whether such a debate has even been launched. But it is not too early to ask what kind of political and economic resources remain in the country to meet a newly perceived juncture of crises."[25]

Three decades later, it's time again to ask what kind of country we want. And that requires asking whether we still have something to prove and are still capable of pursuing a common purpose, especially if it requires personal sacrifice, honest public conversation, and thinking beyond the moment. Carter installed solar panels on the roof of the White House, only to see President Reagan remove them in 1986; renewable energy was no longer in fashion. These days opponents of federal funding for solar energy research, or a myriad of other national-level government actions, can voice their criticisms while using their cell phones or sending a text message over any number of wireless devices. Such technologies benefitted from Earth-orbiting satellite research and the space race—both funded by the federal government—as well as the skilled work of scientists and others educated through the GI Bill.

At the time when the nation committed to those efforts, no one could know what all the benefits would be. But on the way to the moon, we took a shot in the dark: We acknowledged a sense of urgency and the need for concentrated action—and we are better off for it today.

Chapter 2

Is It Too Late to Restore American Ambition?

Over the last decade, America enjoyed the patina of luxury. Easy credit, skyrocketing home values, swank megamansions and opulent megayachts, bigger and bigger TVs at lower and lower prices, a nonstop parade of dazzling new gadgets, the soft comfort of rising stock prices and cheap gas, the extraordinary status of being the world's last standing superpower. Amid the abundance, doubts about the economy's underpinnings and the growing disparity of fortunes were easy to ignore. Who wanted to seriously address the notion that our country was skating on thin ice and losing its edge?

The last few years have been sobering times, slapped by the hardening reality that the party's bill has come due. The Great Recession has dealt a heavy blow, touching nearly everyone, rich and poor. Millions of homes lost to foreclosure, nearly fifteen million Americans out of work in 2010, millions more who stopped looking for work,[1] a 19 percent drop in median household wealth (hitting middle-class earners hardest),[2] and nearly three million bankruptcies filed in 2009 and 2010 alone.[3] Such statistics only begin to depict the wrenching personal trauma many have suffered, provoking dark questions about America's future.

In June 2010, the Pew Research Center gauged the recession's impact on the public. Clearly, the road ahead is long and treacherous. Twenty-three percent of Americans believed that it could take them and their families a decade or longer to recover financially; another 40 percent said they expected that it could take three to five years to recover. In an alarming sign that American optimism was losing its verve, Americans were becoming more skeptical that their children would experience a better standard of living than them. In 2010, only 45 percent of Americans said they expected their children would do better than them, down from 60 percent a decade earlier. And while only one out of ten Americans in 2000 expected their children's living standards would be worse, by 2010 that number had more than doubled to one out of four. In short, faith in the American Dream, a critical expression of the nation's self-confidence, was slipping away.[4]

An unprecedented decade with net zero job growth combined with a mounting national debt and deepening uncertainty over how to reignite job creation has surely hastened fears about America's decline.[5] But it would be far from the first time in recent history when observers fretted over the prospects of the American republic.

In the 1980s, as the federal debt ballooned dramatically and doubts about the presidency of Ronald Reagan deepened, a growing literature circled the question of US economic and political decline. Yale historian Paul Kennedy, in his 1987 bestseller *The Rise and Fall of Great Powers*, posited the notion that the United States, like all dominant powers throughout history, would inevitably succumb to "imperial overstretch." He wrote that with its resources heavily directed toward military purposes and away from more productive investments, the nation would suffer inexorable, albeit relative, decline.[6] Kennedy faced withering criticism from conservatives, yet he insisted that the accuracy of his observations required the test of time; a decade later, on the tenth anniversary of his book's publication, he restated his contention in the *Atlantic*: "Decision-makers in Washington must face the awkward and enduring fact that the total of the United States' global interests and obligations is nowadays far too large for the country to be able to defend them all simultaneously." That was 1997, mind you, nearly six years before the invasion of Iraq.[7]

In 1988, Samuel P. Huntington, the director of the Center for International Affairs at Harvard, was not so willing to place blame on military expansion and external pressures. Nor was he convinced of American decline. The title of his essay for *Foreign Affairs* was "The U.S.—Decline or Renewal?" But he was clear about the source of the economic threat: "If the United States falters economically, it will because U.S. men, women and children overindulge themselves in the comforts of the good life. Consumerism, not militarism, is the threat to American strength."[8]

Pulitzer Prize–winning Barbara Tuchman was more emphatic about the direction the country was taking in her 1987 article for the *New York Times*. Its title: "A Nation in Decline." Tuchman raised questions about the effects of government incompetence and illegality and voiced her dark discontent about public witlessness. With her eye on the Iran-Contra scandal, she wrote that "lawlessness often accompanies incompetence," then wondered why the disclosures of misconduct at the highest levels failed to arouse the public. "Where's the outrage?" she asked, before blaming the distracting visual power of television and the growing "frivolity" of public opinion. Tuchman concluded with her own thinly veiled display of outrage: "If the American people do not grow angry when their sons' lives are sacrificed to official negligence, or when statutes are casually violated by the caretakers of the nation's security, one cannot expect any change to a steadier Government that commands more respect. Anger when anger is due is necessary for self-respect and for the respect of our nation by others. . . . To raise the level of public understanding from frivolity to a readiness to take serious things seriously will require a great and concerted national effort."[9]

Respectful anger, a readiness to take things seriously, a willingness to turn away from the distractions of consumerism, and sacrifice. Are these qualities retrievable from our DNA? Can we revive the national will to make hard choices, even when it hurts?

While the United States remains the world's largest economy—fueled by a history of brainpower, innovation, and massive consumption—it is losing its competitive advantage in science, math, engineering, and other key areas that are driving the twenty-first-century global economy. At a time when emerging nations are building smart new research centers and aggressively pursuing science and technology, we are concerned that the United States is resting on its laurels and underestimating the need for scientific achievement.

Back in the mid-eighteenth century, French political philosopher Charles de Montesquieu pithily observed that "republics end with luxury; monarchies with poverty."[10] This was a thinker who influenced James Madison when he was shaping the US Constitution. We should have considered ourselves forewarned.

Even if the decline of Western civilization has been bandied about for centuries, there's no question that celebrity-driven culture in our era has gradually shifted the nation's focus. The problem is not unique to the United States, of course; one recent British survey detailed teachers' observations that young people's constant exposure to celebrity culture—by way of reality TV, tabloid magazines, celebrity websites, and more—has spawned the belief that education and hard work are not necessary to achieve success.[11]

In the week after President Barack Obama took office, he invited thirteen leading CEOs to discuss and push for his plan to stimulate the struggling economy. One of them, David M. Coate, the CEO and chairman of Honeywell, spoke to the assembled press before introducing the new president. What was on his mind? "We have to make math and science cool again," Coate said, the president at his side. "We need good engineers."

A career in science or math may never have been the "coolest" path to take (although it surely was interesting and an opportunistic way to join the future and participate in creating something new). Even in the 1950s, a career in science felt like a patriotic choice, a competitive response to the Soviets' Sputnik satellite, a practical way to contribute to the country at a time of risk. The widespread worry about the Soviet threat was matched by a postwar sense of responsibility to the nation, and that motivated many young people to pursue science. This was true in the case of author Harris, and it surely helped that increased funding in those years meant increased job opportunities.

Cool or patriotic, it's clear that today's US students aren't grasping that message. In global assessments of math, science, and reading performance, they are slipping further and further behind their peers from around the world. In 2000, American fifteen-year-olds ranked eighteenth out of twenty-seven countries in overall math performance, according to the Program for International Student Assessment (PISA). That's bad enough. But by 2006, the math scores dropped lower, placing US students twenty-fourth out of thirty participating countries. PISA science scores also have fallen, with US students ranking twenty-first out of thirty countries in 2006—well below top performers Finland, Canada, and Japan, and lower than Ireland, Hungary, Poland, and France (just to name a few). What makes the slipping science scores even more disappointing is that this decline was the fourth largest of all the countries.[12]

Not only are US students in a race to the bottom in science, math literacy, and problem solving, but fewer than half the students graduating from US high schools are ready for college-level mathematics and science—a requirement for 96 percent of the country's fastest-growing jobs. In short, America's students are underprepared. This hurts them here at home; it hurts them in the increasingly competitive global marketplace; and it raises increasing doubts about the country's ability to hold onto a high standard of living.

The problem extends beyond core work in science or math. When Harris worked for Columbia University in the late 1990s, he set up a semester program in earth systems at Biosphere 2 with about 120 students and saw firsthand the quality of their written work. He was stunned: There were many college students from good schools who had earned high SAT scores, yet their writing was poor. And this was before texting, Twitter, or Facebook began making proper grammar and spelling practically laughable.

Meanwhile, students in Asia and Europe are gradually surpassing American students, both in performance and commitment to graduate training. By all accounts, both China and India are producing significantly larger numbers of engineering graduates. China, which awarded few if any doctorates in science and engineering as recently as the 1970s, is now graduating more than ten thousand doctoral students each year. While the US totals are more than double this figure, foreign nationals earn nearly 60 percent of the engineering doctorates awarded annually, with the largest student groups coming from—you guessed it—China and India. While the United States benefits from this foreign-born infusion, an increasing number of these students are taking their advanced degrees and heading home—a particularly troubling drain because businesses founded by immigrants tend to generate an extraordinary boost to the economy. (By one 2007 survey, immigrant-founded companies generated $52 billion in sales and employed about five hundred thousand workers. Among the more notable: Intel, Google, Sun Microsystems, Yahoo!, and eBay.)[13]

The ground is shifting, and it's no longer good enough to simply assert American uniqueness and exceptionalism, no matter how patriotic the impulse may be. We need to inform ourselves with facts, even if we don't like what they tell us.

In recent years, Finland has scored at or near the top in math, science, and reading proficiency among the thirty countries taking the PISA tests, which measure critical thinking and application of knowledge. Nonetheless, this tiny Nordic nation of 5.2

million remains humble in its outlook. At a discussion in Arizona of Finland's academic prowess, the principal of one of Helsinki's international schools described the central impetus for its aggressive education policies. "We are a small country," said Lauri Halla. "We can't waste any brains."

Don't waste brains. That's good and useful advice, even if you think you have size on your side. In the twenty-first century, the United States needs all of its brainpower, since we are small compared to the 2.5 billion people in the rising nations of India and China.

Every so often, a major report appears that decries the failure of education and decline of standards in the United States. In 1958, only months after the unexpected launch of Sputnik triggered the space race, *The Pursuit of Excellence* focused on the need for educational excellence in America. What was at stake? "Nothing less than our national greatness." The report, published by the Rockefeller Brothers Fund, was largely the work of John W. Gardner, who later became Secretary of Health, Education and Welfare during Lyndon Johnson's Great Society and founded Common Cause, a citizens' advocacy group. *The Pursuit of Excellence* called for curriculum reform, fresh attention to rewarding the best teachers, and the need for expanded study of science, math, and languages by the more academically talented students. "The crisis in our science education is not an invention of the newspapers or scientists or the Pentagon. It is a real crisis," the report asserted, caused by "our breathtaking movement into a new technological era" with changes so startling as to "test to the utmost of our adaptive capacities, our stability and wisdom."[14]

Strong words and solid proposals, restated twenty-five years later in *A Nation at Risk*. The 1983 report warned of "a rising tide of mediocrity" and called for three years of math and science at every American high school. Its findings were stark. Average achievement of high school students on most standardized tests was lower than when Sputnik launched. The average graduate of US high schools and colleges "is not as well-educated as the average graduate of twenty-five or thirty-five years ago." This dramatic decline "threatens our very future as a Nation and a people. . . . If an unfriendly foreign power had attempted to impose on America the mediocre educational performance that exists today, we might well have viewed it as an act of war."[15]

Now, nearly three decades later, we are forced to ask whether our national complacency has made it impossible to harness our intrinsic talent and reestablish our preeminence in the world. While we address education reform in detail later, it's worth reflecting on the simply stated description of excellence in *A Nation at Risk*. It requires "setting high expectations and goals for all learners, then [trying] in every possible way to help students reach them."[16] Achieving this will require new urgency, a belief in the centrality of hard work, a fresh focus on achieving excellence, and a willingness to sacrifice, even if it's painful. That will require leadership and national will, backed by the power of individual commitment. The alternative will only lead us further down a path toward decline.

Chapter 3

What's So Bad about Good Government?

Y ou know you have a problem when American kids are afraid to eat a peanut butter sandwich. But that was exactly the situation in 2009 after news spread that nine people died and more than twenty thousand others suffered salmonella poisoning caused by a rodent-infested Georgia peanut plant that knowingly shipped contaminated products.[1] It would be somewhat consoling—and parents might have more easily calmed their children—if this were an isolated case of criminal negligence. But the sad fact is that this was a systemic problem caused by the federal Food and Drug Administration's dramatic decline in inspectors and its reliance on self-regulation by private companies to compensate for its overwhelming inability to manage its portfolio.[2] Since 1972, FDA inspections have declined by 82 percent. Between 2003 and 2006 alone, federal inspections by FDA staff dropped 47 percent. By 2009, the FDA had fewer than two thousand inspectors to oversee 136,000 US food processors and warehouses.[3]

This makes no sense. The safety of the American food supply should be beyond question, a no-brainer in government commitment, just the kind of basic protection that all Americans presume they and their families can depend on. After all, we are talking about what we eat. But the poisoned peanuts at the Georgia Peanut Corporation of America (the name would be funny if the failure were not so tragic) illustrate how deregulation fervor and a burgeoning antigovernment mind-set over the last three decades have affected the nation's well-being, indeed its very health.

It might seem convenient to pick one troubled agency to identify a wider failure, but the FDA's troubles are not an aberration or a sudden phenomenon. The 2010 BP oil spill disaster, which suffered from a lack of federal oversight by the Minerals Management Service, is another case in point. Ironically, it was such failures, hastened by a lack of attention and resources, that helped fuel the fire of the Tea Party crowd and paved the path for libertarians like Kentucky senator Rand Paul and other libertarian-conservatives to take office in 2010. Among Paul's targets: abolishing the Department of Education, getting rid of the Environmental Protection Agency, and gutting regulatory control on coal mines.[4]

As much as the economic downturn has created a climate of frustration and anger, few candidates claimed victory with dynamic plans for job creation. Instead, we heard that the federal government, which had failed to stave off a wrenching recession and protect the public from a financial system gone wild, was killing our freedom and stealing our hard-earned dollars. The message from the Tea Party successfully tapped into the country's continuing doubt about the size and nature of the government we want and can afford. With mounting fears about the burgeoning national debt and anger about the sense that the country is slipping out of control, an unsteady and impatient public was listening, ready to take a different tack just two years after President Obama was elected with a promise of change. Republicans and independents voted into office a new Republican majority in the House of Representatives, offering fresh evidence to Democrats that the country remains skeptical that more government is the answer.

This debate over the appropriate scale and value of government is hardly new. In 1978, libertarian and Nobel Prize–winning economist Milton Friedman and his wife, Rose, toured the country to promote their bestselling book, *Free to Choose*. He extolled the failures of government, and he called for the abolition of agencies such as the FDA. A dyed-in-the-wool libertarian who cheered for unfettered capitalism, Friedman believed in "maximum freedom for each individual to follow his own ways, his own values, as long as he doesn't interfere with anybody else who's doing the same."[5] In the case of the FDA, Friedman counted on businesses to protect the public's health because, he argued, they would not want to undermine their reputations or face damaging class action lawsuits. His list of government uselessness was long: as an adviser to Arizona senator Barry Goldwater in the 1964 presidential campaign, Friedman urged abolishing government oversight of the energy, telephone, and airline industries as well as dismantling the Social Security system and national parks. With the election of Ronald Reagan in 1980 (and a spot on his Council of Economic Advisers), Friedman's political influence reached its zenith.[6]

In his first inaugural address, Reagan was very clear about his intended direction for the country. "Government is the problem," he memorably proclaimed with sound-bite perfection, adding that it is "no coincidence that our present troubles parallel and are proportionate to the intervention and intrusion in our lives that result from unnecessary and excessive growth of government."[7] Thus began an antigovernment theme that would carry the nation all the way to its current fiscal crisis.

Government is the problem. It was a line heard so often in the 1980s that it became a virtual mantra, a derogatory tagline, for the Reagan years. This denigration of government was matched with a steady drumbeat about the preferred value of individualism, self-reliance, private enterprise, and unfettered markets. Demonizing government—how it interferes, how it fails to solve problems, how it causes harm to capitalist enterprise—provided the justification for cutting taxes, stripping away regulations, and eliminating or drastically cutting social services. In nearly every speech, the president found a way to underscore his opposition to not merely big or bloated government, but government itself: "The nine most terrifying words in the English language are 'I'm from the government and I'm here to help.'"

Of course, not everyone in the highest ranks of the Reagan administration was confident that the economic strategies made sense. Eventually Reagan's own budget director, David A. Stockman, the thirty-four-year-old whiz kid with oversized glasses and long hair, publicly expressed his doubts. Stockman's disparaging remarks about supply-side/trickle-down economics, stunning in their honesty, caused an uproar in Washington. In an *Atlantic* cover story, he questioned the economic benefit of tax cuts that favored the wealthiest individuals and largest enterprises. "I've never believed that just cutting taxes alone will cause output and employment to expand," Stockman confessed to *Washington Post* reporter William Greider. He described "magic asterisks" that hid actual budget costs and "rosy scenarios" that minimized the impact of deficits. "If the [Securities and Exchange Commission] had jurisdiction over the White House," Mr. Stockman wrote several years later in his memoir, "we might have all had time for a course in remedial economics at Allenwood Penitentiary."[8]

Despite public pronouncements by the president to the contrary, Stockman also doubted that Reagan and his administration were genuinely committed to pursuing budget cuts necessary to avoid a ballooning deficit. How, after all, Stockman wondered, is it possible to increase military spending, cut taxes, and balance the budget?

The answer, of course, is that it wasn't possible—which is why the national debt nearly tripled during Reagan's two terms from less than $1 trillion to $2.6 trillion, an increase that surpassed the debt accumulated by all the nation's previous presidents combined. This from the president who was voted into office with a confident pledge to balance the federal budget—the same president who did not hesitate to describe the horrors of deficit spending in his first inaugural address: "For decades, we have piled deficit upon deficit, mortgaging our future and our children's future for the temporary convenience of the present. To continue this long trend is to guarantee tremendous social, cultural, political, and economic upheavals."[9]

Strong words, intended to rally the nation to an era of fiscal responsibility. Yet the supply-side economics that Reagan pursued—focusing tax breaks on the top income brackets and locating budget cuts primarily in discretionary social programs that affected the most economically distressed—suggested quite different intentions. No wonder Stockman's truth telling provided such a stirring counterpoint to the president's efforts to sell Reaganomics.

In response to the firestorm caused by Greider's "The Education of David Stockman," a story was concocted to tamp down the flames. President Reagan took Stockman "to the woodshed," a metaphorical tale for the budget director to tell the media and endure "self-inflicted public humiliation."[10] (In reality, the personally congenial president was quite forgiving over his budget director's indiscretions; the woodshed experience actually took place over lunch.)

But there is no metaphor that can explain away, or misdirect, the actual numbers resulting from the tax cuts. According to a 2006 nonpartisan study of the Economic Recovery Tax Act of 1981, the nation lost revenue of nearly 3 percent of GDP on average for each of the four years following that bill's passage. This amounted to a four-year loss of nearly half a trillion dollars—$445 billion, to be exact—from the government's resources.[11] And it happened in the midst of a massive military buildup: a total expenditure of $1.9 trillion, representing an increase from 5.4 percent of GDP in 1980 to 6.5 percent of GDP in 1988. The stated goal of tax cutting targeted to the wealthiest Americans was to boost investment, productivity, and employment—in other words, to stimulate growth. Yet the message appeared blithely unconcerned with who might be hurt in the process. Supply-siders, Stockman confessed, "have a happy vision of this world of growth and no inflation with no pain."[12]

Nonetheless, antigovernment advocates reveled in the president's criticisms of bloated government and expanded their influence. They helped solidify a political culture increasingly cynical toward government intervention and hostile toward the productive role that government can play—despite its limitations—in solving the nation's challenges.

One of the most single-minded supporters of shrinking the government was conservative warrior Grover Norquist, whose advocacy group, Americans for Tax Reform, was launched in 1985 with the backing of President Reagan. Norquist is famous for his scorched-earth commitment to cutting taxes and whittling government down, if not stamping it out altogether. "I don't want to abolish government," he has said. "I simply want to reduce it to the size where I can drag it into the bathroom and drown it in the bathtub."[13]

His fierce tactics over the years have deepened the reluctance of Republicans and some Democrats to oppose tax cuts and strengthened the resolve of the conservative wing of the Republican Party to oppose government solutions to the nation's problems. Not only did he help push George H. W. Bush into his "Read My Lips: No New Taxes" promise (which he later recanted), Norquist hosted a weekly Wednesday strategy meeting for key officials in George W. Bush's administration, including adviser Karl Rove.[14] As literature from his antitax group proudly states, since 1986 every successful Republican presidential candidate has signed the group's pledge never to raise income taxes. By November 2010, only days after the elections, Norquist could tout that 235 representatives and 41 senators from the incoming 112th Congress—all Republicans—took that pledge.

By virtually anyone's standards of political gamesmanship, Norquist and his acolytes have been successful crusaders for tax cutting. But it's important to ask, to what end?

It was David Stockman who coined the phrase "starving the beast" to describe the view that taxes should be cut with the specific purpose of forcing drastic reductions in public spending. As the Nobel Prize–winning economist Paul Krugman noted in a prescient 2003 *New York Times Magazine* article about an impending fiscal crisis, "For starve-the-beast tax-cutters, the coming crunch is exactly what they had in mind." Krugman described "starve-the-beasters" at conservative think tanks like the Hoover Foundation who vociferously oppose the programs that emerged under the New Deal and the Great Society. "That means Social Security, Medicare, Medicaid—most of what gives citizens of the United States a safety net against economic misfortune," he wrote.

Adherents of this libertarian doctrine have increasingly included mainstream politicians, the forty-third president of the United States among them. "George W. Bush himself seemed to endorse the doctrine as the budget surplus evaporated," Krugman wrote. "In August 2001 he called the disappearing surplus 'incredibly positive news' because it would put Congress in a 'fiscal straitjacket.'"[15]

Fast forward to 2009 and 2010, a time of fiscal crisis long detached from the flush pleasures of a budget surplus. No one would dare publicly describe the long-gone budget surplus as "incredibly positive news." Yet if shrinking the nation's revenues at a time of expanding military costs in Iraq was the goal—the first time a US president cut taxes during a war— Bush was enormously effective. Not since the Reagan tax cuts of 1981 had the nation experienced such a precipitous, self-imposed drop in revenue. According to the Department of Treasury's own accounting, the 2001 tax bill led to a loss of $323 billion, and the

2003 tax cuts cut revenues by an additional $225 billion for a combined drop exceeding half a trillion dollars.[16] It's been well documented that George Bush arrived in office in 2001 with a budget surplus of $239 billion and over the subsequent eight years proceeded to spawn a budget deficit exceeding $2 trillion. "Starve the Beast became a substitute for serious budget control efforts, reduced the political cost of deficits, encouraged fiscally irresponsible tax cutting and ultimately made both spending and deficits larger," noted Bruce Bartlett, a senior policy analyst in the Reagan White House and a Treasury Department economist who has become an outspoken critic. He calls "STB" a "completely bankrupt notion that belongs in the museum of discredited ideas."[17] (And what about David Stockman? He reemerged in 2010 with dire warnings about debt-financed tax cuts and the need to both raise taxes and reduce spending: "We've had a debt spree for 30 years. The economy has been badly injured. It is sunk under the weight of $50 trillion of debt that we've created publicly and privately."[18])

It's easy to blame President Bush and Vice President Dick Cheney for this profligate behavior. ("Reagan proved deficits don't matter," Cheney reportedly told Treasury Secretary Paul O'Neill in 2002. "We won the midterms. This is our due."[19]) But this budget-busting strategy did not happen in a vacuum; they were able to ride the wave of antigovernment, antitax sentiment to victory, just as the Republicans did in 2010. Consider the climate already back in 2004: In a survey of delegates to the Republican national convention, only 7 percent agreed when asked if government should do more to solve national problems. That's 7 *percent, less than one out of fourteen.* These were not members of a political fringe group living off the grid. These were delegates to one of America's two major parties—active participants in national-level Republican politics—portraying a startling disdain for the role of government.

Douglas G. Amy, a professor of politics at Mount Holyoke who launched a website with the prosaic title Government Is

Good, tries to make sense of this survey: "So even though our nation is faced with a variety of serious problems—even though 30 thousand people die prematurely every year from air pollution and 40 million lack healthcare insurance; even though we have the highest level of childhood poverty among advanced Western nations; even though we face serious threats from economic globalization, nuclear proliferation, and climate change—these conservative activists find government so abhorrent that they don't want it to do anything more to address these issues."[20]

Is it any surprise that when a Democrat regained the White House with an active government agenda, one that included corporate bailouts and a Keynesian spending policy to counteract the financial collapse and recession, that the antigovernment fever approached boiling point? Is it any wonder that politicians from each side of the aisle have struggled to find common ground for government action? As quickly as budget cutters jump on reducing waste, fraud, and abuse as their popular plan for shrinking and improving government, you would think it's never been tried before. And before an election, it's hard to get any government representatives to specify exactly what departments and/or programs they would cut.

In the first year of Bill Clinton's presidency, he launched a national initiative to reinvent government with Vice President Al Gore at the helm. "Our goal," Clinton said, "is to make the entire federal government both less expensive and more efficient, and to change the culture of our national bureaucracy away from complacency and entitlement toward initiative and empowerment. We intend to redesign, to reinvent, to reinvigorate the entire national government."[21] The need was so clear that it had become passé, indeed almost cliché, to describe government as bloated and inefficient, bureaucratic and broken, complacent and wasteful.

So taking a page from private enterprise and the freshest management thinking, the initiative aimed to create more entrepreneurial government organizations, cut red tape, emphasize customer service, empower employees to achieve results. In short, produce better government for less money. Who didn't want a government that worked better and cost less? The resulting review identified cost savings and efficiencies in department after department, program after program, adding up to savings in the billions. And the public's response? Was there any response? Management guru Peter Drucker described "a nationwide yawn."[22]

In hindsight, no one should have been surprised. Because as worthy and constructive as the effort was, it was already up against a rising tide of public disenchantment and a growing belief that government's ills cannot be fixed. In other words, Gore's National Performance Review could patch individual problems with the system, but it could not repair a deepening hostility toward government itself. As much as every American citizen interacts with the work of government each day—and depends on roads, bridges, parks, mail delivery, police and fire departments, schools, drinkable water, breathable air—Americans have been fed a steady diet of doubt and destruction toward the role of government by Republican leadership at least since Ronald Reagan and much more recently.

With government operating as a piñata, an easy target for critics and a hard target to love, it was inevitable that the nation's best and brightest graduates would pursue alternate career paths. That's largely been true even among self-selected graduates who trained in public affairs. Back in the late 1950s, American University's just-founded School of International Service (SIS) counted some 85 percent of its graduates starting careers in the public sector. By 2001, the number had dropped to about 20 percent, with the majority choosing instead private-sector work. According to the Association of Professional Schools of International Affairs (APSIA), less than a third of policy school graduates took government jobs in 1998. The motivations included bigger private-sector salaries, substantial student loans to pay off, frustration over the long process of landing government jobs, greater glamour and prestige attached to private-sector work, and a belief that they could accomplish more and much faster in the private sector.

But there's fresh reason for optimism. Both Louis Goodman, dean of SIS, and Leigh Morris Sloane, the APSIA's executive director, estimate that a growing number of graduates—about two-thirds—are now seeking careers in the public sector or not-for-profit sector. "That compares favorably with the early days of SIS," Goodman said, noting that the school's annual graduating class of three thousand is the nation's largest. That's welcome news for Sloane. "You want to see our best and brightest go into public service because the country needs it," she told us. "The younger generation is more interested in making the world a better place."[23]

That would be a welcome shift at a time of enormous need. It could be a signal of a move away from the belief that the best government is the least government to a conviction that freedom itself is not inextricably tied to unregulated capitalism.

Of course, that may not bode well for the legacy of Milton Friedman. In his 1962 book *Capitalism and Freedom*, he rejected both sides of the inspirational exhortation in President John F. Kennedy's inaugural address: "Ask not what your country can do for you. Ask what you can do for your country." Friedman opposed the implication both that the government is the citizen's patron and that citizens should be the government's servants.

In 2003, Krugman foresaw the economic reality that has hit like a boulder shot from a cannon. "The astonishing political success of the antitax crusade has, more or less deliberately, set the United States up for a fiscal crisis," he squarely asserted. "How we respond to that crisis will determine what kind of country we become."[24]

In our estimation, a renewed commitment to national purpose and government service can usher in a confident new period when our children no longer need worry that their next peanut butter sandwich might be their last.[25] But it will require turning around the deepening levels of distrust, doubt, and anger toward the government. To do so will take a genuine public dialogue, beyond partisan warfare and kneejerk positioning, about the appropriate size and scope of the government we want and can afford. And it will need a new performance-minded culture in the government so that it is seen as part of the solution and not the problem. As we shall explore, that means taking a hard look at the growing disengagement of the public from civic and political life—and the false promises that political leaders have served warm and comfortable to us for far too long.

Chapter 4

Have We Lost Contact with Our Democracy?

In the late 1950s, a wealthy Texan willed the interest of her $20 million estate to help pay off the national debt for twenty-five years. In response, a special US Treasury account was created to accept gifts for the specific purpose of reducing the debt. Several decades later, in 1982, Kay Fishburn, a nurse from New Berlin, Wisconsin, remembered that fund, and she launched Citizens for a Debt-Free America. She and her network of about six hundred people around the country addressed, stamped, and sent out thousands of letters each year urging fellow citizens to make tax-deductible gifts to the Bureau of Public Debt's debt reduction fund. "There's a chance that, given the opportunity, people will do what's right," Fishburn told a reporter in 1990. "It is a demonstration of responsible citizenship." By that time, the Treasury had collected $17.1 million in donations, not exactly creating a ripple in the rising pool of debt. That didn't bother Fishburn. She understood that some of the letter's recipients probably thought the request was a joke—her own children found it embarrassing—but she took the idea seriously, however preposterous it might seem. "Americans pride themselves on getting the job done," she said in a 2010 National Public Radio interview. "So I just assumed it would take off."[1]

Over the years, that account, authorized by Public Law 87-58 in 1961 and called "Gifts for Reduction of Public Debt," continued to attract donations. Kids mailed proceeds from car washes. World War II vets sent money for the country they fought for and loved. Some people mailed $5 or $10 or $17.76. After Ronald Reagan's second inaugural, $1 million in unspent donations was deposited. In 1992, an anonymous donor sent $3.5 million. Some jokers contributed a penny, a clear message about how worthwhile they figured a donation would be. Yet in the five years between 2004 and 2009, the fund attracted more than $11 million, including more than $7 million from just seventeen people.[2]

We live in cynical times. It's hard to imagine that any of these contributors really believed they could make a difference; since 1961, the public debt has ballooned from $290 billion to more than $14 trillion (a number so immense that it's virtually unfathomable). Why did they bother? Didn't they get the message that you just can't trust the government anymore? Had they missed the cries of the angry crowd demanding to know what they're getting for their tax dollars? What era are they living in anyway?

The simple answer is that they live (or lived) in an America where citizenship matters, where the goal is not simply what you get for your money, but what you can do to make things better. "Probably the best $100 I spent in a long time," wrote one man who contributed to the fund. "Makes me feel like I really did something to help the country."[3] It's an old-fashioned notion, it seems, derived from a time when America was a nation of citizens, the extremes did not define politics or dominate the airwaves, and sacrifice was not a dirty word. Americans paid attention to current events, and not just when a war broke out or a scandal erupted. Americans voted, and not just when presidential elections or controversial races caught our attention. Americans participated in the political process by stamping envelopes and making calls, signing petitions and joining committees, even sharing coffee with wild-eyed neighbors in a friendly effort to find common ground. Americans trusted their government. In the overheated pot of contemporary politics, this seems like a long, long time ago. And every year the number of Americans who experienced that America grows smaller.

A 2008 report traced national election data and public attitudes from the early 1960s to the present to capture the changing mind-set of the American public. The result: a depressing downward spiral from trust to distrust and derision. This speaks loudly about the nation's current turmoil and discontent. In 1964, noted the report's authors, William A. Galston and Elaine Kamarack, "a remarkable 76 percent of people said they trusted the federal government to do the right things just about always or most of the time." Eight years later, in 1972, 52 percent still felt that way "despite turmoil at home and an unpopular war." Yet by 1980, following Watergate, the Nixon resignation, two oil crises, high inflation, and rising unemployment, only 25 percent did. The number improved during the 1980s as inflation abated and the economy grew, but by 1994 it dropped to 21 percent. While the level of trust climbed again in the late 1990s and experienced an extra bump following 9/11, it suffered "a precipitous decline" after the government mismanagement of Hurricane Katrina in 2005. By 2008, it had descended to its lowest-ever standing of 17 percent. In almost laughable understatement, the authors concluded that "absent unforeseen events, the next President will confront levels of trust still at or near the nadir." The report's title spoke volumes about the predicament they anticipated for the Obama administration: "Change You Can Believe in Needs a Government You Can Trust."[4]

While we can highlight specific historical moments that intensified the nation's discontent and exacerbated the doubt and distrust, it's useful to consider an underlying trend throughout this period. Surely, the Vietnam War, Watergate, and the wrenching assassinations in the 1960s of a president, his brother, and

Martin Luther King Jr. were among the transformative national events that triggered widespread disenchantment and rejection. But there was a less visible yet arguably more significant generational shift that continues to define the country's unrest and disunity—that is, the gradual fading of political and civic participation, all those community-oriented activities that require cooperation, foster a body politic, and create social cohesion. These are simple things: signing a petition, joining a community group, canvassing your neighborhood, serving on a committee, even contacting (and knowing) your own town's elected officials.

The notion of waning public involvement may seem contradictory, especially at a time when the wired world is buzzing with political passions and hot debate; it's hard to miss the intense emotions driving cable news and the blogosphere. But that slice of enthusiasm masks the wider population's decline in interest and action; it portends a continuing trend of division and disappointment; and it raises serious questions about how a democratic nation sorely in need of participation can solve increasingly complicated and contentious problems.

The most obvious marker of this decline is voter turnout, or, rather, the lack of voter turnout. The most visible expression of public apathy is the shrinking turnout for presidential elections. The last time more than 60 percent of the American voting-age population bothered to vote for a US president was in 1968, and that includes the hotly contested 2008 race with its aggressive registration and get-out-the-vote efforts (56.8 percent cast ballots). Yet that level of interest is practically cause for celebration when compared with the number of eligible Americans who show up for midterm elections: Typically, barely a third can be roused to get up, get out, and vote. And what about midterm primaries? The last time more than 30 percent showed up was in 1966 (31.8 percent); since 1994, not even 20 percent of eligible voters have been interested enough to cast ballots in a statewide primary.[5]

In 2010, with all the fevered media coverage about energized and angry Republicans, only one out of ten cared enough to vote in the primaries. When we drill down from there, the numbers are even more alarming: In a study of primary voting in thirty-five states, Republican voting in a third of those states did not even reach 10 percent of the eligible population.[6] (The participation among Democrats was even lower, which is why Republicans were so enthused about their prospects.) Tea Party candidate Christine O'Donnell dominated the airwaves after her stunning upset over longtime Republican Mike Castle in a Delaware primary for US Senate, yet she attracted only one out of six Republican votes in that primary. That number represents an anemic 4.9 percent of the state's total Republican and Democratic registered voters—or just one out of every twenty voters. The story is often worse in elections for state legislators and local officials.

By any measure, the numbers are a firm slap in the face to the vaunted notion of the United States as a robust democracy. "The nation that prides itself on being the best example of government of, for, and by the people is rapidly becoming a nation whose participation is limited to the interested or zealous few," noted voting expert Curtis Gans.[7] In fact, in an international ranking of voter participation, the United States lands near the bottom of the list, an embarrassing 138th out of 169 countries. That's below Russia, below France, below Mexico and Brazil, below 137 other countries.[8] So much for being a model to the world. Is this any way to run a country? "Not to vote is to withdraw from the political community," said author Robert D. Putnam, suggesting that the declines can be traced to the baby boomers (born between 1946 and 1964) and their children replacing the more engaged electorate that "came of age before or during the New Deal and World War II."[9]

Putnam laid out a persuasive case for this political and social disengagement in his richly detailed work *Bowling Alone: The Collapse and Revival of American Community*. A professor of public policy at Harvard University and former president of the American Political Science Association, Putnam surveyed a wide swath of American life to encapsulate a changed country. This includes political involvement—those face-to-face, everyday inter-actions that required citizens to listen to, work with, and even learn from each other, and not just because they shared the same viewpoint. Like muscles that atrophy from disuse, this failure to connect and communicate has led to the gradual disappearance of a broad cross-section of voters, including voices of moderation.

Who is participating now? Putnam drew on data collected by a Roper survey of social and political trends between 1973 and 1994. He described how self-described centrists or "middle-of-the-roaders" in the 1990s were about half as likely to participate in public meetings, local civic organizations, rallies, or political orga-nizations as they were in the 1970s. Among those with stronger partisan leanings, those who described themselves as moderate lib-erals or moderate conservatives, about a third were less likely to participate in that same period. Among the most partisan, those who described themselves as very liberal or very conservative, less than one-fifth stayed on the sidelines. In other words, the more ide-ologically extreme, the more likely they were to participate. And the middle-of-the-roaders, that large mass? Harder and harder to find. The result, of course, is that "more extreme viewpoints have gradually become more dominant in grassroots American civic life as more moderate voices have fallen silent."[10]

This is the exact problem, Putnam reminded readers, that many of the Founding Fathers worried could destabilize the country. James Madison described groups organized around spe-cific interests or passions to be "mischiefs of faction." Madison's fear, Putnam noted, is that "elected representatives, swayed by these 'factions,' would sacrifice the good of the whole for the pet projects of the few." Sound familiar? Think lobbyists, special interest groups, narrowly focused parties. In 1861, the British political philosopher John Stuart Mill warned of the harm caused by the disengagement from public life. A citizen "never thinks of any collective interest, or any objects to be pursued jointly with others but only in competition with them, and in some measure at their expense. . . . A neighbour, not being an ally or an associate, since he is never engaged in any common undertaking for joint benefit, is therefore only a rival."[11]

You would think that cable news executives at Fox and MSNBC read Mill's *Considerations on Representative Government* when they planned their programming, creating echo chambers that gin up ratings by appealing to political niches and feeding on polarization and opposition. That's turned out to be good for business, even if it's bad for democracy and the country. But that only works because they correctly grasped that the public had become more ideologically divided and disengaged. Once citizens, now mere viewers and consumers, the politically minded can skip the hard and often dull work of democracy, stay home, and enjoy their favorite *passionistas* as they duke it out on TV. Here's how Putnam described the problem in 2000, a reality that has only gotten worse.

> If participation and extremism are linked, there are a number of important repercussions. First, voluntary organizations that are ideologically homogeneous may reinforce members' views and isolate them from potentially enlightening alternate viewpoints. In some cases such parochialism may nurture paranoia and obstruction. In a polarized voluntary group universe, reasonable deliberation and bargaining toward a mutually acceptable compromise is well nigh impossible, as each side refuses "on principle" to give ground. Moreover, political polarization may increase cynicism about government's ability to solve problems and decrease confidence that civic engagement makes any difference.[12]

This does not bode well for participatory democracy. Yet it's a reality that the emergent Tea Party movement has well understood. "Government belongs to those who show up," former House minority leader and Tea Party sponsor Dick Armey told a *USA Today* reporter. "The only people showing up are the small-government conservatives."[13] That's what Delaware's O'Donnell hoped before her unexpected primary win: a small turnout, she said, "definitely works in our favor."[14] This is the way the political world has turned—politicians hoping that the public stays home. As Putnam pithily put it, "Citizenship is not a spectator sport."[15]

Still, the political industry of lobbyists and special interest groups, campaign coordinators, bloggers, consultants, and marketers—the professional machinery of politics—emerged to replace voters no longer willing or able to volunteer their time or energy. While the responsibility of citizenship has been largely transferred to political professionals, citizens-*cum*-consumers can be riled up and persuaded to spend their money. No wonder that as soon as a candidate faces criticism from an "enemy camp," that attack is used to troll for donations. Nor is it coincidence that the task of wooing apathetic voters to the polls has grown more costly, turning politicians into full-time fundraisers and alienating potential voters turned off by big money, corruption, and waste. Between 1990 and 2008, the average price to win a House seat more than tripled from $408,000 to $1.4 million, while the average price to land a Senate slot more than doubled from $3.9 million to $8.5 million, with some individual races costing two or three times more.[16] As Mark Twain wryly observed, "We have the best government money can buy."

In the shift from a population of engaged citizens to one of restless consumers choosing between products, elected officials have played into the rising expectations by promising more than they can deliver. The inevitable result is an increasingly dissatisfied electorate who want, to use a timeworn yet still apt adage, guns and butter. Like children abetted by negligent parents afraid to demand discipline, we are angry when anyone mentions the idea of raising taxes or cutting Social Security or Medicare benefits, and we are frustrated and resentful when we see that the country is struggling to cover its costs and debt is mounting. Confronted with the terrible sense that things are slipping out of control, Americans are blaming the federal government and elected officials for letting it happen.

In a 2010 Pew Research survey, a majority of Americans were clear about their displeasure. A hefty 80 percent of Democrats, Republicans, and independents think that Congress is doing a lousy job—too influenced by special interest money, caring only about their own careers, too unwilling to compromise, too careless with the government's money, and out of touch with regular people.[17] How many think Congress is doing an excellent job? A whopping 2 percent, clearly a group that doesn't own a TV, read a newspaper, listen to the radio, or probably get out of bed in the morning. "Record discontent with Congress—and dim views of elected officials generally—have poisoned the well for trust in the federal government," the Pew report asserted. "Undoubtedly, this has contributed to growing discontent with government even among groups who are generally more positive about it, such as Democrats."[18] This survey group also weighed in on federal agencies, decrying the problem of waste and inefficiency and complaining that the federal government unfairly benefits some groups. They cited the Social Security Administration, the Justice Department, the Department of Education, the Internal Revenue Service, the Food and Drug Administration, and the Environmental Protection Agency for doing a poor or only fair job. And the negativity does not stop with government agencies or Congress: a majority of Americans also said they don't like the impact of banks and financial institutions, large corporations, and the national news media.

Even though the media-fueled notion of a broad-based angry public has taken root, Pew researchers found that the large majority of Americans are more likely to describe themselves as frustrated (56 percent) or even content (19 percent). Who's angry? In 2006, when George Bush was in the White House, one out of five Americans described themselves as angry. In 2010, with Barack Obama in the White House, one out of five Americans were still angry. The difference is that in 2006 mostly Democrats were angry. In 2010, it was primarily the Republicans (and Republican-leaning independents). Among each party's wing: 44 percent of liberal Democrats were angry in 2006 (and only 6 percent of conservative Republicans), while 30 percent of conservative Republicans plus another 27 percent of moderate Republicans were angry in 2010. This does not discount the level of discontent that defined the 2010 election cycle, especially at a time of profound economic turmoil and particularly among a wide number of Republicans, but it does suggest that it's always worth double-checking who is in power and who wants to be.[19]

Worried about an expanding crisis in citizenship and its impact on the nation, the Intercollegiate Studies Institute (ISI) began in 2006 a multiyear study of college students and the general public to assess their civic literacy. First, the ISI gave a sixty-question multiple-choice test focused on basic knowledge of American history, government, founding principles, and market economy to fourteen thousand freshmen and seniors at fifty colleges and universities. The results offer a damning picture of the gap in civic knowledge and the general failure of four years of higher education to close it. The average college senior barely answered half the questions correctly, scoring an average 54.2 percent, just 3.8 percent higher than the average freshman. Less than half knew that the source of "We hold these truths to be self-evident, that all men are created equal" is the Declaration of Independence. Less than half knew that the Bill of Rights explicitly prohibits the establishment of an official religion in the United States. Only four out of ten knew that NATO was formed to resist Soviet expansion. Remarkably, while first-year students from Yale, Duke, and Cornell were among the highest scorers with better than 60 percent correct, seniors at each of these schools performed worse.[20]

The ISI followed this with an abbreviated thirty-three-question test for the general public. The results were not better; yet they were not much worse either, with an average score of 49 percent. Like the previous test for students, this one was not tricked up with complicated or obscure matters of knowledge.

Less than half of Americans could name all three branches of government. Only half knew that Congress, not the president, possesses the power to declare war. Only a quarter knew that the Bill of Rights prohibits the establishment of an official religion. Perhaps most jaw-dropping, this survey included a subgroup who said they had held an elected office—and their average civic literacy score was lower than the general public's, at 44 percent. Among this group, more than a fourth could not name what right is afforded by the First Amendment.[21]

The institute's work was premised on the notion that greater civic learning increases political involvement; the findings suggest that greater civic literacy leads to a greater appreciation for American ideals, free enterprise, and self-government. At a time when the country is confronted with public education's failure to teach many basic academic skills, the ISI's focus on civics and the need for an expanded civic curriculum that includes pre–twentieth century history may seem secondary, even frivolous. Yet we believe this is part and parcel of the necessary tools that can help America regain its footing. The institute cites George Washington's support for higher education that teaches the principles of good government and supports national unity and purpose by producing graduates who could "free themselves in a proper degree from those local prejudices and habitual jealousies which . . . when carried to excess, are never failing sources of disquietude to the Public Mind, and pregnant of mischievous consequences to this Country."[22]

The failure of higher education and earlier schooling in civics not only may discourage Americans from participating in the democratic process, but also hasten the slippery slide into public policy untethered by facts or the moderating influence of history and knowledge. That may sound like an old saw, an oft-voiced complaint emanating from elite circles, but civic literacy as a path to expanded civic involvement and renewed political cooperation may be critical to securing a new generation of Americans willing to solve increasingly complicated problems. Moreover, that expanded civic knowledge can help ensure that we end up with more adequately prepared elected officials.

From a contemporary perspective, it's hard to imagine the intensity of civic activism that defined the World War II home front as American soldiers battled overseas. While 16 million men and women would serve in the armed forces, another 12 million volunteered for the civilian defense corps by 1943. Brandishing flashlights and whistles, block captains helped supervise blackouts and prepare for other enemy threats. Millions more joined the Red Cross, collecting blood donations, rolling bandages, and training for emergencies. When the president discussed a serious rubber shortage, Americans gathered their car mats, old tires, gloves, shoes, hoses, anything made of rubber, enough scrap to equal six pounds for every American. In response to the war bond sale, twenty-five million workers "enlisted" for payroll savings plans.[23]

There was a war to win, a common enemy to battle, a time for sacrifice and shared adversity. That included paying taxes, just as it did in every other time in the nation's history. Just before the war broke out in 1939, the top tax rate was 79 percent. By 1942 it was raised to 88 percent, then raised again in the last years of the war, hitting an extraordinary level of 94 percent. Since there was a war to win, everyone would have to do their part, including the country's wealthiest. Throughout the 1950s until 1963, a period that included the launching of Sputnik and America's mission to the moon, that top income bracket was still taxed at 91 percent and stayed at 70 percent or above until Ronald Reagan became president.[24]

While volunteerism and civic engagement continued in the postwar period, the following generation began to break away from the tough-minded sense of duty that had originated in the country's war for independence. As Putnam describes, the first baby boomers born after 1946 were more individualistic, preferred to be on their own rather than part of a team, and were generally uncomfortable with rules and more tolerant and open-minded. And late boomers, even those born just six years later, "were less trusting, less participatory, more cynical about authorities, more self-centered, and more materialistic," even than early boomers.[25] The world had changed, and they were not their daddy's generation. Far too often, sacrifice was not high on the list of priorities, neither on the personal level nor for country. (To be fair, this new attitude often derived from their parents' desire to compensate for what they missed during the tough war years.)

With the rise of distrust and frustration toward government, the consistent antigovernment drumbeat since the 1980s, the shift from citizens to consumers, and the decline in civic engagement and political participation, it may seem inevitable that our political leaders would fail to expect or demand Americans to make sacrifices for the good of the country. After all, that was no way to win an election; just ask George H. W. Bush after he reneged on his "no new taxes" pledge. That was a lesson that his son learned well, even though the country had to finance two wars in Iraq and Afghanistan, despite the fact that every historical precedent showed a very different reality—that Americans were asked to absorb higher taxes to finance every other major war in the country's history.[26] The president chose not to ask Americans to sacrifice after 9/11, and he was not about to do it by raising taxes. Quite the opposite. In 2008, as the country careered toward its worst recession since the Great Depression and was embroiled in two major military conflicts, the country's top tax bracket hovered at 35 percent, down from the 39.1 percent rate when President Bush took office.[27] What about the lessons of history? "We're an empire now, and when we act, we create our own reality," a senior adviser told journalist Ron Suskind.[28] (As we noted, Vice President Cheney had a different answer when Treasury Secretary Paul O'Neill warned of a looming fiscal crisis intensified by tax cuts: "Deficits don't matter.")

It's hard to argue that we should turn the clock back. Postwar Americans have been fortunate not to endure the terrible sacrifices imposed on the World War II generation. We can only hope that it won't take a dirty bomb or some other major attack on American soil to motivate a fresh conversation about the nature of citizenship and the value of sacrifice—and a renewed sense of shared purpose. Yet rather than asking Americans to roll up their sleeves and chip in to help their country, our politicians seem determined to skip the discussion of sacrifice, too afraid, it seems, to face a temper tantrum from a voting public raised on nothing but good news; indeed, too accustomed to low taxes and minimal responsibility, whether it's good fiscal policy or not. That's not political leadership, nor should it be a path to victory at the polls.[29]

During the 2008 campaign, Joe Biden talked about the link between taxes and patriotism to explain why households earning more than $250,000 should pay more taxes. "It's time to be patriotic," he said. ". . . Time to jump in, to be part of the deal, time to help get America out of the rut." His comments were largely dismissed, or roundly criticized, by no one more mockingly than the competing Republican candidate for vice president. "You recently said paying taxes is patriotic," Sarah Palin said at their one debate. "In middle-class America, where I have been all my life, that is not considered patriotic." Tom Friedman joined that debate in a subsequent *New York Times* column, calling Palin's comment "a terrible statement," noting that her support of costly military and other "government-led endeavors" depends on Americans paying taxes.[30] Suffice it to say, none of this led to a new openness to seriously discuss how the nation's tax policy or defense policy may need to be transformed to offset the rising debt.

All of which brings us back to Kay Fishburn and her Citizens for a Debt-Free America. Beyond reaching out to Americans to make gifts to the debt reduction fund, she calculated that if every American paid about 3 percent of their income for ten years, the country could pay off its existing debt. And she did her part, paying down her share by 1993. Ironically, with the debt many trillions higher, Michael Kinsley proposed something similar in the *Atlantic* in 2010 with the idea that this could be the payback, the big sacrifice, that could set things right for the boomer generation.[31] Military analyst Andrew J. Bacevich offered his version of national sacrifice in the *New Republic*, suggesting that America's military conflicts and war on terrorism could be paid for by an annual surcharge to each taxpayer (except for veterans), rather than financed by borrowed money.[32]

Fishburn, Kinsley, and Bacevich admitted that their proposals were long shots, maybe even utopian. That may be, for the moment, but the time may be fast approaching when the country's survival will depend on hard decisions, personal sacrifice, and genuine cooperation; this will require a renewed commitment to civic responsibility and accountable leadership. Then we can hope that Americans know how to reach their elected officials, not to complain about what's wrong but to ask what they can do to help.

Chapter 5

Can America Prosper in the Twenty-First Century without Classroom Excellence?

T om Davison is a math teacher in Scottsdale, Arizona. But he didn't begin his career at the head of a classroom—or develop his worldview through teaching. Davison earned his first degree from the University of Pennsylvania's Wharton School of Business, then took jobs on Wall Street with Smith Barney and other investment banking firms. You wouldn't expect it, but Davison's attitude about the job that must be done—his job, his students' job—is drawn more from his experience as a farmer working with his brother. "We work. We don't waste time," he told us. "The cow's got to be milked every day."[1]

Davison is intense and determined, the kind of guy you're not surprised to discover was a high school football coach. Back in the 1980s, when he decided that corporate finance was not for him and he wanted to teach math—"I always loved school and learning"—Davison got a second bachelor's degree in thirteen months from a teacher's college. He followed that with a master's degree in math from the University of New Hampshire, earned over three years while teaching in the public schools of Sayre, Pennsylvania. Just as he pushed himself, he pushed his students, serving out detentions when they didn't do their homework. He believed in their capacity for hard work, and he was disappointed when a complaining parent led to administrative pressure to drop the detentions and relax his standards. "I didn't go into education to be mediocre," he said. "It's the old coaches' thing: You are either getting better or getting worse. There's no standing still."

It wasn't until Davison was invited in 2003 to join the newly forming staff at Basis, a public charter school in Scottsdale, that he found his match. The school's accelerated curriculum, emphasizing advanced math and science at both the middle school and high school levels, is based on the belief that students can thrive when presented with rigorous demands. Geared toward college prep, the program begins teaching chemistry, physics, and biology as separate sciences in the sixth grade, Algebra 1 in the seventh grade, and college-level economics in the eighth grade. "They were the only ones I've ever heard who were willing to say they wanted to be the best," Davison said. "[They said] 'We want to be the best school in Arizona, then we want to be the best school in the country.'"[2] In fact, several years after opening, Basis Scottsdale was named by *Businessweek* as the best overall school for academic performance in Arizona.[3] Its sister school, the equally rigorous Basis Tucson, was ranked by *Newsweek* in 2008 as the top public high school in the entire country for college readiness.[4]

The Basis schools—clearly not for everybody—are just a few dots in a sea of educational reform. Yet they are part of a growing movement throughout the nation of educational leaders and teachers searching for new ways to achieve excellence. The purposes are as broad as strengthening America's capacity to compete globally in an increasingly sophisticated twenty-first century—and as precise as enabling every student to achieve his or her academic potential. These schools have emerged at a time of pervasive doubt about our capacity to find solutions to what is a national crisis: declining test scores and standards, decreasing interest in math and science, too many dropouts, a focus on rote-oriented standardized testing over imagination, innovation, and interpretation—and a teaching profession saddled with low pay and low prestige, inadequate support and limited autonomy, and high turnover rates. In fact, a group of military leaders told us that they consider the failings of the US educational system to be a national security risk.

While there has been a long tradition of educational leaders seeking to achieve a combination of excellence and equity in public schooling, innovative activists at Teach for America, the KIPP Academy, and the MAC-Ro program are among those demonstrating that aptitude can be matched with achievement in any community when it's backed by fresh-minded and committed leadership. Their work is rooted in the simple notion that academic success begins with good teachers—that a good teacher can make a meaningful difference in a student's life, even in a bad school in a poor neighborhood. That's common sense. Every one of us who has been inspired by a teacher—that special person who recognized and responded to our individual strengths, who motivated us to do better and go further—knows this. Even those who've lacked that fundamental gift understand it intuitively. And the data backs this up; a good teacher is the single most important factor in spurring achievement, more than class size, dollars spent per student, or the quality of textbooks and materials.

So if we know how crucial teachers are to educational success—and that American students have fallen behind in math, science, and reading performance when compared with their peers around the world—why are so many public schools struggling to respond? Clearly, we need the best people we can to be running America's classrooms.

But that's easier said than done.

We should expect that teachers' colleges provide the training ground to help us achieve that goal. Yet these schools typically offer programs with low admissions and graduation standards, inevitably discouraging many of the best and brightest students from signing up. The results of a 2006 report, "Educating School Teachers," are startling: three-quarters of the country's 1,206 university-level schools of education do not have the capacity to produce excellent teachers; more than half of teachers are educated in programs with the lowest admission standards (often accepting 100 percent of applicants) and with "the least accomplished professors"; and only about 40 percent of school principals, when asked to rate the skills and preparedness of new teachers, thought the education schools were doing even a moderately good job. These controversial findings were not reached lightly or quickly. The report was based on four years of research, including surveys of school principals and deans, faculty members and graduates of education schools, as well as assessments of programs and practices at twenty-eight institutions.[5]

While public schools require teachers to go through a licensing process that emphasizes teaching methodologies, they are typically less stringent about content mastery. That means that a university professor with a PhD degree in chemistry like author Harris has (he has successfully taught introductory classes to incoming freshmen, not to mention more advanced classes) would be ineligible to teach in a public high school. Here's why this is alarming: While researchers have found a direct correlation between teacher effectiveness and their level of subject-matter expertise, nearly a third of middle and high school math, English, science, and social studies classes are run by teachers lacking a major even "closely related to" the one they are teaching. The group that lacks subject mastery climbs to two-thirds in the physical sciences.[6]

Consider the case of Robert Lee, who teaches high school physics at Basis Tucson. Before joining the staff there, he taught physics part-time at the University of Arizona, where he earned his master's degree, and at an Arizona community college. He also worked in one of the university's optic labs, conducting research in solid state physics. While he is eligible to teach in a public charter school like Basis, which is not bound by Arizona accreditation requirements, he would be out of luck if he wanted to move to one of the state's public schools. It's a ruling that makes no sense to him. "Students are excited by content," he told us. "It's not that complex. If the teacher's excited about the material and knows the material, that's the formula for success."[7]

The final report of "Educating School Teachers" was written by Arthur Levine, one of America's leading educational reformers, who was president of Columbia University's Teacher's College for a decade and since 2005 has served as president of Princeton University's Woodrow Wilson National Fellowship Foundation. Levine wrote that "to compete in a global marketplace and sustain a democratic society, the United States requires the most educated population in history." But he frets about achieving this; he notes that unlike other professional schools, such as law or medicine, there is no consensus in education about how long teachers should study or whether they should concentrate on learning theory and methods or emphasize subject knowledge. Put another way, there's no agreed-upon approach to training good teachers.[8]

This predicament is further complicated by the fact that school systems are stuck between worlds. As Levine explained to us, schools were originally developed to serve an industrial economy and now find themselves wrestling to meet the needs of our information age, "where the rules are still being written" and "we are trying to imagine the institutions." Why, for example, do we assume that all students can learn in the same amount of time? With the advent of new technologies and software, why not rethink the teacher's role to facilitate new learning styles? Why not refigure schools based on learning rather than teaching? Levine believes that we are entering a period of experimentation, which will require bold new approaches to learning that move beyond a "nostalgic past" and "a path that is moribund."[9]

One dramatic example is Quest 2 Learn, a new public school in New York City that started with sixth grade in 2009 and draws on the design principles of games and other digital media. The goal is to create highly immersive, gamelike learning experiences that can take advantage of the powerful media kids use outside the classroom inside the academic environment. This experimental approach is based on the recognition that literacy in the twenty-first century is changing, and so too must the tools for learning. In addition to the normal public school funding, Quest 2 Learn has attracted grants from the MacArthur Foundation and the Bill and Melinda Gates Foundation.[10]

But even as intriguing new learning styles are tested and the role of teachers gradually changes, alternate strategies are required to serve the needs of students now, especially in more economically distressed urban and rural areas where teacher quality is often weak. So we are back to the central question: How do we get the best people we can to run our nations' classrooms?

Teach for America, proposed in 1990 by Princeton University senior Wendy Kopp, who then raised $2.5 million to launch it, has implemented an answer. This success story has recruited and placed more than twenty thousand high-achieving college graduates into classrooms in poor communities—and opened the doors for hundreds of thousands of students to discover good teachers, improve their school performance, and head to college. With about six thousand teachers in twenty-nine urban and rural areas, the program is proving that teaching is a route that many idealistic young college graduates from top colleges and universities will gladly pursue when there's prestige and support—and a fierce competition to be among a respected corps. In 2008, nearly 25,000 students with an average GPA of 3.6 applied for 3,700 teaching slots. Even more impressive, at a time when the percentage of students interested in teaching in a public school has continued to decline (down to 31 percent in 2008 from 45 percent just two years earlier), Teach for America attracted applications in 2008 from 11 percent of the senior class from Yale University, 10 percent from Georgetown, 9 percent from Harvard, and 7 percent from the University of Michigan.[11]

And what about the students taught by TFA teachers? A study by the Urban Institute found that high school students in North Carolina performed significantly better on state-required end-of-course exams, especially in math and science, than their peers taught by far more experienced instructors. The TFA teachers' effect on student achievement in core classroom subjects was nearly three times the effect of teachers with three or more years of experience. Jane Hannaway, director of the Urban Institute's Education Policy Center, acknowledged that "we don't know whether it was the strong academic credentials of TFA corps members or some kind of special motivation that came with being a TFA teacher that made the difference, but the results were clear: Students performed better when they had an inexperienced TFA teacher than when they had a veteran educator at the blackboard."[12]

Teach for America has been criticized for placing neophytes in schools, elite graduates who sign up for only two-year stints and are unlikely to stick to teaching for the long haul. Yet the program has inspired a new generation of education advocates, many of whom take what they learn and continue their careers in education as administrators and leaders, even founders of new schools. Among them is Michelle Rhee, a Teach for America alum who became the reform-minded chancellor of the Washington, DC, school district. When she taught through TFA, her students in Baltimore went from the thirteenth percentile on standardized national tests to the ninetieth percentile within two years' time. "People say that kids are disadvantaged because they come from poor homes or whatever," Rhee told *U.S. News* reporter Lucia Graves. "But the bottom line is that, if kids have teachers with extraordinarily high expectations of them, if they work hard and do the right things, they can absolutely achieve at the highest levels."[13]

Carol Peck, former National Superintendent of the Year and a superintendent for sixteen years in one of the most impoverished school districts in Phoenix, shares Rhee's view. "I believe most every student can achieve what we used to think only the top 10 percent could achieve," said Peck, now the CEO of the Rodel Foundation in Arizona and chief advocate for the MAC-Ro math initiative. Putting her ideas into practice, she launched a Math Achievement Club (MAC) in ten elementary schools in 2002 that focused on teaching up to the state standards, which, sadly, was not happening in many of the high-poverty schools. The program, above and beyond the regular classroom instruction, required the active involvement and additional training of classroom teachers and principals. Most important, teachers had to sign agreements that they would teach all the skills in each monthly booklet that was sent home to parents. The parents, in turn, had to sign every page of the booklet and help their children as needed.

The program worked, producing significant gains among students, most of whom came from high-poverty families where English is not the first language. By 2010, the MAC-Ro program had expanded to 168 schools and was serving more than thirty-nine thousand students. "At first we had to twist arms to get schools into the program," Peck told us. "Now we have as big a waiting list as those who are already in." Next up? A plan to take the Arizona program national.[14]

KIPP (Knowledge is Power Program) has also proved how the connection between hard work and high expectations can make the unlikely downright probable. With a focus on college for every child, KIPP (founded by two TFA alums) has evolved since 1994 from two schools into a charter school network of sixty-six schools serving seventeen thousand children in nineteen states and Washington, DC. More than 90 percent of KIPP students are children of color and 81 percent are low income, yet an extraordinary 84 percent of the first students to graduate eighth grade in a KIPP school have gone on to college.[15]

It may seem strange for a program that is primarily fifth through eighth grade to talk so much about college, but it backs up these high-achieving expectations with nine-hour school days, required summer and Saturday sessions, enthusiastic teaching and discipline, music and sports, and a minimum of rules. (Two of them: Work hard. Be nice.) One KIPP school launched in 2001 in an impoverished neighborhood of Washington, DC, referred to its fifth graders as the class of 2009, the year they could be going to college. Talk about proof in the pudding: the students there earned the highest test scores in the city, and in 2009, fifty-eight of the first sixty-two students who finished KIPP are now going to college.[16]

That's impressive, truly impressive.

"Sending your kid to college is the nation's great unifying aspiration," wrote Jay Mathews, an educational columnist for the *Washington Post* who authored a book about KIPP founders David Levin and Mike Feinberg. "It increases life's choices and doubles average incomes. But for every 100 black and Hispanic ninth graders, fewer than 20 earn a college degree—a problem that is only going to loom larger as their share of the population grows."[17]

KIPP's founders, like so many education reformers, focus their attention on the importance of quality teaching as the key to success. In an op-ed in the *Washington Post* several weeks before Barack Obama's presidential inauguration, they suggested "a paradigm-shifting goal—ensuring that within 10 years every child in America will be on track to earning a college degree or completing a meaningful career-training program." They followed that with a call for increasing the respect for teachers, attracting top graduates to the teaching profession, and assessing teachers on their "demonstrated impact on student learning, not whether they hold traditional teacher certifications."[18] These are sensible goals. So is the "Educating School Teachers" recommendation of establishing a norm of five-year teacher education programs "to ensure that future teachers graduate with an enriched major in an academic subject and the ability to communicate that subject matter to young people."[19] Yes, such moves have a high price tag, but not making reforms will be even more costly for America's long-term well-being.

Leonard Fine, a long-time professor of chemistry at Columbia University and author Harris's colleague at Science Foundation Arizona, tells a story about the day after Albert Einstein died. It was April 19, 1955, and Fine was an undergrad and a fledgling chemist. His philosophy teacher, Paul Schrecker, devoted his class that morning to talking about Einstein, who was his friend. In great scientific detail, Schrecker focused on Einstein's profound work in 1905 and how the originality of his thinking spawned a revolution in physics. The moment was an epiphany for Fine, not only because Schrecker knew the legendary scientist, but because he was able to connect him to that extraordinary current of ideas that changed the world. "A great teacher is inspirational and steeped in content," Fine told us.[20]

And a great teacher can change a student's life.

Chapter 6

Don't We Want
the Best and Brightest
to Come and Stay?

The city of Harbin, tucked into the northeast corner of China near Mongolia and Siberia, may seem from an American perspective like the end of the earth, far from civilization and far from the pulse of the future. Once a simple fishing village, it owes its emergence in the late nineteenth century to the Chinese Eastern Railway that linked it to Russia's Trans-Siberian Railway and Vladivostok. Before and after the Bolshevik Revolution, this frontier town became an international trading center with a diverse European population, absorbing a huge influx of white Russians and Russian Jews seeking refuge and a new life.[1]

While Russian history and onion-domed Russian Orthodox churches still influence the city's identity, Harbin today is a bustling Chinese industrial city. It boasts a population of ten million and more than a dozen colleges and universities, including the Harbin Institute of Technology, a highly ranked research university with more than forty-two thousand Chinese students. Founded in 1920 with buildings that resemble Moscow University, the school has benefited from preferential government support and now offers 73 undergraduate programs, 147 masters programs, and 81 doctoral programs.[2]

In February 2010, braving bitter subzero weather, hundreds of college-level computer science students from around the world headed to Harbin, just in time for its extravagant annual snow and ice festival. But they didn't come for fun; they came to conquer their fellow competitors in the "Battle of the Brains," the IBM-sponsored world finals of the ACM International Collegiate Programming Contest, a yearly gathering drawn from thousands of the planet's best young computing minds. While the Harbin Institute of Technology is the oldest in town and among the most demanding schools to get into in China, the 2010 event was hosted by another rising institution, the Harbin Engineering University, which was founded in 1953 and trains another twenty-three thousand undergraduate and grad students.[3]

International observers of American baseball may question why its final championship should be called the World Series, but there's little doubt that the Battle of the Brains is a world contest. The 103 teams competing in Harbin were selected from more than 7,109 teams at 1,931 universities in 82 countries on six continents. Each three-member team is given five grueling hours to solve anywhere from eight to twelve computing problems; the winning team is the one that solves the most problems, with ties sorted out by the amount of time it takes each team to figure out the correct solution (minus penalties for incorrect answers).[4]

In the early years of this brainy competition, American universities could count on sterling results, but the balance was in their favor: the battle was mostly between North American schools. Stanford University, the most successful US entry, picked up the top trophy in 1985, 1987, and 1991. Those heady days flicker like a fading memory. "We're like the worst of the best of the best," said one dejected American programmer after his team from Duke University solved only one answer in the 2006 contest.[5] Any team can have a tough year, but the last American winner was Harvey Mudd College in 1997. Since 2000, the grand prize winners have come from such places as St. Petersburg State University of Information Technologies, Mechanics and

Optics (five times); the Shanghai Jiao Tong University (twice); and the University of Warsaw (twice). The year 2010 was no different. Once again, Shanghai's Jiao Tong University took home the big prize, with the top ten dominated by teams from Russia, China, Taiwan, and Eastern Europe. The best American team finished fourteenth: Stanford University, a team composed of programming students Jeffrey Wang, Jaehyun Park, and Phillip Krähenbühl and their coach, Andy Nguyen.[6]

It would be a wild stretch to suggest that the Battle of the Brains pinpoints the leader of the world or necessarily portends the future of America. Yet by all accounts the teams that prosper are possessed of fierce drive, clear focus, and relentless discipline. To be sure, they have something to prove, big time, and are willing to put in the hours of practice, day after day, month after month, required to reach the top of the game. IBM grasped the benefit of this; it not only attaches its name to the computing contest, it guarantees employment or internship to programmers from the top teams.

It doesn't take a genius to grasp that the quality and quantity of good universities and dedicated, well-trained students has expanded far beyond America's borders. Nor should it require sophisticated logic to realize that it's in America's best interest to attract and keep as many of these talented performers as possible. As Richard Florida, author of *The Flight of the Creative Class*, put it: "If our talent base weakens, our lead in technology, business, and economics will fade faster than any of us can imagine."[7] As we will explore later in depth, the country's prosperity and future growth is increasingly tied to our ability to spur innovative new companies and products, and especially not-yet-imagined new industries.

That's why it's so critical to ask: Who will make this possible? The facts make clear that foreign-born immigrants are intent on expanding their knowledge and career prospects in science, technology, and engineering. About 586,000 foreign students with temporary visas were enrolled in American colleges and universities in 2009; nearly half of those, 259,000, were studying science and engineering. They earned 43 percent of the graduate degrees and 59 percent of all the doctorates in engineering and computer science. Meanwhile, American enrollment in these programs has been shrinking, exacerbating the problem of a shortage of engineers and scientists.[8]

The importance of foreign-born students is not a new phenomenon; they collected more than half of all engineering doctorates back in 1984, when a *New York Times* article asked "Foreign Students: A Boon or Threat?"[9] Even then, the majority of those international students arrived from Asia. In 2009, most of the students came from China and India, with South Korea not far behind, and their numbers are growing. This is in the wake of enrollment declines in the years following September 11, 2001, and the Bush administration's restricted visa policies.

But just as the foreign talent pool provoked a combination of admiration and dread in 1984—some saw the economic benefit, others feared students would "steal" jobs from Americans and drive down wages—today's international students face a systemic resistance with an immigration policy that limits the number of available visas even for highly skilled applicants. The widely voiced plea from business and educational leaders is that US policy must do more than provide a limited number of temporary work visas; they insist that a green card, providing permanent residency, should be attached to every doctoral diploma of a science and engineering graduate. That couldn't be more obvious.

The underlying reason should be plain. It's better that these foreign-born high achievers, trained in America, apply their brains and skill for the benefit of America and the US economy. Their departure means not only America's loss but a gain for China, India, or a growing number of countries determined to enrich their economies and move up the knowledge chain. Back in 1984, American-educated Indian or Chinese immigrants may have struggled to find comparable opportunities in their home countries, but that comparative disadvantage becomes less and less true. They have benefited from the aggressive move offshore of American manufacturing and jobs. This underscores why it's never been more important to open America's doors wider to the best and brightest.

And what say our political leaders? They have failed to successfully connect the dots and communicate why it's so critical that we nourish our economy with the world's best minds. At a time when America's global competitors are increasingly surpassing us, they have allowed internal arguments over terrorism and illegal immigration to undermine the country's long-term progress. Even while our industrial prowess and economic fate grow more shaky, this internecine battle places us all at grave risk. Restrictive policies focused on keeping out problems can also drive out the creativity and energy that have long fueled the country's prosperity.

Consider the data on foreign-born entrepreneurs. Describing this group as an "underestimated resource," Duke University researcher and Harvard fellow Vivek Wadhwa noted that one-fourth of US science and technology companies founded between 1995 and 2005 were led by a foreign-born chief executive or lead technologist. By 2005, these companies generated revenues of $52 billion and employed 450,000 workers. Wadhwa noted that in Silicon Valley, half of the startups were founded by immigrants, and three-quarters of this group had graduate or postgraduate degrees, primarily in fields related to science, technology, engineering, or mathematics.[10]

Given this, we should expect that immigration policy would ensure that these skilled workers stick around. Yet attaining a visa for permanent residence can take as long as six or seven years, if it comes at all. Wadhwa found that in 2006 more than a million educated and skilled professionals were on hold as they waited for an employment-based permanent residence visa.[11] Why? In any given year, no more than 120,000 visas are available for skilled immigrants. Even if you are coming from a highly populous country like China or India, the system limits the number of visas to about 7 percent of the total, or about 8,500. Not all of the best and brightest are willing to linger in that queue. Amid recession and a tightening of job prospects, many of those immigrants may head home and never come back. That has the makings of a disaster for America.

Does this represent a reverse brain drain? That's what Wadhwa and his research team fear. "If the United States doesn't fix its policies and keep these highly skilled immigrants, India and China will welcome them home," he wrote. "So will countries like Singapore, Canada, Dubai, and Australia, which are opening their arms to skilled immigrants. They will start their ventures in Bangalore or Shanghai instead of Silicon Valley and Research Triangle Park."[12] And they will take advantage of increasingly open immigration policies for skilled immigrants in dozens of countries in Europe and Asia bent on nourishing their economies.

In a report on immigration policy entitled "Regaining America's Competitive Advantage," the US Chamber of Commerce argued for eliminating the cap on H-1B visas or dramatically increasing the ceiling. Here's how the report summarized this stance:

> America's greatness rests in its institutions and its historic openness to new people and innovations. Closing the door to highly educated individuals seeking opportunity and who aid the competitiveness of U.S. companies will weaken, not strengthen, our country and will diminish the competitiveness of American employers. In the global economy, investment follows the talent and attempts to restrict the hiring of talented foreign-born professionals in the United States encourages such hiring to take place overseas, where the investment dollars will follow.[13]

They couldn't be more right. We believe that a lack of strategic industrial policy, hastened by a failure of political and business leadership, including the US Chamber, has harmed the American economy and exacerbated the loss of good jobs by encouraging offshoring. Limiting the number of skilled foreign-born immigrants who can help expand the American job base will only further weaken the country's future prospects. Bill Gates, testifying before Congress in 2008, stressed the importance of loosening the visa policy. "At a time when talent is the key to economic success, it makes no sense to educate people in our universities, often subsidized by U.S. taxpayers, and then insist that they return home," Microsoft's founder said. Yet "the current base cap of 65,000 H-1B visas is arbitrarily set and bears no relation to the U.S. economy's demand for skilled workers."[14] Nor, by the way, does it bear much relation to common sense. Can anyone really believe it's reasonable for India (population 1.1 billion) and Iceland (population 317,000) to be granted the same maximum number of visas?

Gates offered the example of Arpit Guglani, an Indian-born computer science student whom Microsoft tried to hire for two straight years, yet failed to help land an H-1B visa to work in Seattle. Surely, following Gates's public mention of this problem, one would think that Guglani became an honored member of the Microsoft family. But no. He ended up taking a job as a technology trend analyst in Singapore, where that country's open immigration policy granted him permanent residence while he was still in New Delhi and put him on a path to citizenship within two years. But Guglani's lost opportunity to work in Seattle still stings. "It's a strange thing, really," Guglani told the *Toronto Star*, "that you bring in people, educate them, and then in the prime of their life, you say goodbye, thank you very much, you're not needed, and they go help a company in another country."[15]

At a time when so many countries and American cities fret over their shrinking populations and their capacity to grow, it's self-defeating for America to tread a path of decline. Have our leaders resigned themselves to a future where Americans will be fighting over a shrinking pie? This can't be the American way. Nor does this restrictive approach recognize how America's ability to attract talent throughout its history has made it possible to secure a comparative advantage. Labor unions have complained about skilled immigrants taking jobs from Americans and driving wages down, an assertion refuted by various studies.[16] Other critics of the H-1B program have focused on cases of abuse, particularly by Indian tech firms that employed people in the United States, then sent them back to India to apply what they learned. But none of these worries offset the central role that these immigrants can play in driving innovation, launching new companies, and expanding the economy—all actions they could be pursuing to the benefit of other countries. This drive is real and verifiable: a study by the Center for an Urban Future described how immigrants were significantly more likely to be self-employed than the American-born population— a trend consistent in every US census since 1880—and, moreover, during the last decade were launching more new businesses than their native-born counterparts.[17]

It seems obvious that Americans, a practical people, would take advantage of the wealth of talent hungry to excel. This is how the nation's prosperity has been built. Imagine a contemporary America—indeed, the modern world—without the benefit of Russian-born Google cofounder Sergey Brin, Hungarian-born Intel founder Andy Grove, Chinese-born Yahoo! cofounder Jerry Wang, and French-born eBay founder Pierre Omidyar, not to mention thousands of historic figures who have enriched our country: Albert Einstein, Andrew Carnegie, Irving Berlin, John Muir, and I. M. Pei, just to name a few.

And the story only begins with the immigrants themselves, who typically pass on their value of hard work, belief in education, and the willingness to face adversity. Consider Benito Almanza, a Bank of America president in Arizona, who was driven to expand his horizons beyond his Mexican grandparents and his American-born parents. They attended only grade school and worked as migrant farm-workers, but they believed in the value of education. Almanza, who also worked the fields during summers and was taught to keep his head down and never look the boss in the eye, attended Stanford University. He struggled with the sense that he didn't belong, but he employed a singular mind-set when he went to work for Bank of America after graduation. "I wanted to outperform everyone else," he told us. Within barely a decade, he had become a manager, the kind who encourages participation and leads by collaboration.[18]

Few Americans need to dig deeply to find touching tales of immigrant achievement in their own family histories. Nonetheless, a deep strain of fear and resistance continues to drive the nation's restrictive approach to immigration, even when it's not in our best interest. This is deeply ingrained in the intricate fabric of America's story, a pattern that replays itself in wave after wave, generation after generation, each time a new immigrant group arrives and begins to influence the larger society. "In almost every generation," author Peter Schrag observed, "nativists portrayed new immigrants as not fit to become real Americans: they were too infected by Catholicism, monarchism, anarchism, Islam, criminal tendencies, defective genes, mongrel bloodlines, or some other alien virus to become free men and women in our democratic society." He reminded that this is a stage in the process: "Again and again, the new immigrants or their children and grandchildren proved them wrong."[19] Yet again and again, with tragically reliable repetition, Americans have viewed the new arrivals as enemies, especially when times are tough. As Roger Daniels described in his rich history of immigration, *Coming to America*, "When most Americans are generally united and feel confident about the future, they seem to be more willing to share that future with foreigners; conversely when they are divided and lack confidence in the future, nativism is more likely to triumph."[20]

In the two generations after 1880, noted Schrag in his insightful work *Not Fit for Our Society*, the perceived closing of the frontier and the western "safety valve," urban corruption, industrial expansion, and depression-driven cycles of economic fear were among the factors "contributing to the surge of anger, xenophobia and imperial ambition." Added to this combustible mix were a "confident sense of racial superiority" and a panic-level fear in some circles of "immigrant-infected racial degeneration."[21] From a present perspective, it's startling to recall that most Chinese were blocked from entering the country for half a century until 1943. President Chester A. Arthur signed the Chinese Exclusion Act in 1882, disallowing both skilled and unskilled Chinese laborers and denying citizenship to any Chinese already living in America, many of whom had played a key role in building the transcontinental railroad but now were seen as threatening competitors for low-wage jobs—and worse. As President Arthur signed the bill, he said that the "experiment of blending the social habits and mutual race idiosyncrasies of the Chinese laboring classes with those of the great body of the people of the United States . . . [has been] proved . . . in every sense unwise, impolitic, and injurious to both nations."[22]

This act was the first national legislation targeting and barring a specific immigrant group, laying the groundwork for a more comprehensive system of quotas based on nationality or ethnicity in 1921 and 1924. While the Chinese bore the brunt of anti-immigrant feeling, they were far from alone. The Reverend Josiah Strong, a leader in the Social Gospel movement and author of an 1885 bestseller trumpeting the ultimate victory of the noble Anglo-Saxon race, described the crisis caused by a dangerous influx of undesirable immigrants, increasingly from southern and eastern Europe: "The typical immigrant is a European peasant, whose horizon has been narrow, whose moral and religious training has been meager or false, and whose ideas of life are low. Not a few belong to the pauper and criminal classes. . . . Our population of foreign extraction is sadly conspicuous in our criminal records."[23] Strong was just one of a growing chorus of voices bent on shutting down America's open immigration policy.

A 1917 act underscored the rising xenophobia and nativist fever, barring immigration or naturalization of peoples from a widening sphere of Asia and the Middle East, the so-called

Asiatic Barred Zone. Passed overwhelmingly by Congress over the veto of President Woodrow Wilson, this was a precursor to the Immigration Act of 1921, which cut the number of entrants from any one country to 3 percent of the total of that country living in the United States in 1910 (the year that the foreign-born population peaked at 14.7 percent). Several years later the Immigration Act of 1924, signed into law by Calvin Coolidge, went further, cutting the number of entrants to 2 percent of the total from any one country living in the United States in 1890 (that was before the major flow of southern and eastern Europeans). Passed by Congress with only six dissenting votes, this legislation created an upper limit of 165,000 immigrants.[24]

Who was in? Germany, Great Britain, and Ireland, with nearly 110,000 slots or a full two-thirds of the total, followed by the Nordic nations of Sweden and Norway. Who was sent a resounding message that they were no longer welcome? Besides a quota of zero for the "Asiatic" countries, Poland's quota was cut to less than 6,000, Italy's quota was cut to less than 4,000, Czechoslovakia's total was 3,000, and Russia's quota was dropped to less than 2,300. By comparison, Italy averaged 200,000 immigrants every year between 1900 and 1910 (and more than 4 million by 1920).[25] The US Congress had spoken about the kind of talent that the country preferred, a quota system that stayed in place until 1965.

The chief author of the 1924 act was clear about his intent. "Our capacity to maintain our cherished institutions stands diluted by a stream of alien blood," explained Washington State congressman Albert Johnson, head of the House Committee on Immigration. And "the myth of the melting pot has been discredited. . . . The United States is our land. . . . The day of unalloyed welcome to all peoples, the day of indiscriminate acceptance of all races, has definitely ended." These were not words delivered in the heat of the moment, but three years later when the congressman could collect his most reflective thoughts.[26]

This history darkly illustrates the ongoing tension between

American ideals of equality, fairness, and inclusion, as well as the intense rivalries among ethnic groups. But it also demonstrates the failure of the country's leadership to recognize the potential skill and brains that existed throughout the world. Those restrictions may have been rooted in a refusal to engage our enemies, a fear of the negative impact they might have on American society, or a legitimate concern about how many immigrants the country can absorb at any given time. Paradoxically, they also demonstrate a perverse kind of confidence that America did not require "their" help to prosper.

To be sure, that thinking needs to be overhauled. That would mean taking advantage of the skills and gifts that can be found throughout the world—and recognizing the urgency needed to make this happen. That includes attaching a green card to every PhD diploma in science, technology, engineering, and math. It also means supporting a proposal for a startup visa that encourages immigrants to invest in America and spur jobs. Cosponsored by Senator John Kerry (D-MA) and Senator Richard Lugar (R-IN) in 2010, the bill would provide a two-year visa for immigrant entrepreneurs who raise at least $250,000 to launch a new business; if they can generate at least five jobs and raise another $1 million in revenue or investment within two years, they can get a green card. The bill also demands lifting the cap on the available number of H-1B visas, a move that may require separating this initiative from the larger issue of comprehensive immigration reform.[27]

This can be accomplished if the country's leaders choose to stop their political gamesmanship (that includes not fanning the flames of xenophobia for political advantage) and acknowledge the economic urgency that cuts across parties. They've done it before, in far more extreme and morally conflicted circumstances, under the assumption that the country's national security—perhaps even its survival—was at stake.

In 1945, in the closing days of World War II, American officials put aside immigration restrictions, even if it meant airbrushing the criminal backgrounds of refugees. President Truman had specifically ordered that anyone found "to have been a member of the Nazi party and more than a nominal participant in its activities, or an active supporter of Nazism militarism" should be denied entry to the United States. Yet members of US military and intelligence operations were determined to capture and bring in German scientists and other specialists involved in the development of Nazi military technology, including supersonic rockets, guided missiles, nerve gas, stealth technology, and other military breakthroughs.[28] Under a cloak of secrecy, they sought to not only exploit their knowledge and skills, but also deny them to the Soviets. This included Wernher von Braun, a member of the Nazi party and the SS who helped build the V-2 missile, thousands of which were launched against Germany's enemies; and Alan Rudolph, determined at the time to be an "ardent Nazi" and later recognized as the director of a V-2 factory that used some twenty thousand slave laborers to build its missiles, many of whom were worked to death.[29]

They were among a group of more than a hundred German rocket scientists and more than a thousand scientists in all who were spirited into the United States, many of whose Nazi pasts provided sufficient reason to reject their eligibility for immigration. But in the quickly unfolding Cold War with the Soviets and the triumph of realpolitik thinking, such facts were glossed over: The scientists' Nazi Party membership and other troubling affiliations were expunged from their personnel records, and they were granted security clearance to come to America and work for the US government. They were part of a program called Project Paperclip, a name taken from the process of clipping the files that would require rewrites. Rudolph, who eventually had his citizenship revoked in the 1980s, was credited with helping design the Saturn V rocket that transported Americans to the moon. Von Braun, typically cited as the father of the American rocket program, has been described on NASA's website as "without doubt, the greatest rocket scientist in history."[30]

Such success provides a powerful basis for an exploration of whether the ends justify the means, a road down which we won't travel here. But however much this program was an aberration amid wartime realities, it highlights how immigration policy has been bent or ignored if Americans believe the stakes are high enough. How urgent are these times? How much does America's future prosperity depend on expanding its immigration policies?

To put this in context, how many young immigrants living in America now may be the next Wernher von Braun—brilliant, talented, capable of shaping a new industry or designing a new technology that expands our horizons and transforms our world—yet only if someone twists the rules or the policy itself changes? A few? A hundred? A hundred thousand? If progress entails learning from our history and making smarter choices than previous generations, then surely Americans are capable of identifying and employing the talent, drive, and potential among the country's newest immigrant groups. Surely national policy should reflect the urgent need to support the best and brightest, not for altruistic reasons but for the practical, indeed the ruthless, necessity of increasing our odds for success.

Take the case of Oscar Vazquez. Under a blistering Phoenix sun in 2009, he rose to his feet and beamed as his fellow graduates at Arizona State University, and commencement speaker Barack Obama heard his story. In 2004, he and three other students from Carl Hayden High School, a predominately Hispanic school in a tough low-income neighborhood of west Phoenix, took part in a robotics competition in leafy Santa Barbara, California. Their teachers, Faridodin "Fredi" Lajvardi and Allen Cameron, entered their underwater robot against the college contestants, figuring it would be better for them to lose big against the very best than perform decently against high school peers. Their robot, which was required to record sonar pings and retrieve objects fifty feet under the water, was built with $800 of donated funds. The robot's design and functionality, which included creating a battery pack on board the system that was capable of operating underwater, wowed the judges. So did the team's ability to explain their thinking.

But they were competing against some powerhouse teams, including MIT, which had spent $11,000 to build their robot. They hoped that maybe, somehow, they might be one of the finalists. And then the seemingly impossible happened: beyond all possible expectations, the Carl Hayden team that simply came to learn and compete was crowned the winner, besting the second-place finisher, MIT.

The following year, freelance writer Joshua Davis published the story of the remarkable victory in *Wired* magazine,[31] setting off a flurry of national media attention, including a long segment on ABC's *Nightline* and interest from Hollywood that led to Warner Bros. studio optioning their story. But the publicity came with a price: Vazquez and his three teammates were all undocumented immigrants, entering the country illegally when they were children. While they were low priority among immigration enforcement, they carried a constant fear that the day would come that they would be deported. Vazquez understood that he was at risk, but he was determined not to let this status slow him down or kill his dreams. He joined the junior ROTC when he was in the ninth grade, applied himself in robotics, distinguished himself as a leader on the winning team, then pursued a college degree in mechanical engineering after the *Wired* article and other pieces spurred more than $90,000 in scholarship funds.

The president applauded after hearing Vazquez's moving story, then shook his hand after he received his diploma. It was a marvelous day, full of hope.

Then came the reality of obtaining employment without proper papers. Though he had a college degree, and though he was smart, skilled, and ripe with potential, the system did not care. Vazquez had another path that he thought could make a difference: he was married to an American citizen and had a baby daughter, also an American citizen. But still he could not obtain a visa after living in the United States for so many years without documentation. So Vazquez made a brave decision, what he felt was his only decision. He was tired of living on the fringe, so he moved to Mexico to apply for a visa in hopes of reentering the United States legally, even though he was aware that he could face a ban lasting as long as ten years.

More than sixty-five thousand high school students, children of undocumented immigrants who were brought to the United States as minors, graduate each year. The total number capable of attending college is estimated at more than seven hundred thousand. Various immigration bills since 2001 have included a path for this group to gain eligibility to attend college and enter a path toward citizenship, yet all have failed to garner the required votes. Many advocates hoped that the 2007 Development, Relief, and Education for Alien Minors Act, better known as the DREAM Act, could finally solve the problem. The bill mapped out a system that would enable high school graduates who came to the United States before they were sixteen to receive temporary residency if they completed two years of college or service in the military within six years. Then they would be eligible to apply for permanent residency. The legislation had a lot going for it, including a devoted sponsor in Senator Dick Durbin (D-IL) and respected cosponsors Dick Lugar (R-IN) and Chuck Hagel (R-NE). Yet the bipartisan effort failed to garner enough votes to avoid the threat of filibuster, stymied by the deepening conflict over comprehensive immigration reform and criticism that it represented amnesty. Oscar Vazquez was one of many thousands who saw a possible end to their nightmare evaporate again and were left to wonder whether the DREAM Act will ever become real.[32]

In August 2010, 361 days after Vazquez self-deported to Mexico and began work at an auto parts factory, he received a letter that granted him a waiver, allowing him to return to the United States and his family. Vazquez benefited from friends in high places, most specifically the intervention of Senator Durbin. Within weeks, he expected to have his social security card in hand to begin looking for a job that would make the most of his passion for mechanical engineering.[33] "Innocent children should not be victims of a broken immigration system," Durbin said on the Senate floor the same month Vazquez returned. But the reason for such expanded legislation goes beyond doing the right thing for individuals like Vazquez. It's good for the country. "If students are here and do a good job in school, why can't you give a chance for those students?" Vazquez asked in 2008. "That's what the country needs."[34]

Immigration is a subject that triggers strong emotions and intense heat. And like a fire, it can grab all the oxygen, making it tough to think clearly about the larger impact. But it's worth returning to the Battle of the Brains to remember the risks of inaction—and why it's crucial that America push hard for excellence. In 2006, Nicholas M. Donofrio, a former executive vice president for innovation and technology at IBM, the contest's sponsor, told *Businessweek*'s Steve Hamm that he worried about Americans' discipline and drive and their influence on innovation: "Are we hungry enough? Or are we going to amble along and take our time? If so, the Indians and Chinese will close the gap and perhaps even surpass us. You can see the passion in their eyes. They're people on a mission."[35]

They're people on a mission. Why shouldn't that passion help build America?

Chapter 7

What Can America Learn from Ireland?

O ver the last two decades, Ireland's young could remain in their home country, work, and even make a good living. They were part of a confident new generation, unburdened by the cruel grip of poverty and despair that had long shaped the history of Ireland. Their experience of trendy Dublin cafes and an influx of foreign workers lured by the Irish boom was a far cry from the bleak and backward world memorialized by such Irish masters as James Joyce (*Dubliners*), Samuel Beckett (*Waiting for Godot*), and Frank McCourt (*Angela's Ashes*). There was ample opportunity, enough to bring back many of the talented Irish expats who had departed the Irish shores in search of a better life in America, Australia, or other distant lands.

But that was before 2008, when Ireland's housing bubble popped, fueled by massive overbuilding, low interest rates, rising incomes, and skyrocketing home prices. And that was before November 2010, when Ireland agreed to a bailout of more than $110 billion from the European Union, the International Monetary Fund, and the European Central Bank to secure its banks and ward off the intensifying threat of bankruptcy—a decision met by cries that this proudly independent country was forsaking its hard-fought sovereignty.

Amid this gloom and double-digit unemployment, the former rosy picture of the country's economic boom took on a much darker hue, and Ireland's young were forced to rethink whether they should stay or go. (In a particularly Irish version of déjà vu, by 2010 more than five thousand men and women were leaving the country each month, the largest exodus since 1989.[1]) Soon, the heady story of Ireland's rise after decades of doubt, decline, and dwindling population was tossed aside by tales of excess— easy money, massively overextended debt, banks gone wild, and the seductive illusion that prices would rise indefinitely.

Sound familiar? Like the United States, Ireland got drunk on real estate and new construction, abetted by bankers seeking quick profits and cozy government officials who paid too little attention to the risks while the good times rolled.[2] By one estimate, some three-fourths of the loans made by Irish banks were tied to property, construction, and land speculation; this portion of the loans represented more than twice the size of the economy of this small nation of 4.2 million. "We put up our hands and admit it," the new governor of the Central Bank of Ireland told the *Financial Times*. "The regulator simply didn't do the job."[3]

In fact, one niche bank, the Anglo Irish Bank, became one of Ireland's largest, with a loan portfolio exceeding $100 billion and concentrating on real estate. It lent primarily to a small number of high-flying developers. But as the property market slowed and international credit tightened in 2008, nervous customers began withdrawing their assets. Government leaders, fearing Anglo's total collapse and the danger of collateral damage, decided to guarantee Anglo's deposits and most of the debt of five Irish banks—eventually nationalizing Anglo and creating a separate "bad bank" to absorb the toxic assets at a steep discount. This bold decision, made in the crucible of crisis, came at a high price: angry citizens, nervous EU bondholders, and a dazed world watched as the Emerald Isle faced a high-stakes battle to fund its massive debt and remain solvent.[4]

In a scene that could have been in Washington, DC, one protester commandeered a cement mixer and drove it to the government's gates in Dublin. Emblazoned on the truck was a sign: "Toxic Bank Anglo."[5] He expressed the anger of a nation that saw decades of hard-earned progress swiftly trashed by greed, leaving the country saddled with a grim mix of tax increases and cuts in pay, pensions, and public spending. The Fianna Fail government, determined to reduce its debt from 32 percent of GDP down to the Eurozone limit of 3 percent of GDP, announced a four-year plan that included $14 billion in spending cuts and $7 billion in tax increases. On the hit list: raising the sales tax, cutting the minimum wage, and slashing government payrolls. "There are occasions," Prime Minister Brian Cowen said in announcing the deeply unpopular measures in November 2010, "when the imperative of serving the national interest transcends other concerns, including party, political and personal concerns." Clearly, amid calls for his resignation, this was one of those occasions. "The size of the crisis means no one can be sheltered from the contribution that has to be made," Cowen later said at a news conference."[6]

We may wish to imagine that Ireland's woes are not harbingers of America's future. After all, Ireland lacks the scale of the US economy to absorb and cushion its financial trauma; its leaders made a fateful decision to guarantee all the bank deposits before knowing the toxic depths; and they were compelled to follow requirements imposed by their EU partners, rather than act independently to shape their fate. But there is another dissimilarity that is worth considering: Ireland's leaders faced the threat of bankruptcy head on, even when the austerity measures meant hardship for everyone and the outcome was unclear. What Ireland is doing, noted Columbia University economist Jeffrey Sachs, "is so much tougher than anything the United States has even started to contemplate."[7]

As a result, we believe that Ireland, past and present, offers the United States and comparably sized US states a useful example of how a country both struggles through crisis and positions itself for success. For as traumatic as the last several years have been for Ireland, it's possible to envision Ireland regaining prosperity because of the policy-driven progress that the country achieved beyond the bubble, not only in the last two decades, but also dating back two generations to the 1960s. Even amid the shock, Ireland's economy continued to benefit from strong exports in pharmaceuticals, processed foods, and medical equipment and other high-tech products. Moreover, the painful crunch on jobs, wages, and rents helped to attract a new wave of foreign investment looking for a competitive edge, hitting a seven-year high in 2010.[8] As David Gardner of the *Financial Times* noted, "Most of the positive features that predate the property bubble are still in place: a small, open, low-tax economy with an educated workforce; strong European and Atlantic links; and an Irish diaspora acting as an enabling network."[9]

So let's rewind. How did a modern Ireland happen? For anyone over forty, a world-class, revitalized Ireland was a place they may have imagined but doubted they would ever see. Yet since the mid-1990s, Ireland morphed into an economic powerhouse and a magnet for talent. Its annual growth averaged a dazzling 8 percent between 1994 and 2004, more than twice the US level, and its per capita GDP climbed to 135 percent of the EU average. This boom was driven by goods exports and services rather than an overheated property market. Home to hundreds of international businesses, Ireland lured roughly one-quarter of all US foreign direct investment, ranked as the world's leading software exporter (ahead of the United States), and boasted plants from nine of the world's top ten drug companies. Moreover, Ireland's total labor force during the boom period rose nearly 50 percent to 1.9 million; this included some of the best and brightest who had previously left their native land for opportunities in America and elsewhere—a remarkable turn of fortune for a nation long suffering a brain drain. [10]

To explain Ireland's evolution, the phrase "economic miracle" was often used—as if it happened by supernatural force or sheer Irish luck. But the truth is that the unleashing of the Celtic Tiger followed decades of hard and focused work, a national will to succeed, a commitment to educating its people at the secondary and college level, a pragmatic policy of low business taxes and economic openness, and an influential industrial policy that remained in place despite changes in government and the inevitable shifts of political persuasions.

When one of the authors, Harris, was asked in 2001 to initiate and lead Science Foundation Ireland (SFI), it followed a yearlong study by a group of business, education, and government leaders appointed by the prime minister and deputy prime minister. Rather than coasting during the boom times, these Irish leaders were already wondering whether their heavy involvement with American multinationals put them at risk since US businesses could easily move their operations to Eastern Europe or Asia to lower costs. The group was looking for creative ways to enrich Ireland's global relationships in China, India, and elsewhere to help sustain the country's prosperity and focus on excellence. The group's job was to examine how an infusion of government funding could best improve Ireland's long-term competitiveness and growth.

The resulting National Development Plan 2000–2006 committed more than $1.5 billion in funding for research, technological development, and innovation programs. That was an enormous sum for a country of Ireland's size but a hearty indication that its leaders understood that major public investment in R&D was crucial to their country's future. SFI's portion totaled approximately $1 billion, with a goal of supporting world-class scientists and engineers from Ireland and around the world to help launch research programs and pursue ideas that could spawn knowledge-based businesses, create jobs, and generate exports. And not only did they agree to allow an American to launch and head up SFI, they gave the team a virtual "blank slate" to design the agency in a way that team members thought would best achieve its goals. Harris and his team focused on building partnerships between Irish universities and multinational corporations and funded more than 450 research projects in the first five years.

This long-range investment did not happen in a vacuum. Memories of stagnation and poverty were still causing anxiety in the late 1990s. Ireland's economic achievements took many serious observers by surprise. In 1988, editors of the *Economist* asserted that Ireland was "heading for catastrophe."[11] They had good reason: unemployment was hovering around 17 percent, and per capita income lingered at a mere 60 percent of the average of the fifteen countries then comprising the European Community.[12] The country was in such dire circumstances then, saddled with massive public debts, that it teetered near bankruptcy. Despite efforts to transform itself, Ireland was still struggling to escape its history of isolation and poverty.

Flash forward just six years to 1994: how the world had changed. A British economist at Morgan Stanley, comparing Ireland to the go-go economies of Asia, called it the Celtic Tiger.[13] (The moniker stuck.) Then in 1997, Ireland graced the *Economist*'s cover with a remarkable title: "Europe's Shining Light." And by 2004, the magazine confessed that it had sorely miscalculated back in 1988, influenced by Ireland's "awful cocktail" of high unemployment, high inflation, and public debt: "Surely no other country in the rich world has seen its image change so fast."[14]

So how did Ireland do it? How did it transform itself from an isolated country that often saw itself as singularly oppressed to a new land of opportunity? In those boom years of the 1990s, Ireland finally reaped the benefits of the foundations it had been building for decades: a strong educational system, aggressive and business-friendly economic strategies, partnerships with nations rich in knowledge-based businesses, and, above all, highly skilled talent. Multinationals seeking a home in Europe needed well-educated workers, and they were drawn to Ireland's low corporate taxes, educated and English-speaking workforce, and appealing quality of life. (Even now, despite their new hardships, they have refused to increase corporate taxes in order to continue to attract foreign multinationals.) As Europe moved toward a single, integrated market in the late 1980s, Ireland received EU structural funds for social programs, roads, and other regional development to increase the eventual cohesion—funds that surely enhanced Ireland's economic appeal.[15]

First and foremost, Ireland's growing prosperity was achieved through pragmatic action and good strategic policy. The country benefited from an intimate political culture in which citizens knew their political leaders and demanded responsiveness, competence, and clearly articulated goals. Ireland's leaders— politicians, bureaucrats, educators, and business people—were determined to establish a high standard of living for the Irish people. Their policy decisions were driven by a shared will and a galvanizing sense of urgency; that national unity made it possible to sustain a long-range vision. Through education and a belief in the idea that being rich is better than being poor, the country made necessary changes. At the same time, as the country began to relish the fruits of its progress, Ireland's bureaucracy and the salaries of its public officials grew significantly—making the current job and wage cuts that much more painful.

But getting to that moment took two generations and more than a few missteps. For most of the nineteenth and twentieth centuries, ravaged by famine and marked by misfortune, Ireland struggled with an economic reality so bleak that leaving often seemed to be the only good option. In 1922, the year after achieving sovereignty from Britain, Ireland was a closed, agrarian society comprising fewer than three million people. Its population fell slightly every subsequent decade until the 1950s, when a startling four hundred thousand people—one-seventh of the entire population—left the country.[16] Talk about careering down the wrong road: dominated by Britain for hundreds of years, wracked by revolutionary and civil wars between 1916 and 1922, its leaders supported inward-focused nationalism and opposed free trade and foreign investment while lacking a well-developed industrial sector. This may have been a reflexive and understandable response to British rule for this developing country, but it surely misunderstood the limits of self-determination; it was as if a sovereign Ireland was unable or unwilling to pursue economic policies that could expand and invigorate the nation.

By the late 1950s, Ireland's new leaders, supported by the public, laid the foundations for Ireland's transformation. Determined to turn the tide against stagnation and emigration—and join the recovery of other postwar European economies—they offered their plan to expand Ireland and its worldview. *Economic Development*, published in 1958, described a dramatic policy about-face that supported foreign investment, free trade, productive investments, and economic growth over fiscal restraint. That year, controls on foreign ownership of businesses were lifted, following an earlier move to provide businesses tax relief on exports. Helping drive the goals of *Economic Development* was Ken Whitaker, the report's chief author and a fresh-thinking civil servant who served as Secretary in the Department of Finance between 1956 and 1969.[17]

This new openness continued in the 1960s: Import tariffs were lowered, trade agreements were negotiated, and the government expanded its role in providing social services, education, telecommunications, and other infrastructure. And in the 1970s, Ireland joined the European Economic Community, which helped boost the country's confidence by opening its economy beyond the United Kingdom as well as providing an infusion of public funds. For the first time since independence, Ireland experienced increases in population, employment, and national income.

In 1970, the Irish government also established the Industrial Development Authority (IDA) to seek out new industries from overseas. The IDA was the first dedicated state agency in the world determined to build a modern manufacturing base by attracting major foreign investment. The IDA played a central role in Ireland's drive for success, providing a clear point of contact for foreign firms and maintaining a consistent industrial policy whatever the political philosophy of the government in office. New multinational companies—more than 450 of them by 1975, representing two-thirds of the country's total industrial output—took advantage of Ireland as an export platform to serve Europe and other markets.[18] Detached from the politics of the day and scandal-free, the IDA earned the trust and support of companies, government leaders, and the general public.

In a 1978 interview with *Time* (a year that Ireland's economic growth reached 6.5 percent, the highest in western Europe), the IDA's first chief executive, Michael Killeen, was described as the "Pied Piper for industry." Killeen, recalling that four of his uncles and aunts left the west of Ireland to find work in America, served up a textbook description of the role that the IDA played for Ireland. These lessons still resonate in Ireland and beyond: make industrial development a national commitment that attracts the best talent; give companies incentives to export and expand; and create a business-friendly environment that enables companies to earn a return on their investment.[19]

In a country that lacked much of a wealthy class yet has always supported private ownership, these principles faced limited opposition. The IDA's success secured it an honored place in Irish society and deepened the belief that government work is a path of pride. No wonder: "The population is rising for the first time in modern history," *Time* noted in 1978. "No longer can it be said that Ireland's greatest export is men."[20] And despite some serious turbulence in the years that followed—including high inflation, rising government debt, and inadequate employment opportunities for newly graduating students in the 1980s—these strategies helped Ireland become a global leader.

These days, leading companies in information and communications technology (Intel, IBM, Hewlett-Packard) each employ four thousand to five thousand people in Ireland. They are among the building blocks that can lure new international companies and help Ireland regain its footing. Intel, which opened shop in 1992 and played a key role in Ireland's boom, has invested more than $7 billion at its largest operation outside the United States. Its ultimate decision to locate a wafer-fabrication plant just outside of Dublin, on a 360-acre site that was a former stud farm, resulted from the IDA's critical early decisions to focus on companies representing the future, including the computer industry, pharmaceuticals, medical technology, and international services.[21]

When Intel announced plans for a European plant in 1989, the IDA and its chief executive, Kieran McGowan, understood that this high-end manufacturer would be a bellwether catch. They were determined to show their best face, and they hired consultants to create a contact list of qualified and interested engineers to present to Intel. While some of these candidates were local, many of them were Irish emigrants who had relocated to California. They helped the IDA highlight Ireland's rich international heritage—Ireland counts some 40 million people with Irish roots in the United States alone—and were among the returning emigrants who took positions as senior engineers when Intel Ireland opened its doors.[22]

While those emigrants may have originally fled Ireland to find good jobs, they benefited from solid schooling. That would not have been possible without the commitment of foresighted leaders to educate Ireland's young. Two generations ago in 1967, Ireland's minister of education, Donagh O'Malley, boldly introduced free secondary school education, a move that had not been authorized by the finance minister or the rest of the Irish cabinet. O'Malley complained that that one in three of Ireland's citizens were cut off after primary school from learning a skill and other benefits of advanced education. "This is a dark stain on the national conscience," he said.[23]

His visionary initiative created a link between educational

investment and economic growth, ultimately making it possible for knowledge-driven companies to find the talent they needed in Ireland. To that end, Ireland since the 1960s has pushed to make an already demanding K–16 education system more rigorous, formalize workplace education, and match student abilities to the needs of advanced global enterprises.

The results are powerful: Between 1965 and 1980, the number of students participating in both secondary and university-level education doubled. In the following twenty years, the number in university-level tripled again, a more than sixfold increase in thirty-five years. By 1995, through the combined efforts of Ireland's universities and institutes of technology, Ireland had more students per capita with science-related qualifications than any of the other thirty countries in the Organisation for Economic Co-operation and Development. Its quantity of science and engineering graduates aged twenty to thirty-four is the highest in the world—and more than double the US total.[24] By 2005, 48 percent of the Irish population had attained college-level education, compared with less than 40 percent in countries such as the United States, United Kingdom, Spain, Belgium, and France, and less than 25 percent in Germany.[25]

With this kind of talent available, the IDA was able to offer leading companies a workforce that few other countries could match—and combine it with the lowest standard corporate tax rates in Europe. By 2008, Ireland's corporate rate was 12.5 percent, up from 10 percent, to establish a uniform corporate rate for old and new companies. Corporate income taxes account for about 13 percent of all tax revenue in Ireland, compared to 6 percent in the United States. Low taxes, high productivity, and low labor costs enabled US companies that opened shop in Ireland to achieve high after-tax returns on investment. Ireland, in turn, benefited from more businesses, a larger tax base, and greater employment.[26] It's no wonder the Irish have fiercely resisted European pressure to raise the corporate tax, convinced that this incentive for investment has given the country a critical competitive edge.

The Irish economic strategy has been closely followed. Frank McCabe, a former Intel vice president and general manager for Intel's Ireland operations as well as a former Shannon Development chairman, told us that Chinese leaders began taking note of Ireland back in the 1970s.[27] They periodically sent fact-finding delegations; the future Chinese leader Deng Xiaoping, a former Maoist who became a free-enterprise advocate, was among them. These groups were interested in learning about Ireland's business-friendly strategies for attracting multinationals. They visited the Shannon regional development area as guests of Shannon Development in an effort to understand the world's first industrial duty- and tax-free zone. (Beginning in 1980, drawing on the Shannon model, Deng Xiaoping launched similar Special Economic Zones in China that loosened economic controls and offered foreign investors tax incentives to spur trade.)

In recent years, the tables turned. Ireland officials began to visit China and India, looking to help sustain growth by partnering with leading firms and research centers. And as Ireland's economic stature rose with higher-end enterprises, so did wages and other costs, reducing its appeal as Europe's low-cost choice. Ireland has had an increasingly tough time competing for that mantle with China, India, Thailand, Poland, South Africa, and other low-wage developing countries. That motivated Ireland to reposition itself again, to take advantage of the hard work required to become an educated, knowledge-driven economy; a country capable of providing a skilled workforce; and a creative environment for technologically advanced foreign investment. It's a sad irony that it's taken the current economic trauma—especially the downward press on wages and the high unemployment—to improve Ireland's competitive position.

Nonetheless, Ireland has plenty of competitors on this flattened global landscape, ready to pounce as it struggles to cut costs and expand its tax base. But it has already demonstrated the willingness to change direction, summon its collective will, and pursue a long-range economic policy that can buoy its fortunes.

Several years ago, in what now seems like a surreal view through the looking glass, Ireland created a National Development Plan for 2007–2013. This self-described roadmap, the largest and most ambitious investment program ever proposed for Ireland, involved stepping up the country's commitments for education and research, discovery and innovation. This was born in those flush times, with the expectation that such times would last; the price tag was €184 billion. Yet the plan, titled "Transforming Ireland: A Better Quality of Life for All," was also a sign that Ireland was not content to sit still or coast. The document's opening words were both a description of expectations and a challenge to less motivated nations: "Within the next seven years, our economy and our society will undergo a transformation almost as radical as the changes we have experienced in the past decade of growth and development. . . . To optimize our choices for a better long-term future, we need a roadmap clearly marking out the challenges we face."[28]

The roadmap Ireland is now pursuing is a far different and more challenging one than the report's creators pictured. Yet the Celtic Tiger years launched a culture of confidence and innovation in this "James Joyce society"—still hardly believable, but true. The country's current survival mode combined with the global economic downturn will test the depth of Irish resilience. But there are clear lessons that America and its states can take away: Fund R&D, partner with business, establish good government, think beyond the moment, and stay focused and strategic—as if your life depends on it.

Because it does.

And there is another lesson: The United States is careering to the point when it too will be forced to make painful changes by foreign countries that help finance our debt. Even though we can criticize the choices the Irish government made to maintain the country's solvency, it clearly faced its crisis rather than hide behind empty rhetoric or simply blame the opposition and ignore it.

As a global rival, Ireland offers a tough reminder that the

world is increasingly populated by emerging countries that will do what is necessary to take more business and jobs from an unprepared and complacent America. As we will discuss, while US leaders focus on ideological battles with each other, they are missing the big picture: The development of the global economy —and the intensifying competition between nations—will not stop and wait for America to figure out what it takes to lead again.

Chapter 8

Do We Still Care about Jobs and Making Things?

In the Go-Go/Dot-Com 1990s and the No Money Down 2000s, it might have been easy to miss the expanding underbelly of globalization, even if you had the nagging suspicion that your paycheck wasn't stretching as far or your job (if you still had one) seemed less secure. If you were part of that greatest generation born before World War II or a boomer who came of age in the 1970s, you may have still savored the postwar afterglow of American economic superiority. Free trade and free markets may have seemed like the inevitable product of a prosperous, open America willing to share its economic ideals and vision with the developing world, which would then benefit as emerging countries grew richer and more able to buy American goods. As globalization's great advocate Thomas L. Friedman would say, millions of Chinese and Indians and Brazilians will be lifted out of poverty, benefitting from a flatter, more interconnected, and more technology-driven world market. But even with "plenty of good jobs out there in the flat world for people with the right knowledge, skills, ideas and self-motivation to seize them," he warned that American democracy depends on a "broad and deep middle class"—and that a country faced with a growing population of rich and poor and a shrinking middle would spur economic and political instability.[1]

We suspect that more people heard the first part of Friedman's message than the second. But not anymore, not when more and more middle-class Americans are wondering whether the American Dream has faded forever or, worse, if they will be able to keep their family fed, clothed, and housed this year, next year, and the year after that. As we have noted, that fear and frustration is being played out on the political battlefield, especially among those who gravitate to the extremes. But across the political spectrum, it's also raising fresh doubts about the policies and values that the country has pursued in recent years. Has America sold out its workers and sold off its national sovereignty, and what role should government play to create a more secure economic and political future?

Friedman is far from the only voice insisting that globalization and greater global competitiveness could create havoc in America (if the middle class shrinks), especially if the country does not enrich its commitment to education and innovation, ingenuity and entrepreneurialism. In a 2006 *Newsweek* article entitled "How Long Will America Lead the World?" Intel cofounder and former CEO Andy Grove bluntly told Fareed Zakaria that America is "going down the tubes, and the worst part is nobody knows it. They're all in denial, patting themselves on the back, as the *Titanic* heads for the iceberg full speed ahead."[2] Grove followed that in 2010 with his own heat-generating article in *Businessweek*, insisting that "the U.S. undervalues manufacturing" and has accepted "the idea that as long as 'knowledge work' stays in the U.S., it doesn't matter what happens to factory jobs." That thinking is wrong, he wrote. "Not only did we lose an untold number of jobs, we broke the chain of experience that is so important in technological evolution. As happened with batteries, abandoning today's 'commodity' manufacturing can lock you out of tomorrow's emerging industry."

And who's responsible? He says that "job creation must be the No. 1 objective of state economic policy." Citing several high-performing Asian countries, he said that "the government plays a strategic role in setting the priorities and arraying the forces and organization necessary to achieve that goal," and that includes "targeting the growth of manufacturing industries." As for business leaders, "all of us in business have a responsibility to maintain the industrial base on which we depend and the society whose adaptability—and stability—we may have taken for granted." He proposed an extra tax on the "product of offshored labor." If that sounds protectionist, even if it stokes a trade war, he said, "so be it."[3]

It's a mind-set that matches Ernest "Fritz" Hollings, South Carolina's former Democratic governor and senator who left Congress in 2005 after thirty-eight years but has continued to advocate his dearly held views. "The outsourcing and free trade charade are destroying the economy," said Hollings, the former chairman of the Senate commerce committee. Just before Christmas 2009, as the recession and unemployment deepened, he published this little sugarplum: "Who is against jobs in the United States? The big banks, Wall Street, the Council on Foreign Relations, the Business Roundtable, the United States Chamber of Commerce, the National Retail Federation, Corporate America, the President of the United States, the Congress of the United States. Everyone is crying for jobs, but no one seems to understand why there aren't any. And the reason for those opposing jobs is money."[4] As in money needed to finance ever more expensive elections—what Hollings described to us as "the cancer of money"—and money made by shifting production overseas.

Hollings, who delivers barbed bromides wrapped in a silky Southern drawl, is a longtime proponent of industrial policy geared to saving American jobs. He was never reluctant to press his political colleagues to raise tariffs, adjust taxes, and apply other levers of government to stem offshoring and stop the dumping of foreign imports in the United States. In 1960, even before he came to Congress, then Governor Hollings showed up at presidential candidate Jack Kennedy's Georgetown apartment to advocate for tariffs to protect troubled South Carolina textile mills. In the 1980s, he navigated two textile industry bills through Congress before President Reagan vetoed them both. But by 1993, when President Clinton pushed the North American Free Trade Agreement (NAFTA) through Congress despite opposition from the organized labor that helped elect him, Hollings knew the writing was on the wall. Convinced that NAFTA would further hasten job loss, he watched with frustration and sadness as Clinton feted Fortune 500 CEOs and other deep-pocketed corporate bosses in giant tents on the South Lawn of the White House. "I can see those white tents now," he told us. "We cried, but he got the money."[5]

As much as old-fashioned senators like Hollings believed in protectionism, the political tide by the mid-1990s was no longer coursing in their direction. Gone were the days when manufacturing was seen and valued as the nation's lifeblood. Wall Street financiers and free marketers were now in charge, reaping ever greater profits for their shareholders, themselves, and their political allies. Between 1988 and 2005, the financial sector's profits skyrocketed to an average of 3.3 percent of GDP, nearly triple the average from the decades dating back to 1929—and, at their peak, they had climbed to a massive 40 percent of business profits. Determined to keep their party going, the financial industry poured $1.8 billion into political campaigns and another $3.4 billion into lobbying between 1998 and 2008.[6] Is it any wonder that the fevered focus was on making deals and making money rather than making things?

And what a song they sang. Akin to religious faith, the ideology of free trade and free markets had become sacrosanct among the political class, even as America's foreign rivals were expanding their comparative advantage with a combination of lower-cost production and minimal worker regulation, government subsidies, restricted markets, and carefully planned industrial policies determined to back winning industries. Yet this fervent faith, which snugly fit in with globalization's backers and was fanned by a deregulated climate for multinational operations, paid little heed to a burgeoning crisis in America. In the new decade of the new millennium, the country was facing what is increasingly being called "the lost decade,"[7] defined by flat or declining real wages for middle-income earners, an enormous increase in wealth for the top 1 percent, job creation at its lowest level since at least the 1930s, rising poverty, and massive consumption. All of this was buoyed by a river of cheap credit funded by global trading partners (and American financiers taking their cut of the action). The thinking and values that brought us to this dangerous time couldn't possibly survive, could they?

Well, such faith-filled glories die hard, even when facts refute them, even when reality cracks you in the face and changing direction may actually seem like the only possible option. Consider the case of George W. Bush, circa 2008. In the waning days of his presidency, Bush confessed that dire economic realities required him to put aside his faith in an unfettered free market and intervene in the private sector. The words, unusually frank, followed his judgment that it was too risky to allow General Motors, Chrysler, and a rich handful of the nation's largest financial institutions to fail. "Well, I have obviously made a decision to make sure the economy doesn't collapse," he told CNN correspondent Candy Crowley in a December 2008 interview. "I've abandoned free market principles to save the free market system."

Yes, the logic was tangled—if you've abandoned free market principles, is the resulting system still a free market? (It's no wonder the apoplectic conservative blogosphere tore through that question with great abandon.) Yet for a brief and painful moment, Bush offered a sharp-focus picture of the American crazy dance: take one step forward to fix the crisis, then take one step back and say we shouldn't really be doing this. It would be funny if it were not so tragic.

For while the bailouts in 2008 and 2009—including AIG, Bear Stearns, Goldman Sachs, Citigroup, Bank of America, General Motors, and Chrysler—represent the largest combined commitment of federal dollars ever to buoy troubled private companies, they are only the most recent examples of government leaders intervening in the private sector to stave off a perceived economic disaster. Richard Nixon tossed a lifeline to Lockheed Aircraft and the Penn Central Railroad. Jimmy Carter bailed out a near-bankrupt Chrysler. Ronald Reagan and George H. W. Bush backed up the savings and loan industry. And George W. had previously demonstrated a willingness to bail out a troubled industry; after September 11, he stepped in to soften the blow to a broken airline industry.

What makes these moves fascinating is how they undercut the oft-voiced free market axiom that it's not the role of government to step in and pick winners and losers. Clearly, history has shown that this old saw does not hold up to scrutiny, especially when the perceived threat of catastrophe looms. The more we peel away the surface belief in allowing unfettered markets free rein, the more we see that the federal government has always taken an energetic role in shaping the economy, whether it be in deciding tax policy, tariff and trade policy, or, yes, industrial policy. Ask subsidized American farmers. Ask small businesses that rely on federal loans and grants. Ask corporate CEOs who watched as government policy allowed foreign import dumping and then responded by moving their operations offshore. Ask a treasure trove of firms from Intel to Hewlett-Packard and IBM that prospered because the government formed a fifty-fifty public-private partnership that helped save a troubled semiconductor industry in the 1980s.

Yet the crazy dance persists, and not only at the precipice of disaster. As if piecemeal policy and ad hoc decision making were a way to minimize the government's role in shaping the economy. As if the government weren't charged by the Constitution to use economic instruments to "provide for the general welfare" of the nation. One step forward, then two steps back to disavow any suggestion of government meddling in the affairs of business and the private sector. It would almost be laughable if the end result were not a failure of vision and policy that has left our manufacturing sector decimated, our middle class increasingly insecure, and our future nervously dependent on creating innovative new companies and products—indeed, new industries—to replace the jobs and industries that may never return.

How did this happen? At the heart of every conversation about implementing a coherent industrial policy is the simple notion that it's in the country's best interest to expand the collaboration between government and the private sector. Yet this has long been treated as an ugly stepsister to American values, an unwanted reminder of the messy tension between opposing beliefs: on the one hand, that of course government must take an active role in planning and policy to ensure a prosperous economy and healthy society; on the other, that business should pursue its interests without government interference. This conflict between some in the public and private sectors has undermined honest dialogue and the development of smart and strategic policy. As a 1983 report from the Congressional Budget Office wryly and accurately noted—the humor was probably inadvertent—the notion of industrial policy "represents not so much a policy as a debate" over how to handle the country's long-term industrial problems.[8]

And the conversation often stops before it begins. Here's how: Opponents complain that industrial policy smacks of centralized planning—i.e., socialism—and that the government is ill-equipped to make such decisions and should not be meddling in the rightful concerns of the private sector. Sounds good, if we were living in a hermetically sealed world where innovation did not depend on the combination of public and private support for R&D, tax policy did not favor industries or benefit multinationals who exit the country, defense funding did not finance an international arms business and global operations well beyond the requirements of national security, and the competitive land-scape was not increasingly shaped by strategic global rivals who rely on state support to advance long-term economic objectives (and advantage) in everything from advanced batteries and solar photovoltaic cells to rare earth minerals for sophisticated magnets, laptops, and hybrid cars.

To our country's current misfortune, our political leaders have for decades failed to get beyond panic-driven or piecemeal decision making in order to establish strategic, coherent industrial policy that can serve the best interests of our states and nation. To do so requires a clear-eyed look at the nation's significant decline in manufacturing, the rise of offshoring, and the ascendancy of China. It means getting past short-term policies that flip-flop from one election cycle and one political party to the next. It entails conscious planning that links industrial policy and economic growth to education and training, research and development, innovation, and global competitiveness. It means taking a fresh look at a more sensible corporate tax policy that would encourage firms to stay on American soil and other incentives that could drive innovation and growth. And it demands acknowledging that our business leaders have actively pursued moving their major manufacturing overseas to benefit from other countries' industrial policies.

This is a story of opportunity lost, because our growing dependence on foreign benevolence was far from inevitable. Our global competitors have taken advantage of American CEOs' obsession with short-term profits, while our politicians, Democrat and Republican, espoused their fervent belief in free trade and free markets—and then reaped the gains when financing their next election. In the process, they failed to establish industrial policy that would slow the outsourcing of jobs; bolster support for critical R&D work; or secure higher-paying, higher-skill industries on American soil that strengthen the long-term viability of the US economy and the middle class.

The data underscore the precarious reality. Since 1992,

imports have quadrupled, while exports have failed to come close; the trade deficit in goods and services has ballooned from a comparatively tiny $39 billion in 1992 to a peak of $760 billion in 2006 (which dropped in 2009 when the recession dramatically slowed consumer expenditures).[9] Meanwhile, by 2005, manufacturing employment had slipped below fourteen million jobs, less than half its total in the 1970s. That's 9 percent of total employment in the United States, down from 25 percent in 1970. While other developed economies have also experienced this consolidation, none have fallen as dramatically as the United States. Germany's industrial share is still about 23 percent, Italy's is 22 percent, Japan's is 18 percent, France's is 16 percent, and Britain's and Canada's are each 12 percent.[10] And since December 2007, more than two million additional manufacturing jobs have disappeared, with the total now below twelve million, underscoring that this trend is not abating anytime soon.[11] Yes, we can chalk up some of this consolidation to technological advancements and an impressive rise in productivity, but the fact is that American manufacturing has been increasingly unable to compete against rivals in Asia, Mexico, South America, and elsewhere.

That's bad news for America, especially as these competitors climb to more technologically advanced levels—exactly the high-tech, higher-paying positions that should be within the grasp of Americans. For the first time in decades, median income actually dropped, providing genuine reason to worry when—or if—wages will return to help revive the American Dream now that debt-fueled consumption can no longer keep the party hearty. As Robert Kuttner noted in his 2007 book *The Squandering of America*, the productivity of American workers was up 19 percent between 2000 and 2006. Yet the total increase in wages for 124 million nonsupervisory workers was $200 million, an embarrassing $1.60 per worker. He contrasted that with the bonuses paid to the top five Wall Street firms during that time: $38 billion. What about the top 1 percent of earners? By 2007, they were collecting more than 23 percent of all income, nearly triple their take in the 1970s.[12]

This shift should be a source of distress for the entire nation, not only the millions of workers who lost their jobs or those who are still working but struggling to feed their families. This is a national tragedy and a genuine crisis for the future of the country. America has served as the productive center for the world for more than a century, yet today it is increasingly unable to maintain an economic and industrial core that can sustain a middle class. Those individuals at the high end who have benefited disproportionately should recognize that a society severely divided by wealth will become increasingly angry and corrosive; it is in their interest to have a strong, vibrant middle class.

Let's take a moment to consider the path that led to this current dilemma. From the country's earliest years, the framers of the US Constitution recognized the centrality of economic policy and planning. From Article 1, Section 8: "The Congress shall have Power To lay and collect Taxes, Duties, Imposts and Excises, to pay the Debts and provide for the common Defence and general Welfare of the United States." In 1791, Alexander Hamilton, appointed by George Washington as the country's first Secretary of the Treasury, laid out a first industrial policy in his "Report on Manufactures," providing a strategic statement to transform a largely agrarian America into an industrial power: "Not only the wealth, but the independence and security of a Country, appear to be materially connected with the prosperity of manufactures. Every nation, with a view to those great objects, ought to endeavour to possess within itself all the essentials of national supply."[13] Hamilton, who fought with Thomas Jefferson over the future president's belief in the primacy of an agrarian society, favored tariff protection and government intervention to support the country's infant industries and build its infrastructure. His ideas inspired Henry Clay, Abraham Lincoln, and other advocates of an economic policy approach known as the American School; this promoted economic independence by supporting high tariffs to protect industry, government investment to build roads and other infrastructure to aid transportation, and a national bank to promote the development of growth industries. Even amid the Civil War, Abraham Lincoln committed funding to build a transcontinental railroad to California and supported the land-grant Morrill Act to promote the role of universities in spurring economic development. As author Clyde Prestowitz noted, "The railroad led to the creation of huge new markets and cities and transformed the country into a true continental powerhouse of a nation."[14] By the end of the nineteenth century, the United States surpassed the long-dominant British empire and became the world's industrial leader.

This anti–free trade, pro–industrial development policy continued into the 1940s, reaching its zenith during World War II, when demand for military supplies spurred massive new production. The United States became the largest manufacturer of arms in the history of the world, building nearly three hundred thousand airplanes, nearly four hundred thousand pieces of artillery, forty-seven million tons of artillery ammunition, forty-four billion rounds of small-arms ammo, eighty-seven thousand warships, and eighty-six thousand tanks. In the process, workers' wages doubled, and the nation experienced a full-employment economy (including a majority of women and many African Americans who previously had been denied access).[15] The Marshall Plan in 1947 not only helped rebuild the broken economies of former enemies Germany and Japan, it also created the conditions for expanded production and trade for US goods. So did the creation of the World Bank, the International Monetary Fund, and the General Agreement on Tariffs and Trade. By the end of the war in 1945, Prestowitz wrote in *The Betrayal of American Prosperity*, taking advantage of "industrial policy, infrastructure policy, protectionism, and continuous government intervention in the economy to encourage industrial development and direct war production, the United States emerged as an unprecedentedly powerful hegemonic colossus."[16]

American industrial preeminence—experiencing a virtual monopoly for nearly three decades after the war—now benefited from a self-serving new commitment to free trade (as well as a Cold War posture that ensured a continuing military buildup around the world). Throughout the 1950s and 1960s, American prosperity expanded, hastened by the GI Bill, which provided a path for millions of returning veterans to go to college, start businesses, and buy homes. "Made in the USA" was the tag that consumers around the world wanted, whether it was cars or electronics, furniture or metals, jeans or guitars. American exports steadily increased, creating a huge trade surplus. But the heady combination of free-trade confidence and industrial superiority was not to last, not as our international competitors in Europe and Japan were experiencing renewed economic strength and our basic industries were aging and losing their competitive advantage.

It didn't take a genius or especially well-honed observation skills to realize in the mid-1970s and early 1980s that America's industrial base was eroding. If you were living in western Pennsylvania near Pittsburgh, as author Beschloss was, you could see that steel mills up and down the Ohio River were closing and town after town was struggling with dramatic job loss. Beaver County, for example, which had blossomed in the early twentieth century as a home for steel manufacturing and attracted sizable immigrant contingents of Italians and Germans, was no different than many Rust Belt cities in the Northeast or aging textile towns in the South. At the peak, unemployment rocketed to 28 percent and more than 120,000 manufacturing jobs disappeared throughout the Pittsburgh area as major steelmakers such as US Steel, LTV Corp., and J&L shuttered their plants.[17] Their way of life, once a source for poetry and symbol of American prowess, was changing—and no matter how severe unemployment's attendant problems were (rising alcohol abuse, spouse abuse, and divorce among them), there were few signs that national policy was going to sustain troubled mills or stem the relocations to nonunion states or lower-wage destinations offshore. Was this simply capitalism's creative disruption, an inevitable fact of life?

In 1982, authors Barry Bluestone and Bennett Harrison hit the nail on the head with the influential book *The Deindustrialization of America*. They described deindustrialization as a "widespread, systematic disinvestment in the nation's basic productive capacity."[18] They emphasized that this process was not the result of "mysterious market forces,"[19] but a conscious response to increasingly global competition (including Japanese imports) and real or anticipated declines in profit. They placed the blame on shifting priorities. "Controversial as it may be," they wrote, "the essential problem with the U.S. economy can be traced to the way capital—in the forms of financial resources and of real plant and equipment—has been diverted from productive investment in our basic national industries into unproductive speculation, mergers and acquisitions, and foreign investment. Left behind are shuttered factories, displaced workers, and a newly emerging group of ghost towns."[20]

What was happening during the 1970s and at a faster pace in the 1980s was the most profound change in the structure of the US economy since the rise of the industrial revolution a century earlier. It was a defining, transformative period—and one that could have spurred a sense of national urgency, much like Sputnik had done several decades earlier. In a special issue focused on economic revitalization in 1980, *Businessweek* rang the bell. Calling for "fundamental change" to maintain the country's economic viability and respond to "diminished leadership," the magazine's editors said "the goal must be nothing less than the reindustrialization of America. A conscious effort to rebuild America's productive capacity is the only real alternative to the precipitous loss of competitiveness of the last 15 years."[21] Their lament would sound almost quaint, if it were not so relevant to the loss of productive capacity that has continued to this day and leaves America increasingly vulnerable economically.

In the early 1980s, a window cracked open for an honest conversation about the nation's economic policy. For a brief period, the idea of a conscious national industrial policy and a strategic partnership between government and industry was not viewed as heresy within the business community. Nearly all presidential candidates weighed in with government initiatives that they believed could spur economic growth, typically tying their ideas to the issue of social justice. But after Reagan's trouncing of Walter Mondale in 1984—winning forty-nine states and 58.8 percent of the vote—industrial policy as a concept and focus of debate lost all traction.

Which isn't to say that de facto industrial policy wasn't already happening. Between 1981 and 1989, Reagan nearly doubled defense spending to its highest-ever levels. And even while national leaders rejected a consciously articulated industrial policy, the country was already intervening, as one Aspen Institute study put it, like "a brain-damaged octopus." A 1982 Urban Institute study identified 329 discrete "program aids to business," delivered by twenty-nine different agencies and primarily directed to agriculture, transportation, energy, and maritime industries, as well as small and minority-owned firms. It was noted that these subsidies did not reflect "comprehensive national objectives" but rather resulted from lobbying by distressed industries, groups, and regions. Not only was there no indication that this federal support would evaporate under Reagan, his administration actually expanded the funding by $44 billion in its first two years.[22] Yet the president's staff knew the crazy dance well: one ad hoc step forward, two steps backward to say you didn't really mean to do it.

Still, in 1985, business leaders were talking about the importance of serving their country. Sam Walton, America's top retailer, sang the praises of his company's commitment to a "Buy American" campaign intended to help reduce the country's enormous trade deficit, which had jumped nearly 80 percent since 1980 and surpassed $100 billion for the first time. He sent a letter to more than three thousand domestic manufacturers and wholesalers expressing Wal-Mart's desire to buy more American goods, then issued a press release acknowledging the dangerous direction the country was heading. "We cannot continue to be a solvent nation as long as we pursue this current accelerating direction," he asserted. "Our company is firmly committed to the philosophy by buying everything possible from suppliers who manufacture their products in the United States."[23]

Fine words they were, an inspiring recognition of the constructive role that the nation's largest retailer could play. Walton was backed up a month later by Wal-Mart's president, David Glass. "As a company, we are tremendously concerned with the trade deficit," Glass told the *Washington Post*. "We see a tremendous erosion of manufacturing jobs in this country as manufacturers accelerate the movement to go offshore to make their goods. None of us will believe what this country will be like five to 10 years from now if we continue to let this happen."[24] This too was a strong message, one that captured the fearful mood in many towns and cities that were struggling with the concrete consequences of a decline in manufacturing. At that time, in 1985, Wal-Mart was estimated to rely on foreign manufacturers for a mere 5 percent of its products. Imports from China were at parity with US exports.[25]

That small amount seems like a fairy tale now, a snapshot from another planet where Americans still produced their own goods, Americans could buy their own products, and American corporate leaders proudly expressed their belief that the country would be better off because of it. Patriotic promises were pitted against the pressure for increased profits; the brutal drive to cut costs propelled Wal-Mart and many other US companies to seek low-wage workers outside America. By 2005, Wal-Mart relied on one foreign country for more than 70 percent of the items it sold. According to a PBS *Frontline* report, more than 80 percent of Wal-Mart's six thousand suppliers were based in China.[26] Wal-Mart, once hailed in the business press for its determination to help stem an erosion of American manufacturing and American jobs, had become China's eighth-largest trading partner. The company that Sam built was no longer a symbol of concerned stewardship of the American economy; it had become part of the problem. This became increasingly true after Sam Walton died in 1992 and the company faced sluggish sales and a dramatic drop in its stock price.[27] In its unending determination to drive down the price of goods, Wal-Mart, according to Charles Fishman in *Fast Company*, had not only forced American manufacturers to offshore their factories to low-wage countries, it also helped feed the American hunger for cheap goods.[28]

And it worked. Big time. Americans became drunk on cheap stuff. The seductive attraction to cheap *everything* distracted Americans from the reality of what was required to accomplish this—offshoring manufacturing to lower-wage destinations, which hastened the erosion of America's manufacturing base and its jobs. *We may not have a job, but at least we have a cheap flat-screen TV. We may not be able to afford healthcare, college, or a house, but our iPods are great.*

While Wal-Mart is an obvious example of a company that failed to practice what it originally preached, we don't intend to dwell here on the decisions of the world's largest retailer. Rather, we believe that Wal-Mart is symptomatic of a deeper reality that has put America at grave risk. Consider the vicious circle: Buyers put pressure on their suppliers to produce goods at lower prices. Those suppliers are compelled to open shop in China or Mexico or other low-wage locales. That offshoring drives down US wages, creating more pressure on consumers to buy cheap products. This increases exports from China and speeds the race to the bottom. The numbers show how precipitous the slide is: by 2008, the US trade deficit with China had escalated to $268 billion, and the overall imbalance in goods trading skyrocketed to $840 billion.[29]

We could have demanded that our elected officials provide leadership by shaping corporate tax policy and other incentives to encourage job-producing enterprises to stay in the United States. Yet these leaders hastened this departure by refusing to strengthen the competitiveness of troubled industries and enabling multinationals to offshore operations and cut their tax responsibilities. If they experienced any pangs of doubt, they could remind themselves that many of those same businesses did not forget them when they needed to finance their next election.

Where was the political leadership to say that adding a levy on the price of imported TVs, bicycles, computers, or even jeans might be good for America if it meant that American industries could still afford to hire American workers? Over the last two decades, politicians and economists alike have generally praised the benefits of globalization, emphasizing the classic adage that a rising tide lifts all boats. Economists have emphasized the idea that free trade provides mutual gains and an opportunity to benefit from innovation and higher-order work. But recent evidence undermines the comfortable certitude of this position.

While globalization has expanded opportunity throughout the world and established greater economic and cultural integration, it has hastened the decline of American economic preeminence and created alarming vulnerabilities in our economic and national security. The erosion of manufacturing jobs and evaporation of whole industrial sectors has not only propelled a growing number of workers into lower-wage service jobs, it has created growing dependence on foreign manufacturing and foreign suppliers for even highly sensitive military items such as smart bombs, naval radar systems, and night goggles.[30]

Ralph E. Gomory, a mathematician and economist and the president of the Alfred P. Sloan Foundation, hit the issue squarely when he testified before Congress in 2007. "In this new era of globalization, the interests of companies and countries have diverged," he said. "In contrast with the past, what is good for America's global corporations is no longer necessarily good for the American people [or] the American economy." Gomory, coauthor of the controversial book *Global Trade and Conflicting*

National Interest, came to Washington to stress the importance
of expanding science and technology education. He detailed the
conflicting values and questionable thinking that have widened
the growing split between national and business interests:
"Today, most companies emphasize, to the exclusion of nearly
everything else, corporate profitability and shareholder benefit.
By measuring themselves only on profit in a globalized world,
American companies may be able to succeed, but America the
nation and American workers cannot."

Gomory argued against proponents of free trade who rely on
the presumption of mutual gains even as productivity increases.
"There is nothing in either common sense or economic theory
which says that improvement in the productivity capabilities of
other countries is necessarily good for your country," he told the
House Committee on Science and Technology. "This observation
holds true even if these productivity shifts are brought about by
the free and unfettered actions of corporations. . . . For a long
time it was an article of faith that whenever a productivity shift
occurs the U.S. will automatically be certain to export unproductive low paying jobs, while our workers are moved up to
more productive, more highly paid positions—and for an equally
long time, this was, indeed, a reasonable description of the productivity shifts that the U.S. experienced." But "at some point
further development of the newly developing partner becomes
harmful to the more industrialized country."[31]

In other words, those firms with American-branded names,
secured by American-backed military, could reap greater profits
from their overseas operations without any attending benefits for
their home country. Consider the case of General Electric, surely
an American company by history and HQ. It generated a worldwide profit of $10.8 billion in 2009, yet, according to CNN, it
paid a whopping total of zero dollars in the United States because
its American operations tallied a loss.[32]

Is it any wonder that nearly every volume-minded manufacturing operation has felt pressured to move its operations over-

seas for low-wage workers? The economist's beloved notion of comparative advantage possesses diminishing value when emerging countries can offer foreign firms a seductive cocktail of low wages, rising productivity and skill, and massive incentives. The Chinese paid attention to the success of Ireland and other countries in attracting investment; they applied their state-controlled system to provide foreign firms with subsidized land and buildings, low-interest loans, and even fully funded R&D labs to minimize operational expenses. In the process, American firms have cut their costs and gotten access to the huge and growing Chinese consumer market. They've also gotten cheap access back into the American market. That may be good for the short-term bottom line, but, as Henry Ford understood in 1914 when he instituted $5-a-day wages for workers, it's only good as long as Americans still have income to buy those goods.

The alarm bell has been ringing, even in some unlikely quarters. Princeton economist Alan Blinder, a self-described free trader "down to his toes," estimated in 2007 that as many as thirty to forty million service jobs could be outsourced to India, China, or elsewhere in the coming decades. This transition, he said, will be "large, lengthy and painful" for "millions of white-collar workers who thought they were immune to foreign competition," made worse by "a poor social safety net to cushion the blow for displaced workers." His prediction earned him the titles of "heretic" and "apostate" by some of his fellow economists.[33]

Back in 1994, British businessman Sir James Goldsmith testified before Congress on free trade policy and the ruthless pursuit of profit: "So if . . . you have freedom of movement of capital, freedom of movement of technology, and you can employ people forty or fifty times cheaper, who are skilled, and you can import their products back anywhere in the world, that is the basis of global free trade. How can those investments, how can these transnational companies who have $4.8 trillion of sales invest anywhere other than where it is cheapest and where their return is greatest?"[34] Patriotism, in other words, once a matter of honor, becomes hopelessly antiquated among increasingly place-less and restless global players. But here's where businessman Goldsmith meets citizen Goldsmith: "I believe that when you get to a system whereby to get the best corporate profits, you have to leave your own country, you have to say to your own sales force, 'Goodbye, we cannot use you anymore, you are too expensive, you have got unions, you want holidays, you want protection, so we are going offshore,' you destroy your own nation. This is the real short-term investment, because that is like making a profit on the deck of the *Titanic* playing cards, and in a clever, as opposed to a wise way."[35]

That's where government must come in—political leaders who talk straight to the American people and explain why the country must take tough steps to secure its long-term future. This will take sacrifice, they would say. The price of some cheap goods may go up. The country may face enhanced strife with some of our trading partners who've grown accustomed to our open markets. But free trade has done us harm, and free markets are a myth. Our competitors around the world have grown stronger while we have clung to outmoded and wrongheaded ideas about the role of government in the economy. Yes, we made a mistake. We forgot about our history. We believed that we could sustain preeminence just because we are Americans. We forgot that our economic success required active political leadership and sustained government commitment. But it's not too late to get back on our feet and fix it. We must have the courage to look honestly, act boldly, and put America first, even when it's hard. A great nation demands no less.

Of course, we don't kid ourselves about the level of courage, honesty, and openness that defines the current political environment. Nor would we suggest that this approach has often led to victory. When Fritz Hollings ran for president in 1983, he imagined that he could ride a wave of honesty straight to the White House. "In the last few years, we have stalled, lost our unity, lost our purpose, and stopped pulling together for the common good," he said when he launched his campaign. He talked about rising deficits, burgeoning unemployment, reckless defense spending, and the need for fiscal discipline and sacrifice. Unable to raise enough money with his centrist message, Hollings pulled out of the Iowa caucuses and tallied 4 percent in New Hampshire before ending his race.[36]

Hollings lost that battle, but nearly three decades later he's still fighting the war. "We properly tried to spread capitalism in the Marshall Plan, but in doing so we've given away the store. And we've still got the Marshall Plan going," he told us with a laugh. "We act like we're in charge. The Chinese are in charge of international trade and the economy. They've taken us to the cleaners."[37]

America has been hurt by failing to take concrete steps that would reassert the country's commitment to domestic production amid intensified global competition. We do not believe that most of the jobs that have left America will be returning—and that's why we will explore in the next chapter the critical role of innovation in securing the country's future competitiveness and economic security. But there are initiatives that can help, without erecting major trade barriers. This includes reducing the corporate tax, which at about 35 percent is among the highest in the world and nearly double the international average of 18 percent; that only intensifies the impulse to pursue lower tax options offshore. A corporate tax rate of 15 percent can be a magnet for investment and an incentive to keep jobs here. And it should be treated like a flat tax. No games. No deductions. A plan must also include increasing support for R&D at the federal and state levels and provide tax breaks for companies that boost investment in R&D and related capital investments. Yet such steps cannot replace the need for a more comprehensive look at the country's tax structure and economic goals, not only to raise revenues to address the nation's mounting debt but also to strengthen its competitive position globally. We cannot turn back the clock, but we can act like adults to create the conditions that will reinvigorate the country's creative drive. America was the birth of a grand experiment; we cannot lose our capacity for risk taking and experimentation now.

Chapter 9

Have We Lost Our Edge for Innovation?

Roger Angel plays with fire. As the founder of the Mirror Laboratory at the University of Arizona's Steward Observatory and one of the world's leading astronomers, he often can be found in a laboratory under the school's football stadium. There, employing a two-hundred-ton rotating furnace fired at temperatures that exceed 1,100 degrees Celsius, his team of scientists and engineers transforms molten glass into highly complex and extraordinarily fine optics for telescopes. Angel's inventive designs for some of the world's largest telescopes are expanding our ability to gaze at stars and possibly identify life-bearing planets in distant galaxies. His design for the Giant Magellan Telescope, created with seven huge mirrors arranged like the petals of a daisy, will use advanced adaptive optics to capture images that are ten times sharper than those from the Hubble Space Telescope. The largest in the world when it comes online, the telescope will rely on computers to make a thousand adjustments to the mirrors every second to eliminate most of the atmospheric blurring.

This has been Professor Angel's passion and his life's work.

But in recent years Angel, trained at Oxford and drawn to Tucson in 1973 by the clear desert sky, began to feel like he was looking in the wrong direction. At his wife's urging and with his own deepening fear of disaster caused by global warming, the London-born astronomer shifted his sights from the sky to the earth. It was time, he decided, to apply his mind and employ his skill to help save the planet.

Professor Angel, a 1996 recipient of a MacArthur Foundation "genius" grant, has never been reluctant to take risks in his work. Nor is he the kind of guy who's afraid to chase a wild idea if it can lead to a dramatic, game-changing solution. Exhibit A: constructing a giant sunshade to deflect the sun's impact, which Angel realized would cost trillions and represented a last-chance response to global warming. Exhibit B: sending some six hundred satellites up in geosynchronous orbit around Earth to collect sunlight twenty-four hours a day, convert it to microwaves, and beam the energy back to Earth. This approach to cut carbon emissions would produce three thousand gigawatts of electrical energy, Angel estimated, but it would also prove enormously costly to launch. (People at NASA, he admitted to a gathering at MIT, thought the idea was "stupid."[1]) So Angel found an alternate ground-based solution, one that draws on his natural impulse to pursue big answers—even if it requires facing skeptical funding sources more accustomed to proposals that tweak existing systems. As Angel told us, "I'm not fixing one piece in the supply chain. I'm changing the whole chain."[2]

Angel's idea, drawing on his experience with optics, involves concentrating solar rays that are a thousand times brighter than natural sunlight with the use of specially designed reflective mirrors. The concentrated energy then passes through a glass sphere onto photovoltaic cells that are twice as efficient as traditional ones. If Angel's prototype works as expected, its mass-produced cost matches or betters the $1 price per kilowatt for fossil fuel–based electricity. Angel calculates that a hundred-square-mile area can produce enough electricity to power the entire nation.

If he's right, Angel and his newly formed company could provide a transformative technology to cut the use of fossil fuels. If he's right, Angel and his partners will have demonstrated how a sense of urgency, brains, and hard work, combined with the desire to step out of one's comfort zone and tackle big problems, can help change the world. Sitting in his office cluttered with papers and books, Angel clutches an example of the exquisitely designed glass ball through which concentrated sunlight will beam. He describes his approach to problems, drawing on his background as an astronomer. "What I've learned in my career is more of a systems approach," he explains. "There's no single magic bullet that's going to solve the problem. But when you are trying to make a better telescope than anyone's ever made in the world, you don't do it by tweaking an existing one. You think of a new architecture."[3]

We see Roger Angel's solar project as exactly the kind of bold, paradigm-shifting work that government policy and programs must support to help spawn new industries and products, tackle the major challenges that our globe faces, and compete successfully against nations that are ramping up their investment in R&D and raising the quality of their K–12 and university education. It's the reason why Science Foundation Arizona invested $2 million to help finance the early stages of Angel's project, a critical combination of two universities, private industry, and state and federal funding.

Put another way, Science Foundation bet on Professor Angel to help release his creativity. We believed it was a solid bet because of his track record of innovation in astronomy, the quality of his university partners, and his urgent desire to find a solution to cut carbon emissions and US dependence on fossil fuels. His success will be good for Arizona, where he is launching a new company among a growing collection of solar-related firms, and it will be good for the country.

Big problems require big and imaginative responses. President Eisenhower made the judgment after the launch of Sputnik in

1958 that the country could not risk losing its technological superiority, so he expanded funding for basic research and math and science education. The Defense Advanced Research Projects Agency (DARPA), formed within the Defense Department and originally known as ARPA, communicated America's fresh commitment to world-class science and engineering. Even after the spinoff of NASA in the first year, ARPA pursued high-risk R&D and new technologies that had the potential for big payoffs with disruptive capabilities. As much as this focused on military weapons and systems, the federally funded research spurred breakthroughs with technologically advanced applications far beyond defense, including work with time-sharing computers, microprocessors, parallel computing and programming, and the evolution of the Internet.[4] This investment seeded work (and high-paying jobs) at IBM, Intel, HP, and other leading tech companies such as Microsoft and Dell.

Eisenhower's strategic leadership to a perceived existential threat laid the foundation for industries and companies that are still changing everyday life more than half a century later. Would there be Google or Amazon, YouTube or Facebook without Sputnik and DARPA? Highly unlikely. Eisenhower, rather than choosing a shortsighted and potentially lethal response to the initial hysteria sparked that October night, pursued an uncertain yet promising path of innovation instead. It's a lesson for us today.

Clearly, Eisenhower benefited from a shared sense of urgency, just as President Kennedy did when he proposed his massively expensive and highly risky mission to the moon. The threat was both existential and originating from a well-defined source. But it's worth pausing to ask: Have we drifted so far from a shared sense of the dominant threats that we face today, or is the bigger dilemma that we have lost the ability to find solutions about which we can agree?

Identifying innovation as crucial to America's future can sound like a mere platitude. Don't we all support creativity and educational excellence, new products and industries, more high-paying jobs, and efforts to answer to some of our most vexing problems? How hard can it be to find common agreement about innovation's importance? As a report from the Organisation for Economic Co-operation and Development put it, "Much of the rise in living standards is due to innovation—this has been the case since the Industrial Revolution. Today, innovative performance is a crucial factor in determining competitiveness and national progress. Moreover, innovation is important to help address global challenges, such as climate change and sustainable development."[5] Does anyone doubt that innovation is critical to the nation's economic prosperity?

So while innovation may comfortably join the list alongside Mom and apple pie as a value that we all believe in, it's at risk of becoming a mere slogan, a relaxing buzzword that comforts us with the soothing notion that everything's fine. Yet just like the gleaming superhighways that have fallen into disrepair, America's path to innovation has begun to look slipshod, in need of fresh attention. America's reliable position as the global innovation leader has grown precarious, hastened by the rising intensity of emerging nations, a failure to implement a coherent and strategic national policy, limited state policies that lean too heavily on federal R&D support, and corporate-funded R&D that is overly focused on short-range results or heading offshore. Once again, we face the uneasy reality that the United States has rested on its laurels and grown complacent with its presumed preeminence.

In fact, a growing body of evidence suggests that America's status as an innovation leader is slipping. A 2009 study by the Information Technology and Innovation Foundation (ITIF) ranked the United States sixth out of forty leading industrialized nations in innovative competitiveness and "dead last" in improvements over the last decade in such metrics as innovation capacity, entrepreneurship, IT infrastructure, economic policy, and economic performance.[6] Dead last. That's *fortieth out of forty*. And even if this judgment were too harsh or otherwise exaggerated, it's a tear in the armor of self-satisfaction, an uncomfortable counterpoint to unwavering assertions that we are the world's innovation leader. How did this happen? Consider this from Stephen Ezell, a senior analyst for the ITIF. This performance "is a direct reflection both of other countries' articulation and aggressive implementation of national innovation strategies, and the United States' corresponding lack thereof," he wrote. "And while the United States remains near the top of the world's most innovative countries, it remains so based primarily on residual innovation strengths, not new capabilities it has assembled over the past decade."[7]

Other analyses confirm the slippage. In one assessment of R&D investment as a percentage of GDP, what is known as "R&D intensity," the United States ranked seventh behind such countries as Japan, South Korea, Finland, and Sweden. In a 2006 study that benchmarked innovation, the United States ranked a startling twenty-second in the amount of investment as a percentage of GDP focused on nondefense research.[8] That report's basic theme: US industries are not benefiting from national strategies and coordinated partnerships in the way that many foreign-based corporations are. To be fair, total US money spent on R&D still represents a third of the world's share, with an estimated $402 billion in 2010, essentially the same as Asia and nearly double that of Europe.[9] Nonetheless, since the mid-1990s, the US share of world R&D investment has been falling, largely the result of a drop in federal investment to levels well below its 3.5 percent average annual growth between 1953 and 2004.[10]

Of course, the issue is not just throwing dollars at the problem. It's connecting with the smart and talented; building teams that cut across disciplines to solve complex problems; creating strategic partnerships that link public and private interests; facilitating knowledge transfers and speeding up the patent process; developing organizations and policies that encourage speed and flexibility; and ensuring that the support reaches to a state and local level, where the work is really happening. And it means reawakening a sense of urgency and commitment to strong, decisive action.

Our growth as a nation of innovation has been fueled by bold policy decisions, not ad hoc policies geared to finding quick fixes for the budget crisis of the moment. It's worth recalling that the United States led the world in education for a long, long time. This happened because the country initiated mandatory education through high school in the first decade of the twentieth century to support growth and cultivate the talent that industry needed. By mid-century, the GI Bill not only helped build a stable middle class, it democratized our universities. In a relatively short period, nearly 25 percent of our population obtained college degrees—far beyond the number of college grads in the rest of the world, where only a small percentage even held high school degrees.[11] This created a unique "knowledge advantage," a fact that we did not celebrate or fully appreciate as a nation. These days it's as if we no longer care what it took to achieve these successes—or refuse to acknowledge the changed competitive landscape.

According to Adrian Slywotzky in *Businessweek*, Bell Labs, long one of the crown jewels in the corporate research world, has pared away its basic research to focus on more short-term commercial targets. The storied lab, buoyed by a virtual monopoly and relatively predictable profits from its corporate parent, Bell Telephone, provided a brilliant picture of scientific achievement: the invention of the transistor in 1947, the invention of the photovoltaic cell in 1954, the creation of the UNIX operating system in 1969, the development of cellular telephone technology in 1978, and six Nobel prizes for work that originated from its scientists (including Steven Chu, the Obama administration's Department of Energy secretary).[12]

By 2009, though, a downsized, more narrowly focused Bell Labs offered a quite different vision, what Slywotzky said was emblematic of a broken link in the business model. "With upstream invention and discovery drying up, downstream, industry-creating innovation is being reduced to a trickle," he wrote, adding an ominous observation about the need for new industries to spur job creation. "The effects of the massive scaling back of American science and engineering research in the 1990s and 2000s may just be beginning. Unless reversed, it is likely to have its greatest impact a decade from now, when the missing discoveries of a generation earlier would have been expected to come to commercial fruition."[13]

Jeong Kim, president of the current Alcatel-Lucent Bell Labs, was clearly stung by the criticism of Bell Labs. In a response to *Businessweek*, he questioned the article's notion that Bell Labs is gone—staff cuts were not as deep as suggested, he insisted. Kim defended the Bell Labs of today by emphasizing the increasingly interconnected nature of R&D. "No longer are there monolithic research organizations that do everything," he wrote. "Increasingly a model for research organizations, one that Bell Labs researchers exemplify, is based on a collaborative ethos that is increasingly global, increasingly open to partnerships with universities, government, and other institutions, and more responsive to the needs of industry."[14]

Bell Labs may indeed be following the widening reliance by corporations on outside collaboration. As corporate R&D has become more narrowly focused, the role of government investment has grown more important. Researchers Fred Block and Matthew R. Keller documented the trend by analyzing award-winning innovations cited in *R&D Magazine* between 1970 and 2006. What they discovered was a seismic shift: While large firms were solely responsible for 80 percent of the innovations in 1970, two decades later a majority of the innovations depended on collaborations between government agencies, federal laboratories, research universities, and private firms. By 2006, seventy-seven of the eighty-eight innovation awards had received government support.[15]

While private industry is playing a less central role in American innovation, US corporations also are increasingly spreading their bets on innovative research work in other countries. In 2008, former Intel chairman Craig Barrett told a conference that Intel splits its venture capital investments in half between the United States and Asia, a far cry from when 90 percent of the processor maker's venture capital money was focused in America. "Anyone in the audience from the United States who says that the Chinese or Indians are not entrepreneurial, not creative, that they don't want to rival the United States in business startups, has not been to India or China," Barrett said.[16] He was one of about five hundred business, government, and academic leaders assembled in Washington, DC, to review the impact of a 2005 National Academies report, *Rising above the Gathering Storm*, which focused on K–12 math and science education, science and engineering research, science and engineering higher education, and other incentives for innovation.

Norman Augustine, the former chairman and CEO of defense contractor Lockheed Martin and chair of the group that wrote the report, came bearing news. "A number of significant events have taken place since 'Gathering Storm' was released," he told the crowd.[17] Yet Augustine, who prides himself on his world trekking —dog sledding in the Arctic, exploring volcanoes in Antarctica, snorkeling on the Great Barrier Reef—explained that the progress was primarily happening in other countries. Foreign governments are expanding support for science and engineering research, enhancing science and math education, and investing in higher education. As for the United States? "It would be a cruel outcome if the 'Gathering Storm' report were to motivate others to become more competitive while we did little," Augustine said.[18]

Cruel indeed. But is it inevitable?

While the United States resists strategic national policy, global competitors are advancing, determined to eat our lunch. A United Nations investment report estimates that more than 21,500 multinationals are based in the emerging world. Adrian Woolridge, writing for the *Economist*, argued that emerging countries are becoming "hotbeds of business innovation," experimenting in everything from new and cheaper products and services, to new systems of production and distribution, to altogether new business models. Woolridge noted that Fortune 500 companies are aggressively exploiting this growing dynamism, operating ninety-eight R&D facilities in China and sixty-three in India as of 2010. And the major players are not just dipping their toes, Woolridge reported: General Electric's healthcare research center in Bangalore is its largest in the world; Cisco is spending more than $1 billion for a second headquarters, also in Bangalore; and Microsoft's R&D facility in Beijing is second only to its HQ in Redmond, Washington.[19]

No big surprise here. Gone are the days when old-school arguments of patriotism and the value of "made in America" held sway. As we've noted, more and more United States–based R&D is moving offshore, taking advantage of state-funded incentives offered in China and other locales for facilities and staff, seeking proximity to the production process, developing products specifically geared to that local market, relying on an emerging class of trained researchers and well-funded universities, and even collecting new ideas on innovation from the on-the-ground realities of emerging markets.

In the case of China, this is all according to plan—a fifteen-year plan launched in 2006, in fact, pithily titled "Medium to Long-Term Plan for the Development of Science and Technology." This state plan aims to clearly and expeditiously orchestrate China's drive to become an "innovation-oriented society" by 2020, developing capabilities for "indigenous innovation" by 2020 and being a leader in science and technology by 2050. By the end of the fifteen years, the plan calls for R&D investment to nearly double to 2.5 percent of GDP and to limit reliance on foreign technology to 30 percent. As researchers for *Physics Today* explain it, the plan addresses Chinese leaders' recognition that they can no longer rely on a "market for technology" growth strategy used over the last several decades, which lured foreign firms with the promise of market access in exchange for technology transfers (an approach which has in recent years flouted World Trade Organization regulations). The Chinese have used this strategy not only to expand their knowledge base and capacity for producing higher-value goods, but also to modernize their military hardware.[20]

Whether the Chinese are capable of hitting their marks on schedule, they've clearly got a plan. And, at a time when the momentum for innovation heads offshore, where goes America? We may oppose state-controlled capitalism, but that doesn't mean we should ignore how the Chinese are marching toward world leadership—unencumbered by the tragic whimsy of a US political system in which funding can be axed for purely partisan purposes and herk-a-jerk election cycles make strategic long-term planning nearly impossible. Added to this unhappy picture is a cynical electorate unmoved by the risks of inaction and unconvinced that politicians are able to transcend partisan differences for the common good.

The harsh recession that began in 2008 offered a teachable moment to emphasize the importance of public-private partnerships throughout US history. Beyond bailing out troubled financial firms and automakers to help rescue a deeply troubled economy, this was a chance to shape the public's commitment to innovation and economic development. It's not that President Obama hasn't tried. In a report presenting a national innovation strategy, he described the links among job growth, education, and innovation—and backed this up with a long list of proposals, many of which were contained within the 2009 American Recovery and Reinvestment Act. This included proposals to expand federal R&D funding by $18.3 billion to 3 percent of GDP; double the R&D budgets of the National Science Foundation and several other federal science agencies; make the "research and experimentation" tax credit permanent to provide businesses additional incentive; invest in improving the nation's infrastructure (roads, bridges, the electric grid, broadband access, high-speed trains); and provide support for clean energy solutions.[21] The president also announced in 2009 a campaign to increase student literacy in science, technology, engineering, and math called "Educate to Innovate," backed by more than $4 billion in federal grants to schools and $260 million from private firms. "We are going to show young people how cool science can be," he said, then watched a robot built by high school inventors that was capable of scooping up and tossing moon rocks.[22]

These were meaningful commitments, and only a tiny sampling of the huge handful of ambitious ideas offered in the president's innovation agenda. Yet rather than creating a stirring narrative to rally the nation, they have been drowned out by partisan bickering that typically stops the conversation before it gains traction. Consider the America COMPETES Act, originally passed in 2007 by unanimous consent in the House as part of President Bush's competitiveness initiatives to fund science and technology agencies, including the National Science Foundation, the National Institute of Standards and Technology, and the Department of Energy's Office of Science. In 2010, the bill was up for reauthorization; its intent was simply stated by Bart Gordon (D-TN), chairman of the House Science and Technology Committee: "Research leads to innovation; innovation leads to economic development and good paying jobs. Creating good jobs is the goal of this bill, and it is what our country needs right now."[23]

Yet that message didn't get through: Despite endorsements by more than 750 organizations from across the political spectrum, the previously bipartisan legislation was voted down multiple times by the Republicans, even after its price tag was nearly cut in half and its time frame reduced from five years to three. How did this happen? Without detailing here all the arcane legislative maneuvering used to complicate the process, one of its opponents inserted an antipornography amendment cracking down on federal workers found viewing pornography on their office computers. Democrats agreed to the provision even though the bill then required a two-thirds majority to pass because they feared voting against an antiporn measure would be used against them come election time. It's the kind of political game playing that has the rancid air of leaders fiddling while Rome burns.

The net effect of this sad dithering may not be felt right away. But imagine for a moment if we are looking back at 2011 in 2030. We may describe these years as a signal moment when the country did not grasp the stakes of inaction and the promise of innovative new industries never materialized. We may well remember this as a poisonous political period that hastened the move of R&D offshore, triggered the decline of government support in spurring game-changing innovations, and enshrined 2011 as a milestone in the permanent decline of jobs and real wages. Rather than the moment when the country came together to support an innovation agenda and spur long-term growth, this may be remembered as the era when the momentum for innovation finally departed from the shores of America forever.

As disturbing as the current climate is, it's far from the first time we've had to lay down a marker and assert what's important. In the mid-1980s, when one of the authors, Harris, was part of the National Science Foundation's chemistry division, President Reagan was discussing eliminating NSF from the budget. In 1987, Harris was asked by then NSF director Erich Bloch to direct a newly forming program of Science and Technology Research Centers. This followed a turnaround by President Reagan, who was persuaded by Bloch to nearly double funding at the NSF.[24] Reagan got the message that this could be a keystone for building the country's economic competitiveness, and he announced his commitment to basic research and the new centers at his State of the Union in 1987. "How well prepared are we to enter the 21st century?" he asked Congress. "In my lifetime, America set the standard for the world. It is now time to determine that we should enter the next century having achieved a level of excellence unsurpassed in history. We will achieve this, first, by guaranteeing that government does everything possible to promote America's ability to compete. . . . The Congress will soon receive my comprehensive proposals to enhance our competitiveness, including new science and technology centers and strong new funding for basic research."[25] (The antigovernment president had spoken: government should do everything possible to promote America's ability to compete. Should it be any different today?)

These centers were unique, specifically designed to support university-based research in science and technology that cut across disciplines at a time when academics were discouraged from stepping outside their own fields. The science and engineering projects were expected to spur transfers of knowledge, taking advantage of strategic partnerships between universities and industry. The first centers received as much as $4.3 million in the first year, with the possibility of grants continuing for as long as eleven years. But the investment went well beyond dollars; in some cases, it represented the critical support needed to launch a researcher's project and, more important, transform the trajectory of his or her career.

Leroy Hood, a now legendary inventor and scientific entrepreneur, was one of the program's first recipients. His biotechnology center, based at the California Institute of Technology, was one of eleven Science and Technology Centers (STC) chosen from a flood of 323 applications. Its stated purpose—to create new possibilities for understanding, diagnosing, and treating diseases at a molecular level—involved bringing together disparate researchers to create new techniques and technologies in genetic engineering, protein chemistry, and data analysis. The center was granted $4 million in its first year.

This was by Hood's own description "the most catalytic and transformational" funding he ever received, a chance to pursue big science and systems-level thinking at a time when purists in university biology were urging him to put aside his interest in technology and engineering. This from a scientist who invented the automated gene sequencer, which enabled the Human Genome Project, and who is a cofounder of more than a dozen biotech companies. Among them are Amgen and Applied Biosystems, which alone employ more than fifty thousand people with market capitalization exceeding $100 billion. "The STC program got me thinking about cross-discipline environments, about strategic partnerships, about K–12 science education, and about systems approaches to things," Hood told us. "Would I have ended up in the same place without the STC? Maybe the answer is yes, but, boy, I think it would have been delayed by a long period of time, if in fact I ever got there. There are certain critical points in your career where you either gel and take on these things or you end up getting stuck with what you have done in the past."[26]

If innovation is defined by the creative work that takes place in the lab, its ultimate fulfillment also depends on the imagination and drive to communicate an idea that connects with funders, however long it may take to build those relationships. By that measure of creativity + communication + drive, Leroy Hood embodies one of innovation's premier achievers. In 1992, backed by Microsoft's Bill Gates, Hood left Caltech to create the cross-disciplinary Department of Molecular Biotechnology at the University of Washington in Seattle. In 2000, he launched the pioneering nonprofit Institute for Systems Biology. His success makes it looks easy. But Hood, who has been called the father of biotechnology, has a remarkable capacity to keep pushing forward no matter how often he hears the word "no." That was true in the late 1970s when nineteen instrument companies rejected his commercializing vision for how instruments would transform biology, and it remains true now as he pushes to expand the boundaries of his integrated systems approach. His latest idea aims at nothing less than revolutionizing medicine—to enable physicians to predict a person's predisposition for disease based on his or her genetic makeup and employ their knowledge of defective genes to block the harmful effects.

Given Hood's track record, you might expect that US financing sources would be falling over themselves to back his work. Yet he has traveled the globe to find a home for a new institute for systems biology, pursuing funding prospects from Israel, Ireland, Canada, and Korea, in addition to seven major universities. Eventually, a friend at the accounting firm PricewaterhouseCoopers mentioned that the Grand Duchy of Luxembourg wanted to diversify beyond financial services and was interested in getting into biotech and medicine. In a matter of weeks, Hood landed a five-year, $100 million-per-year commitment from the tiny European country with the promise of building strategic partnerships and spinoff companies that may expand the global nature of medicine. In the end, all Americans may benefit from Hood's energetic global effort and cultural exchange. But it's remarkable that at a time when innovations were so central to the nation's future, public resources were not available to keep Hood at home.

Perhaps we shouldn't be surprised. Americans are drawn to tales of the lone tinkerer working in his garage or lab or basement—Alexander Graham Bell, Thomas Alva Edison, Henry Ford, Steve Jobs, and Steve Wozniak, just to name a few. They exemplify the up-by-the-bootstraps vision of the American Dream, where a combination of hunger, imagination, and elbow grease can reap remarkable rewards. This image of a singular inventor feeds our cherished belief that one man or woman can truly make a difference, and it has legitimately inspired generations of innovative and entrepreneurially minded students to take seriously the idea of a career in math, science, engineering, or design. It also connects with free market devotees convinced that this independent and distinctly American path should not be undermined by government intrusion. Yet at a time of intensifying global competitiveness, resistance to coordinated federal and state support for innovators can only further slow American innovation's momentum.

Perhaps the relationship between discovery and policy will always be fractious, an inevitable tension between the creative high-wire act of invention and the hard mechanics of policy making that depends on the promise of tangible results. More ominously, as rich as America's frontier-expanding history is, we may have reached a point where our leaders and citizenry are losing their collective ability to pursue big missions. We hope that's not true and remain buoyed by the fact that the greatest triumphs may always depend on the unexpected imagination of individuals who refuse to limit their thinking.

We began this chapter with the potentially transformative solar energy project of Roger Angel; his unconventional solar work made it tough to land funding from such federal agencies as the Department of Energy or the National Science Foundation. In the early days of federal funding for science after Sputnik, America was unique in the world for its bold support of young researchers with strong ideas and great potential. That risk taking has grown less common, tempered by a conservative peer-review system and large, centralized federal agencies that are more disconnected from researchers. This may be the inevitable outcome of a nation that has more than doubled in size and now exceeds three hundred million people. But these are not times for complacency or conservative research, which is why Harris and Science Foundation Arizona's board believed it was critical to back Angel's bold ideas. We believe that every state should have in place a strategic research entity to make smarter use of federal funding and more effectively connect research and industry at the local level. That will depend on an intensified national focus on the role of innovation and R&D and, as we will see, require rebuilding a healthy relationship between the federal government and individual states.

Chapter 10

Will Our States Be Part of the Solution?

Holmes County is one of the poorest counties in Mississippi, the poorest state in the country. Sumter County is one of the poorest counties in neighboring Alabama. Both counties are part of the Southern region known as the Black Belt, originally a reference to the rich dark soil in parts of Alabama and Mississippi and gradually broadened to include a crescent of Deep South land from Virginia to Texas defined by predominantly black populations, persistent poverty, and a history of slavery and slave plantation agriculture.

Still today, Holmes and Sumter struggle with per capita income barely half the national average and a third of their residents living below the poverty line. Still today, not everyone enjoys the most basic standards we expect in America, including indoor toilets and running water. To no one's surprise, both counties faced dwindling populations between 2000 and 2009, increasingly unable to provide gainful employment. The Sumter County town of Emelle is practically a ghost town now, population 31—the inevitable misfortune of harboring the nation's largest toxic waste dump and an ongoing environmental danger.

Several decades ago in 1987, while reporting for the *Virginian Pilot*, one of the authors, Beschloss, visited these two counties and a dozen Southern states to understand why some places were thriving as others were falling behind, indeed why some were at risk of disappearing forever. At the time, the media was full of reports about the economic boom in Sun Belt states—stories that offered welcome relief from the grim tales of the Midwestern Rust Belt. But this coverage typically missed the growing disparity between urban and rural areas and the concentration of growth in a limited number of states and urban areas. At the beginning, Beschloss expected to focus on the decline of manufacturing as companies that headed south for cheap labor were again on the move for lower-wage options overseas. He knew he would document prospering locales like Atlanta and North Carolina's Research Triangle, where forward-thinking leaders focused on improving schools, enhancing infrastructure, building partnerships, and creating a business-friendly climate to attract investment. But what he didn't anticipate was how central a role racial attitudes and resistance to federal authority played in identifying which communities were trapped by the past and destined for failure. It was a wake-up call when he met local leaders who were unrepentant and unconcerned about how their decisions were hastening the downward spiral of their communities' fortunes. Today, as we face growing tension between the federal government and increasingly vocal advocates for expanding states' rights, Holmes and Sumter counties offer a warning sign. We are at a fork in the road. Will we engage the future or be trapped by ideology that limits opportunity?

More than fifty years ago, Holmes and Sumter angrily opposed school desegregation efforts by the federal courts. As in so many other counties in their region, the white leadership resisted *Brown v. Board of Education* in 1954 by treating the Supreme Court's direction to proceed "with all deliberate speed" as a ticket to drag their feet. Even after Alabama federal judge Frank Johnson passed a desegregation order in 1964, many were emboldened by Alabama governor George C. Wallace, who responded with his infamous "Segregation, today. Segregation, tomorrow. Segregation, forever." As federal pressure mounted, local whites took matters into their own hands, setting up private white academies and abandoning the public schools.

More than four decades later, little has changed: whites attend the private schools and blacks represent virtually 100 percent of the public school population. Not only has that led to underfunding of the public schools, it also created an antagonistic environment that severely undermined their ability to attract outside investment and advance economically. "Those federal court decisions were intolerable," said a local attorney who, ironically, was also the chair of Sumter's industrial development board. "After [Judge] Frank Johnson committed his ignoble act, we said to him, 'The hell with you. We'll set up our own school.'" They did all right, ensuring that blacks *and* whites suffered the consequences ever after. "We have a lot of advantages, but who can get past our disadvantages?" admitted one local businessman. "Our internal problems are tearing us apart." Another local sagely summarized the enduring conflict like this: "As long as he's got his boot on my neck, he can't move either."[1] His focus, while local, neatly defines the predicament in national politics: the "can-do" spirit has been replaced by pride in checkmating the adversary, even when both parties suffer.

Nearly a century and a half after the end of the Civil War, in which eleven states seceded from the Union, extreme talk of states' rights has been bubbling up again with a new fervor. What has long been considered anti-American—in fact, taboo—is now dancing dangerously along the edges and into the mainstream. In 2009, Texas governor Rick Perry refused to reject the idea of secession at an April 2009 antitax protest in Austin. "We've got a great Union," he told reporters. "There's absolutely no reason to dissolve it. But if Washington continues to thumb their nose at the American people, who knows what may come of that?"[2]

Nothing more than a cynical ploy to curry favor with the

state's more extreme elements? Perhaps. But a week earlier, Perry stood alongside Texas state legislators, proudly praising a states' rights resolution asserting Texas sovereignty under the Tenth Amendment of the US Constitution over all powers not specifically granted to the federal government. "I believe that our federal government has become oppressive in its size, its intrusion into the lives of our citizens, and its interference with the affairs of our state," Perry said.[3] According to the *New York Times*, more than thirty states passed so-called sovereignty resolutions that interpreted the Tenth Amendment to mean the right of state control in any instance when the Constitution does not expressly grant that power to the federal government. Conservative advocates in four states—Alaska, Idaho, North Dakota, and South Dakota—pushed full measures through their legislatures that underscored their anger at perceived federal overreach. More extreme resolutions asserted that US leaders were engaging in criminal behavior, but there was surely a limit to their scorn; few state leaders were willing to declare that their states should give back their share of the $787 million federal stimulus money.[4]

This deepening tension between the states and federal authority, while always a part of the American dynamic and a reminder of the Constitution's vibrancy, is gathering strength and taking on a darker hue as state legislators struggle with budget deficits not seen since the Great Depression and confront the threat of bankruptcy. Amid the rhetoric of freedom, patriotism, and tyranny, combined with wild talk of secession and nullification, we can understand the deep frustration with a world that appears to be flying out of control. The proponents of the measure are clearly people who are determined to take action and no longer trust the feds to make the right moves. But this divisive road must always be traveled with great caution; after all, the Tenth Amendment provided the constitutional basis employed by states to justify slavery, and then, a century later, oppose the civil rights movement to end racial segregation and voting discrimination. In a scan of the states' current predicament, as the jangle of economic and political interests battles over a shrinking pie, it's hard to imagination how this heated mind-set will soon grow calmer.

Still, at a time of killer deficits and rising distress, we should demand that reason prevail. At its most basic, we should expect that recession-saddled state leaders will focus on the cuts and changes (spending and policy decisions) that can bring their states' budgets back into balance and support economic development. Ideally, a time of crisis represents a moment to clarify what matters most—to define the set of values that are critical to the progress and prosperity of a state. Surely this should be the time to transcend self-interest and ideology to serve the best interests of the state, to ensure that its economic wellbeing is served as the state's finances are put in order. And we believe that in a moment of crisis, strategic thinking that is not simply ad hoc and short term is especially crucial.

Easier said than done, of course. Arizona offers an unusually strong example of a legislative hothouse invigorated by the emergence of the Tea Party and its history of libertarianism. As the state struggled with more than $3 billion in deficits—responding with massive cuts in education and social services, reductions in healthcare for poor children, closing of state parks and highway rest stops, selling off state buildings,[5] and raising the sales tax to generate additional revenue—the more extreme legislators saw their chance to play a winning hand. State senator Russell Pearce, a Republican from the Phoenix-area town of Mesa and a former deputy sheriff, had been trying for years to push through harsh illegal immigration bills before he finally succeeded in 2010 with the controversial SB 1070, which requires police to check suspected undocumented immigrants and arrest them if they lack proof of legal status. By his own description, Pearce had been advocating legislation that would be so unpleasant that illegals would "self-deport."[6] His cause was strengthened by the failure of federal policy to take responsibility for immigration reform—more than a decade of foot dragging.

Pearce, who takes inspiration from a painting of John Wayne

he keeps in his home, has been determined to change the dynamic in the state.[7] He and others have complained harshly about a rise in immigrant-related violent crime, exacerbated by the increasingly violent drug cartels south of the border. In fact, while Pearce and others talk of an alarming rise in kidnappings, killings, and even beheadings, FBI data from local police agencies show that crime rates in the state's border towns have remained essentially flat and that violent crime rates statewide have fallen.[8] What is sure is that Arizona, much like its neighboring border states, has seen a dramatic increase in its foreign-born population—more than tripling to 933,000 in the two decades since 1990 and primarily from Mexico. Arizona's southern neighbor is more than a source of immigration, both legal and illegal: it's also the Grand Canyon State's major trading partner, a source for nearly $6 billion in exports in 2008 alone.[9]

But enriching ties with Mexico was the last thing on Pearce's mind. In 2008, before Obama's election or the emergence of the Tea Party movement, Pearce's acerbic states' rights message was crystal clear. In an interview on National Public Radio, he said, "I want to take back America, one state at a time."[10]

When Harris, the other author, came to Arizona in 2006 after five years in the cool climes of Ireland, he knew its legislature was divided and the state overreliant on land speculation and real estate to drive its fortunes. But his experience overseas, working closely with motivated leaders to attract world-class scientists and enhance the quality of its R&D, inspired him that a similar impact could be made in the United States at the state level. The timing seemed perfect. The state was flush with resources and optimism, buoyed by record tax receipts and a booming economy (just between 2000 and 2007, the economy grew by 35 percent, twice the national average).[11] Arizona had unseated Nevada as the nation's fastest-growing state, climbing in 2006 to a population of more than six million. The popular Democratic governor, Janet Napolitano, with a budget surplus of more than $1 billion, pushed through full-day kindergarten in the majority Republican legislature (agreeing to across-the-board income tax cuts in the bargain) and was selected to chair the National Governors Association with a focus on innovation, school reform, and global competitiveness. She won reelection that November by an earth-scorching twenty-seven-point margin, winning every single county in the state. Educator Michael Crow, a longtime colleague of Harris, had become president of Arizona State University with a fierce drive to build the New American University, a concept aimed to expand the collaboration between the university and its surrounding community and pursue a rich system of cross-disciplinary programs geared toward complex twenty-first-century realities. This fit closely with Harris's belief that the country would benefit from a modern application of the land-grant Morrill Act, which inspired close working relationships between the business and academic communities to solve problems and create wealth.

Harris was impressed by the governor's enthusiasm. Their first meeting in 2004, scheduled for ten minutes, lasted more than an hour, caught up in talk about the policy lessons Arizona could take from Ireland. This was not just idle conversation; Napolitano, Crow, and a group of Arizona business and education leaders later trekked to Dublin to experience how Ireland focused on diversifying its economy and how government, industry, and university leaders worked together to achieve common goals for the country.[12] In late 2005, they approached Harris about running a newly forming public-private partnership, which became Science Foundation Arizona (SFAz), funded by a combination of motivated private donors and the state. Napolitano herself told Harris that she wanted to enrich Arizona by enhancing its commitment to innovation, education, and economic development, strengthening its strategic leadership, and expanding the role of science and technology to help diversify the state's economy.

Over a series of dinners, Harris was persuaded by the governor, state legislators, and business leaders such as Don Budinger, who founded the education-focused Rodel Foundation, and real estate magnate and philanthropist Jerry Bisgrove. Harris questioned the bench strength of the state's leadership and wondered about the level of mistrust within the legislature, but how could he say no? This was an opportunity to demonstrate that a laserlike focus on science and research could have a substantial impact on Arizona's economic development, expand its pool of high-paying, knowledge-based jobs, and help reduce the state's overreliance on real estate and tourism. Here was a chance to show how state-level investments in R&D that provide seed money for cutting-edge research and emerging companies—and that build partnerships between existing universities, state government, and private industry—could be a critical driver of advances in everything from solar energy and biotechnology to aerospace and mining. Harris couldn't turn this down, especially after he got the go-ahead to establish a board of directors selected for their expertise rather than their political connections.

A supportive governor. A business community that understood the need for diversifying the economy. University and research partnerships that had the potential to make catalytic breakthroughs. Public pronouncements that sounded just the right tone. "Science Foundation Arizona was created to catalyze a new operating model for government, industry, and education to effectively work together and propel Arizona into a twenty-first century rooted in innovation and discovery," Governor Napolitano said after Bisgrove's Stardust charitable fund committed $25 million and another nonprofit pledged $50 million to match state support.[13] Everything looked good and right. Oh, how times would change. Could Harris have known that in less than three years the governor would be gone, crunching budget deficits would rock Arizona, and a new crop of legislators would take advantage of the moment to push their own agendas?

In this first decade of the new century, Arizona was not the only state pursuing R&D-minded initiatives that could add jobs, lure talent, carve out innovative and lucrative new fields, and reduce dependence on federal programs and support. In response to President Bush's rejection of federal funding for stem cell research beyond twenty-two adult stem cell lines, California voters passed a $3 billion bond referendum to launch the California Institute of Regenerative Medicine. By far the largest, it was among stem cell research programs initiated by more than a dozen states. Florida legislators committed $310 million to build a new facility in Palm Beach County for Scripps Institute and leapfrog the state's position in the bioscience research field. Michigan's legislature, in an effort to diversify its economy, appropriated $400 million in 2006 and agreed to spend about $2 billion over ten years to create the Michigan 21st Century Jobs Fund. Its targets: applied research in life sciences, alternative energy, advanced automotive, and homeland security and defense.[14] Around the nation, governors and other forward-thinking state leaders grasped that they had to commit money and brainpower to economic development that could attract outside investment, spur new industries, and expand their job base—or risk watching from the sidelines as other states passed them by. They recognized that in the competitive fight for the best jobs, you're either moving forward or you're moving backward.

From the beginning, Harris understood that he needed to demonstrate success with the science foundation, especially since some skeptics in the legislature questioned why the state was using public money for the benefit of private enterprise. That meant matching state support with private dollars, then investing those resources to attract, keep, and create technology jobs and companies. By 2010, three years after its launch, SFAz showed progress, generating 1,151 direct jobs, 16 new companies, 84 patent filings, 11 technology licenses, and 760 science-related publications. It also supported 223 graduate research fellows and tallied 163,000 students and 2,900 teachers involved in its K–12 STEM (Science, Technology, Engineering, and Mathematics) education programs. A Battelle survey documented that $50 million in state funding generated an additional $152.8 million in matching support from the private sector or outside Arizona.

That's more than $3 for every $1 of state funding—"new wealth brought into the state by SFAz's research activities," the report noted, adding that the "multiplier effect" had spurred an additional $178 million and 1,490 more jobs for the state over the three-year period. "It is not just the cumulative totals in measures of innovation that make SFAz stand out, but its greater productivity in translating research funding into innovation."[15]

Beyond the data, SFAz could point to the seeds of transformation: scientists turning algae grown under the desert sun into jet fuel, for example, or an unlikely alliance between defense contractor Raytheon and the Arizona Cancer Center applying battlefield technology to analyze the surface of the face and detect early-stage melanomas. Three years on, legislators who had supported the launch of SFAz in 2006 could see how the state's partnership with private industry was making a difference and was consistent with the best practices laid out by the National Governors Association (NGA) and the Pew Center on the States. "The innovation imperative—for both companies and economies —isn't a fad," asserted the NGA's 2007 "Investing in Innovation" report. "Wise states avoid a flip-flop approach to their R&D investments. They strategically erect structures that will survive new administrations intent on making change for change's sake. They institutionalize the idea of long-term investment so that it can survive economic downturns."[16] It was crucial to put in place a sound economic ecosystem, in other words, that can serve the needs of this generation and the next.

Excellent advice it was, a melody written in 2007 that played so well to Harris's vision. Yet this strategic thinking was about to face a head-on collision with an economic crisis and a wild-riding set of state leaders more than ready to use the country's shifting fortunes to advance a very different agenda. As much as innovation-oriented governors and like-minded supporters believed they were strengthening their states' independence and growth through creative investments and partnerships, these frustrated antigovernment advocates saw their chance to change the music. Theirs was a take-no-prisoners game, whatever the facts, whatever the consequences, even if it meant everyone moved backwards. It conjures an unsettling reminder of the tragic missteps of Mississippi and Alabama.

In the month after Governor Napolitano exited the state in January 2009 to become the president's secretary of homeland security, it was like a light switched off. The shift was that clear from light to dark, from confidence to confusion. Jan Brewer, a Republican, ascended to the governor's office after serving as secretary of state. Ironically, Brewer had introduced numerous ballot proposals over the years to create a lieutenant governor position in Arizona to be next in line to replace the governor if he or she left the office. (Arizona is one of only six states without a lieutenant governor.) Her reasoning, explained in a 1994 op-ed to the *Arizona Republic*: The duties of the Arizona secretary of state "do little to prepare that officeholder for the statewide leadership role required of a governor," and "Arizonans deserve to have a governor that will continue the same general policies as the one [voters] elected."[17]

While Brewer's lengthy résumé included several decades in the state House and Senate and as chair of the county board, the newly installed Republican governor brought a very different perspective than the one voters elected several years earlier. Her Democratic predecessor often took a hard line with the predominately Republican legislature, vetoing bills dealing with antiabortion issues, gun rights, school choice, and illegal immigration. Arizona was about to undergo a seismic shift, and not only because the state was facing a deficit of more than $3 billion in 2009, one of the nation's highest in percentage terms. At a time when we would expect a focus on budget balancing, revved-up legislators saw their chance to push their personal projects—and not just in the arena of immigration policy, which grabbed the national headlines. For a while, it wasn't clear how or if Science Foundation Arizona would survive the attacks.

"Good evening, fellow extremists!" That was Republican state senator Sam Crump's welcome to an April 2009 Tea Party rally near the Arizona Capitol, punctuated with a raised clenched fist. Two months earlier in February, as the legislature was trying to reach agreement on a fresh round of budget cuts, Crump decided to take the process hostage and demand that $22.5 million for SFAz be swept from the budget if the leadership wanted his vote and those of four other freshman GOP congressmen. The Speaker of the House, the president of the Senate, and newly installed Governor Brewer each spoke privately to this group and urged them not to block the budget from passing, but they ignored the state's leadership. Here's how Crump described it to the Tea Party crowd: "We took on a fight along with our fellow patriots against the 21st Century Fund [which funds SFAz], which is nothing more than corporate welfare, and we've saved you $22.5 million this year and another $50 million the next two years. Unless we keep this Tea Party and this second revolution going, they are going to keep raising your taxes and keep overspending until we do something about it."[18] The ambitious state congressman got himself a cheer—who wants their taxes raised, and who supports overspending?—but the coming months portrayed a quite different reality than the one he offered his supporters that hot Arizona day.

Crump, an attorney by trade, told his "fellow patriots" that the funding for SFAz is "a scam" that the state should not pay. While he was taking pride in disregarding a law so essential for business, more than a few legal experts insisted that existing contracts are not something to be treated so lightly. At a time of economic insecurity, how productive is it for state legislators to communicate that they won't take responsibility for funds promised and already paid? As then Attorney General Terry Goddard acknowledged, this could discourage firms from relocating to Arizona. As a Tucson weekly newspaper put it, "Yanking funds that have already been promised to people—is that a sure-fire way to encourage economic development, or what? Nice work, guys. It's good to know that your principled opposition to corporate pork outweighs the principle that businesses that sign contracts with the state ought to be able to trust the state to follow through."[19]

With $18.5 million already obligated, SFAz sought to secure an emergency private loan to pay more than a dozen education and research grants, keep scientists and other researchers working, and avoid losing projects that were already being wooed by other states. And it wasn't just Harris and SFAz that worried about Crump's move. Remarkably, both Governor Brewer and House Speaker Kirk Adams privately urged Harris to file suit against the state to reclaim the funds. SFAz did just that in May, claiming that the state had reneged on its contracts and the foundation was owed $18.5 million. In June, a superior court judge found in favor of SFAz, yet he asserted that he could not force the state to pay the judgment. The Arizona Supreme Court then agreed to hear the case in October. In the weeks leading up to that date, Senator Crump showed no signs of regret. "These contracts shouldn't have been entered into in the first place," he told the *Arizona Republic*. "I am pleased that, thus far, we have not paid them."[20] Governor Brewer and the legislature disagreed, and they repaid the money before the case came to trial.

At a time of fiscal crisis, it's a state's responsibility to make tough decisions about where it wants to put its limited resources. Crump could have raised a legitimate conversation about whether it's the government's role to fund such a program given the financial emergency. But beyond what we see as an ethical lapse in this instance, the state's growing ideological warfare seems certain to raise the level of toxicity and create a depth of divisiveness that will be harder and harder to repair. Moreover, at a time when companies are thinking hard about where to locate their operations, Arizona's legislators risk fostering the state's race to the bottom. Its economic progress has already suffered from overdependence on the real estate market and a reputation for poor schooling, with one of the lowest levels of per-student spending in the country. To paraphrase the Mississippi businessman noted earlier, Arizona may have a lot of advantages, but will potential investors get over the disadvantages? We believe they can, but it will take the dedicated work of the state's most visionary business leaders to redirect this downward trajectory.

Yet it's in this context that the aggressive push to drive away undocumented immigrants seems certain to exacerbate the state's struggle to recover from the deep recession—and therefore particularly badly timed. Russell Pearce was emboldened by his success in passing SB 1070 and his rising national attention, unmoved by the risks of rising distrust between law enforcement and the state's one-third Hispanic population or the flood of costly boycotts and lawsuits from the US Justice Department and others. He was already upping the ante: In a direct attack on President Obama, he cosponsored a "birther" bill that would require candidates for US president to prove they are natural-born citizens if they want a spot on the Arizona ballot in the next election. Convinced that "illegals" slip into the country to bear their children, he pushed a so-called anchor baby bill that would give the state authority to deny citizenship to children born to undocumented immigrants. (What did Crump think of this? "Russell Pearce for President!" he tweeted on Twitter.)

Pearce, who has expressed admiration for a 1950s deportation program called "Operation Wetback" and characterized opponents to SB 1070 as "anarchists," has asserted that he's neither racist nor mean-spirited in his desire to ensure greater security. But even if we take him at his word, such spotlight-grabbing moves exploit the swirl of fear and paranoia that a time of economic insecurity breeds. Whatever honest intentions may be behind such bills, they are creating a picture of Arizona circa 2010 that has all the makings of a Wild West push to the extreme. Or worse, mythology aside, they've taken the serious work of creating a twenty-first-century innovative state and turned Arizona into a backward-looking national joke. Consider this in the *Christian Science Monitor*: "Legal scholars laugh out loud at Republican state Sen. Russell Pearce's proposal and warn that it would be blatantly unconstitutional, since the Fourteenth Amendment guarantees citizenship to anyone born in the U.S."[21] Or this from Jon Stewart on *The Daily Show*, in a nod to Supreme Court Justice Brandeis's description that states are the laboratories of democracy: "It turns out Arizona is the meth lab of democracy." Stewart, after describing how SB 1070 requires legal immigrants to carry proof of citizenship papers at all times, noted that this is "the same thing that free black people had to do in 1863. Lord knows that didn't cause any residual anger."[22] Stewart's Comedy Central colleague Stephen Colbert proffered this in response to Pearce's suggestion that his goal is to make life so difficult for illegal immigrants that they'll leave on their own: "It's the same strategy I use to keep deer out of my garden. . . . If this law fails, we should think of sprinkling Arizona with wolf urine."[23]

Beyond the comedy shows, even the conservative-minded *Arizona Republic* grasped that the birther bill was a road too far. "The proposed legislation . . . is worse than a foolish waste of time. It suggests Arizona is a place where any crackpot whim can be enshrined in law. What is Arizona? A state of rugged individualists or a swamp of breathless fanatics? If legislators fall for this one, they'll be trading in our Stetson for a tin-foil hat."[24] The bill was eventually withdrawn after failing to pass the House, but the damage on Arizona's reputation was already done.

Though Pearce's more determined backers may not care what Jon Stewart, Stephen Colbert, the *Christian Science Monitor,* or anyone else in the mainstream media thinks, the state is saddled with the multimillion-dollar costs of boycotts and lawsuits; some enterprises are expressing their opinions by uprooting their businesses and taking their dollars to other states. ECOtality, a company involved with electric cars and other clean technologies, decided to move its corporate headquarters and top executives from Tempe, Arizona, to San Francisco. When asked if recent legislation made a difference, a spokesman said, "How could it not?"[25]

Ironically, the state's loss has provided political gain, at least in the short term. When the US Justice Department filed suit against the state in July to stop the bill's enforcement, citing the federal government's "preeminent authority to regulate immigration matters," it dramatically strengthened the governor's standing in the polls before the November election against Democrat Terry Goddard. Governor Brewer was seen as taking on the feds, earning her newly minted status as a states' rights icon fighting against big, intrusive government. National polls found widespread support for SB 1070 from a majority of Americans, underscoring the sense that the federal government had failed to do its job on immigration policy.

Arizona, like so many states, may be dealing with a rising contempt for federal authority and federal policies, including healthcare legislation and immigration. More extreme elements may succeed in increasing the pressure to chip away or usurp federal power. Secession talk, unhinged from its longtime stigma, may rise in volume in the coming years, especially as economic uncertainties create greater fear. When rage and resentment dominate the discourse, the nation begins to look like it's coming apart at the seams.

As much as Jon Stewart built a laugh around Justice Louis D. Brandeis's call for states to serve as laboratories, it's useful to revisit the justice's comments in 1932, another time in the nation's history fraught with supreme dangers—social, economic, and political. (That was the year that thousands of jobless World War I veterans, demanding their cash bonuses, confronted troops armed with bayonets and tear gas in the streets of the US capital.) Brandeis's words are to be cherished, a hearty expression of confidence in America's democracy. "There must be power in the states and the nation to remould, through experimentation, our economic practices and institutions to meet changing social and economic needs," he wrote. "Denial of the right to experiment may be fraught with serious consequences to the nation. It is one of the happy incidents of the federal system that a single courageous state may, if its citizens choose, serve as a laboratory; and try novel social and economic experiments without risk to the rest of the country."[26]

We believe the future of the country depends on backing our best instincts and ensuring that the principles that bind us matter more than the day-to-day issues that pull us apart. On July 4, 2010, *Wall Street Journal* columnist Peggy Noonan penned a touching reminder of the profound feelings that drove Thomas Jefferson as he crafted the Declaration of Independence. Her comments underscore why we must cheer for bold ventures yet demand reason and reserve when our most enduring experiment is placed at risk. "The tenderest words in American political history were cut from the document they were to have graced," Noonan began, and later she described the pain Jefferson felt in separating from Britain. "Poignantly, with a plaintive sound, Jefferson addresses and gives voice to the human pain of parting: 'We might have been a free and great people together.'" She continued:

> What loss there is in those words, what humanity, and what realism, too. . . . Jefferson was thinking of the abrupt end of old ties, of self-defining ties, and, I suspect, that the pain of this had to be acknowledged. It is one thing to declare the case for freedom, and to make a fiery denunciation of abusive, autocratic and high-handed governance. But it is another thing, and an equally important one, to acknowledge the human implications of the break. These were our friends, our old relations; we were leaving them, ending the particular facts of our long relationship forever. We would feel it. Seventeen seventy-six was the beginning of a dream. But it was the end of one too. "We might have been a free and great people together."[27]

As dissension and distrust course through the country and a growing collection of state leaders feel empowered by thoughts and feelings, indeed legislative actions, that deride the value of national government, it's useful to dwell on the price and pain of separation.

As troubling as 2010 was for Arizona and the country, when angry voices of doubt and derision dominated, it's worth remembering that people are more than unbending, unthinking stick figures and therefore are capable of change. This is true despite the hardening of positions amid the constant pressure to pick sides. While Science Foundation Arizona was targeted for destruction by its ideological critics, the Republican governor worked hard to get beyond the conflict and publicly expressed her commitment to its role in securing world-class research, innovative technologies, and high-paying jobs—then backed that up with financial support. Privately, she sought advice on how to make science a more critical piece of the state's economic development. Sam Crump, meanwhile, who angled to expand his political platform by running for US congressman, garnered only 5 percent in the Republican primary,[28] providing fresh fodder, perhaps, for reflection on a more productive way forward. The experiment of democracy is complicated, messy, and often painful, but still capable of invigoration. In December 2010, a little more than a year before Arizona would celebrate its first century of statehood, several hundred Arizona leaders and citizens from every political persuasion gathered together to set a new global agenda that they hoped could advance the state's competitiveness and drive its progress and prosperity.

Chapter 11

Can Our Cities
Show the Way Forward?

D etroit is America's poster child for urban dysfunction, a
metaphor for failure and self-destruction, a grim vision
of entropy. But beyond what the city represents in the American
psyche, its concrete, on-the-ground reality is more alarming. The
vertigo-inducing facts give the terrible sense that Detroit's downward spiral is only going to get worse. The highest unemployment
in the country, more than a third of its citizens below the poverty
line, per capita income at half the national average, the nation's
highest violent crime rate, a dwindling population less than half its
1950 peak of 1.85 million—all underscoring its shrinking tax base
and increasing inability to fund basic city services.[1]

The demolition of homes and the implosion of the city's
housing market make it tough for even the most jaded observers
to suspend their disbelief. Over the last decade, thousands of
derelict houses have been torn down, leaving whole city blocks
largely empty or gutted, pockmarked with the detritus of abandonment and disuse. In the first year after his 2009 election,
Detroit mayor Dave Bing pledged to tear down another ten thousand structures by 2014, highlighting the need to shrink the foot-

print of a 139-square-mile city that neither the police nor fire departments could adequately serve.[2]

All that pales, however, in comparison to the ongoing negotiation over what still remains: In 2003, the median price of a Detroit home was $98,000. By 2010, the median price dropped below $8,000—well under the price of even the cheapest car—and in some cases realtors were selling homes for a dollar. As a 2010 report analyzing the fiscal troubles of the city soberly noted, "Remaining businesses and individuals are challenging property tax assessments on parcels that have lost value and, in some cases, can not be sold at any price." The report's overall summary is grimmer still: "The 'Great Recession' that began in December, 2007 has exacerbated the effects of population loss, poverty, and disinvestment on the City of Detroit. The tax base, already stressed, has deteriorated significantly, as the number of businesses and jobs has declined, unemployment has increased, and population has dwindled."[3]

Is this the end or the new beginning for this once great city? It depends on whom you ask. Today Detroit's casinos employ nearly as many people as the automakers still do. But contained within the despair over the city's fate is a drive to radically rethink its future. This includes transforming large swaths of the now fallow city into green parks and gardens, a kind of twenty-first-century back-to-nature movement that squarely acknowledges that manufacturing is no longer the city's destiny. Rather than clinging in vain to its industrial forefathers, the city's advocates are seeking to extend Detroit's reach by acknowledging its diminished status, shrinking its footprint, and redirecting its course. They have fallen so far, it's hard to imagine that they will escape their downward spiral, but their actions suggest an awakening to the necessity of dramatic change, however belated. The effort itself offers a hard lesson to Detroit's urban industrial peers and a nation in search of a new direction.

Clearly, that means stripping away nostalgia and looking at facts squarely. Consider: among the eyesores already demolished under the mayor's plan is presidential aspirant Mitt Romney's childhood home, a 5,500-square-foot structure in the long-exclusive Palmer Woods neighborhood, which is struggling to stave off the same deterioration that has enveloped the rest of the city. Romney's family lived there for twelve years until 1953, before his father went on to become head of American Motors, governor of Michigan, and US Secretary of Housing and Urban Development. As recently as 2002, the house sold for $645,000, then suffered foreclosure, abandonment, and disrepair.[4] This was one more indication that no quarter of the city is free from the centrifugal force of decline—the sad fate of a city that became dependent on a single industry.

Detroit's unraveling did not happen all of a sudden. This was the city known as the Arsenal of Democracy, the dynamic hub for the country's massive World War II military production. The name was coined by President Roosevelt in his fireside chat of December 29, 1940, when he gravely detailed the Nazi threat of world domination and the urgent necessity facing America. "We must be the great arsenal of democracy," he asserted. "For us this is an emergency as serious as war itself." And FDR made clear that manufacturing would be at the center of this effort, since "it is the purpose of the nation to build now with all possible speed every machine, every arsenal, every factory that we need to manufacture our defense material. We have the men, the skill, the wealth, and above all, the will."[5]

Indeed, the country did. By March of 1942, *Time* described the "miracle" of war production and cited Detroit's auto industry as its "miracle worker." Hyperbole aside, a vast machinery was in motion, covering miles and miles of industrial landscape previously devoted to the automobile and its assembly line production. *Time* noted, "Endlessly the lines will send tanks, jeeps, machine guns, cannon, air torpedoes, armored cars," taking advantage of "many of the world's smartest manufacturing brains concentrated in Detroit." In one massive plant, which extended more than half a mile in length and was capable of containing more than seventy thousand workers, Ford would soon produce a four-motored, thirty-ton bomber every hour. In another, Chrysler assembly lines were producing trainloads of olive-green tanks. General Motors was turning out arms of all kinds, while Packard and Studebaker were making airplane engines; Hudson, antiaircraft guns; and Nash, engines and propellers. And the manufacturers were still ramping up, fueling *Time*'s breathless, optimistic prose: "Once Detroit's conversion to war is complete, when the lines are all moving with the precision of timing and economy of motion that Detroit borrowed from the morning stars, they will pour out such a flood of war machines as no man has ever imagined. The one-time auto industry will employ a million men & women, twice as many as it ever did, who will make a billion dollars' worth of armaments a month. If Armageddon is to be decided in Detroit, Armageddon is won."[6]

Thankfully, Detroit played a crucial role in beating back Armageddon, but saving itself was quite another matter. While the Motor City reestablished its previous purpose as a center for car production after the war, little more than a decade later, it was losing its grip. The same publication that praised its wartime genius was now describing a grim march toward the cliff. *Time*'s account from 1961 offers a picture remarkably similar to the present day: "Detroit's decline has been going on for a long while. . . . The U.S. Government lists Detroit as an area of substantial and persistent unemployment. . . . Blight is creeping like a fungus through many of Detroit's proud, old neighborhoods. Vast areas have been leveled for redevelopment projects that have not materialized. . . . Its problems run so deep that they can be solved only by the effort of labor, management, government and citizenry—working in a spirit that once made Detroit the symbol of economic dynamism."[7]

At that time, a full half century ago, more than a few Detroiters were sure their best days were ahead of them. For many, it was true, their destiny defined by the sexy Ford Mustang, the sleek styling of the Chevrolet Impala, or many other muscular beauties that captured the nation's imagination and fueled profits. But beyond the seductive showrooms and glittering promise of next year's model, Detroit the city was struggling to hold together.

If there was any doubt, the riot in July of 1967 was a turning point: a destructive week of arson and looting triggered by an aggressive police raid on an after-hours bar that left forty-three dead, hundreds injured, thousands arrested, and a smoldering city at war with itself. In the tumultuous years of 1967 and 1968, Detroit was one of dozens of urban centers ripped by riots, social unrest, and racial strife, but it was arguably the worst. Viewing the terrible damage concentrated in the city's most impoverished neighborhoods, Detroit's mayor, Jerome Cavanaugh, said, "It looks like Berlin in 1945."[8] The conflagration hastened the exodus of whites to the suburbs north of Eight Mile Road, scared away business and investment, and exacerbated the violent crime, drug dealing, and urban blight that continues to infect the city today.

The two-decade rule of Mayor Coleman Young, Detroit's first African American mayor, elected in 1973, didn't help the racial conflicts and economic disparities exposed by the riot for the world to see. Here's how the cowriter of Young's 1994 autobiography, *Hard Stuff*, explained the challenge of managing a city that saw nearly 90 percent of its white population exit: "While his antagonists have tediously complained that Young introduces race into every issue, the fact is, as a public servant with a manifest black constituency, he is duty bound to identify any racial impositions upon the citizens under his charge. That's what big-city administration has essentially become in the segregated, suburban-oriented, two-nation modern society—the defense and promotion of the minority cause."[9] Put another way, Young was managing a city under siege, from the inside and out. Not exactly a recipe for constructive action.

Whatever thrill the nickname Motor City once afforded, it became a burdensome symbol of a city unable to redirect its fate—as goes General Motors, so goes Detroit. While Detroit the

city and Detroit the Big Three automakers were seen as synony-
mous—and eventually a depressing marker of bloated and failed
leadership—this Rust Belt capital was facing the same collapse of
manufacturing that has starved so many other industrial towns.
The numbers depict the hard facts of industrial decline, a choked
reality defined by overdependence on a dominant industry. In
1947, Detroit tallied 3,272 manufacturing firms employing
338,300 workers. By 1982, the number had dropped to 1,508
manufacturers employing 106,000, and by 2002, the US Census
Bureau counted a mere 647 firms with 38,000 employees, one-
fifth the number of companies in 1947 and nearly one-tenth the
number of jobs.[10] Investors, jobs, and people were exiting the
once-great city.

This path was not inevitable. Jane Jacobs, the famed student
of cities, described a dynamic Detroit of 1880 that produced and
exported a surprising range of goods—from paints and varnishes,
to steam generators and pumps, to medicine, furniture, and
sporting goods. "This was the prospering and diverse economy
from which the automobile industry emerged two decades later,"
only to be stifled by the exporting power of the car, she wrote in
The Economy of Cities. As much as that industry built a modern
Detroit, it posed a grave danger: "A very successful growth
industry poses a crisis for a city. Everything—all other development work, all other processes of city growth, the fertile and creative inefficiency of the growth industry's suppliers, the opportunities of able workers to break away, the inefficient but creative
use of capital—can be sacrificed to the exigencies of the growth
industry, which thus turns the city into a company town."[11]
Jacobs's focus here was on Detroit, but it's a sobering reminder
of why a diversified economy is so crucial for every metropolis to
unleash its potential—and why some American cities are geared
for long-term prosperity and others are on the road to Detroit.

At any given time, whether the national economy is promising or
plummeting, individual cities portray a wide disparity of fortune

and misfortune; they offer useful indicators and insights for assessing the country's prospects. Like the rest of the planet, America is becoming more urban; four out of five Americans live in cities today. And as strong as Americans' attachment may be to their country, we believe that their connection to their city is even stronger. Just think how fiercely sports fans feel about their home teams, even after moving elsewhere. They may live in America, but they reside, every day, for good or bad, in New York or Los Angeles, Chicago or Detroit, Phoenix, Austin, or any one of more than 366 metropolitan areas with a population of at least fifty thousand. (Last on that list, according to 2009 US census data: Carson City, Nevada, population 55,157.) That connection, when it translates into cooperative, purposeful action, means that even the most troubled towns possess the capacity to turn things around. Just look at what happened in Pittsburgh.

Against the backdrop of Detroit, Pittsburgh is riding on a fast track to the future. Rather than cling desperately to its industrial heritage and risk drowning, the city's leadership took advantage of its history of strategic cooperation, legacy of civic-minded philanthropy, and belief in its ability to change course. In a nod to the city's economic turnaround since the collapse of the steel industry, President Obama picked Pittsburgh to host the 2009 G20 summit. The world's leaders debated their response to the international financial crisis, and they learned how one American city acknowledged its troubles, took stock of its strengths, and charted its way out of an economic mess. In a single sentence, *Newsweek* summarized the story that the city's planners dreamed the world would hear: "It was a rusting steel-making behemoth that, through struggle, pain and creativity, retooled itself as a surprisingly vibrant, 21st-century leader in education, computer science, medical research, sports entertainment and boutique manufacturing."[12] While this golden tale glosses over the city's continuing struggles to right its course, it correctly grasps that Pittsburgh, unlike so many of its urban industrial peers, has escaped the painful fate of merely managing decline.

As much as Detroit is tied to the auto industry, Pittsburgh has been defined by its long history as a steel town. Like Detroit, it was a central hub in the rise of a great industrial nation, with all the benefits and attendant miseries. In 1868, seven years before steel magnate Andrew Carnegie opened his first mill, Pittsburgh was already decried as "hell with the lid off." This demonic description by *Atlantic* writer James Parton stuck because it aptly defined the physical reality that plagued natives and visitors alike. "Smoke, smoke, everywhere smoke!" Parton wrote. "The entire space lying between the hills was filled with the blackest smoke, from out of which the hidden chimneys sent forth tongues of flame, while from the depths of the abyss came up the noise of hundreds of steam hammers."[13] As recently as the early 1940s, daytime was typically dark as night; drivers needed headlights and pedestrians relied on streetlamps to find their way. Leading corporations threatened to abandon Pittsburgh, described as a "used-up city," unattractive and economically unpromising.[14]

That began to change after financier Richard King Mellon, one of America's richest men and a Pittsburgh scion from one of the city's dynastic families, teamed with mayor and longtime Democratic boss David L. Lawrence. The Republican-Democrat duo brought together many of the city's public- and private-sector leaders to revitalize the dilapidated and polluted central city. Mellon, chairman of Mellon Bank, could make things happen: He held dozens of corporate directorships; was on the board of General Motors, Gulf Oil, and other Fortune 500 companies; and had already formed in 1943 the Allegheny Conference for Community Development, an organization of business and political leaders that still influences the region's economic development. Launched in 1946, their Renaissance Project focused on cleaning the acrid and dirty air, building river dams to stem frequent floods, razing hundreds of old buildings and slums, clearing away unsightly railroad yards, and erecting new skyscrapers and parks. And that meant keeping together the complex coalition of interests for the larger purpose. "This is a Pittsburgh project, not a Democratic or a Republican project," Lawrence insisted.[15] In 1958, *Life* described "Mellon's Miracle" in a promotional feature about Pittsburgh's gleaming revival: "What does a city do when slums and soot and apathy sap its vitality . . . when real estate values fall and business moves elsewhere? This is the problem of many cities . . . and it's being tackled magnificently by Pittsburgh."[16] The city's glimmering Gateway Towers and verdant Point State Park remain visible reminders of that effort, which by the mid-1960s encompassed some fifteen hundred acres, nineteen urban renewal projects, and sixty new buildings.

Pittsburgh's renaissance became a national model of urban redevelopment, but its local import is greater: it's a revered reminder of the city's commitment to strategic cooperation. This is more than living history; renaissance has become a key piece of the city's sense of identity and civic pride. "That was a real model of the public and private sector working together," Dennis Yablonsky, executive director of the still-thriving Allegheny Conference, told us. "That legacy is an important part of the Pittsburgh story. It's in our DNA."[17]

The belief in the city's capacity to work together and fix problems was sorely tested with the collapse of steel manufacturing in the early 1980s. The region was hit by the loss of more than 150,000 jobs and the exodus of more than 100,000 of its residents. It could have suffered the same grim fate as its Midwestern cousin, unable to disconnect from its deep focus on a dominant industry. At that time, the city's leaders were talking about taking advantage of their universities and shifting toward a knowledge-based, high-tech future—a vision that seemed then quite fantastical to one of us (Beschloss). After all, this was one of the least mobile populations in the country, a staunch working-class culture deeply wedded to its gritty industrial history and way of life. The city's morale was as low as the jobless totals were high. Did Pittsburghers really have the agility, wit, and will to shift into this alternate world?

Perhaps the better question is, did Pittsburgh have another option? This was not a case of incremental decline, which unwinds with the deluded promise that things might revert to "normal." The quick, catastrophic collapse of the steel industry —devastating whole towns and families throughout the region— was the kind of bell-ringing event that left little doubt that glory days were over. The region faced a clear choice: change or die. As a result, the city benefited from this painful wake-up call; its survival was at stake. "It all happened so severely, there was no doubt about the problem," Yablonsky said. "This is a tough-minded place. It will take a punch and figure out how to hit back pretty quickly."[18]

Pittsburgh needed the building blocks that could make the change to an alternate, more diversified economy possible—and the ability to identify those assets. And the leadership to take advantage of them. To the city's great fortune, the focus shifted to what is often described as "eds and meds." Heading that list were Carnegie Mellon University, the University of Pittsburgh, and the University of Pittsburgh Medical Center (UPMC). They were not only significant drivers of the city's revitalization, their leaders often working in tandem to spur economic development, but all have become highly ranked, globally relevant players in their own right, capable of attracting major funding, talented newcomers, and innovative firms seeking to tap into their resources.

While their Pittsburgh roots are deep, each of these institutions was limited in scope three decades ago. While Carnegie Mellon and Pitt were well-regarded regional schools in the 1980s, they evolved into world-class research universities and magnets for excellence. Combined, they attract more than $1 billion in annual research funding, a tenfold increase since the 1980s. Half of Pitt's freshmen are in the top 10 percent of their high school class. A third of Carnegie Mellon's students come from more than a hundred different countries, many drawn by its track record in computer science, robotics, and biotechnology.

UPMC, forged from the merger of several regional hospitals in 1990, is now the region's largest employer, with fifty thousand employees. As one of the world's largest academic medical centers, it's become an $8 billion healthcare powerhouse with medical centers in far-flung locales around the world.[19] It's only fitting that in 2008 the UPMC initials were affixed atop the sixty-four-story US Steel Tower, the city's tallest building and now UPMC's headquarters.

In the days leading up to the G20 summit, the heads of Carnegie Mellon, Pitt, and UPMC were interviewed by then *Newsweek* columnist and Pittsburgh native Howard Fineman before an audience of international journalists. To no one's surprise, they painted the virtues of their respective institutions. But they also detailed an unusual level of cooperation that colors their success and Pittsburgh's progress. Amid the intense global competition for investment and funding, this could read as simple city boosterism—their particular song and dance. Yet their partnership offers a strong counterpoint to urban peers and national leaders who fail to put aside partisan differences to identify and pursue their common purpose.

Literally neighbors in this compact city, the leaders of Carnegie Mellon, Pitt, and UPMC have collaborated on more than five hundred academic centers and projects in a wide variety of disciplines, from education, robotics, and computer science to biotech and medicine. They were early adopters of the idea that research universities are a key to economic development. "We knew that we needed to cooperate and find ways to harness the [academic] power for our own good and the good of the community," Mark Nordenberg, Pitt's chancellor, told the crowd. Jared L. Cohon, Carnegie Mellon's president and a Cleveland native, was asked why his hometown had not accomplished what Pittsburgh has. "They've never figured out how to work together—quite the opposite," he said, referring to Cleveland Clinic and Case Western Reserve University. "It's in stark contrast to what you find here: a private university working very comfortably with a public university and both of us working very eagerly and productively with our major medical center."[20]

As critical as these building blocks were to the city's reemergence, their presence alone was no guarantee of success. The city and western Pennsylvania region benefited from a series of long-range initiatives, including the 1985 Strategy 21 economic development report, the result of a partnership between then Pittsburgh mayor Richard Caliguiri, the presidents of CMU and Pitt, and Allegheny County commissioners. This push was part of an evolving public-private consensus, reinforced nearly a decade later when the Allegheny Conference combined with CMU president Robert Mehrabian to reassess the region's agenda: capitalize on existing strengths by supporting advanced manufacturing and technology, financial services, and energy; leverage university-based research to spur new businesses and commercially minded R&D; rebuild the downtown cultural zone that had fallen into disrepair; enhance the city's natural assets along the riverfront to create a more appealing destination; and revitalize dead and rusting mills for new purposes.[21]

Unlike many newer cities still building alliances, Pittsburgh could count on the support of its leading families and their well-funded philanthropic foundations. Steel magnate Andrew Carnegie symbolized this philanthropic impulse, using his vast fortune to build libraries, schools, and museums, including Carnegie Mellon University and the Carnegie Museums of Pittsburgh. The names read like an historical register of the richest Americans: Carnegie, Mellon, Heinz. Add to this the Pittsburgh Foundation, created in 1945, composed of more than thirteen hundred individual donors dedicated to the community. With assets exceeding $6 billion, they annually contribute to the region more than $300 million, not only an important financial boost but also a source of stability amid wrenching change. They have helped sustain traditional cultural institutions—the opera, the symphony, the museums, the libraries, the downtown cultural district—but also invested in the infrastructure of economic development.

And the results from this decades-long refocus? The city can tally more than five hundred biotech and sixteen hundred information and communications technology firms. It has held onto the headquarters of US Steel and numerous other Fortune 500 companies; added thousands of jobs from top specialty steel makers such as Allegheny Technologies; and expanded cutting-edge manufacturing in robotics, life sciences, and energy. Its downtown cultural district, no longer home to porn and pawn shops, boasts sparkling new theaters and galleries. The riverfront features a smart new stadium, bike paths, and trails for outdoors lovers, while a South Side brownfield site formerly owned by Jones and Laughlin Steel has been transformed into a stylish collection of shops, restaurants, and cinemas. An area once owned by US Steel and home to the Homestead Strike's bloody clash between steelworkers and Pinkerton agents is now a massive open-air mall for shopping, dining, and living. And while the unemployment rate escalated and the real estate market crashed nationwide during the Great Recession, Pittsburgh remained relatively stable, bettering the national averages. As for icing on this high-fiber cake, the *Economist* picked Pittsburgh as the most livable US city in 2009 and *Forbes* did the same in 2010, based on its arts and leisure scene, job prospects, safety, and affordability.[22]

These examples illustrate the city's economic evolution, but they might not be the best signal that Pittsburgh has become a brain center and is prepared to generate a productive and fruitful future. That can be seen in 2009 data collected by University of Pittsburgh researchers Sabina Deitrick and Christopher Briem: Nearly half of Pittsburgh's workers aged twenty-five to thirty-four have earned at least a bachelor's degree, well above the national average of 35 percent. That places this young generation of workers among the top five metro areas nationwide, just behind Boston, San Francisco, Washington, DC, and Austin. The findings are even more impressive when examining the percentage of workers aged twenty-five to thirty-four with a graduate or professional degree: Pittsburgh sits at the top of the list, virtually tying Washington, DC, with 21.5 percent. In stark contrast, Pittsburgh workers over fifty-five and especially those over sixty-five—those most likely to have counted on steel jobs when they came of age and lived through the industry's collapse—have schooling well below the national average.[23]

Here's how Deitrick and Briem explained these facts to their fellow citizens in the *Pittsburgh Post-Gazette*: "Pittsburghers have moved beyond their once-embedded industrial-town psyche. The tradition of working in the mill ended when the mills closed. Since then, subsequent generations of Pittsburghers have been urged to get an education. The shift has taken decades, but our youngest have come of age with an emphasis on higher education few Pittsburghers had in the past."[24] That means young and educated people are finding reasons to come and reasons to stay, a welcome sign after more than a generation of accomplished (and not so accomplished) young residents headed elsewhere for opportunity.

The region continues to struggle with an aging population, more deaths than births, a long-dwindling population, and an inability to lure sizable numbers of immigrants—all factors that hark back to its troubled past and raise lingering questions about the region's long-term health. But in spring 2010 Pittsburgh experienced a bump in its population, the first overall increase since 1990. The city's advocates are hopeful that this uptick will turn into a trend, providing the city one more indication that its renewal is progressing. As Tom Waseleski, editorial page editor of the *Post-Gazette*, told us, "You could solve a lot of the problems of the place with another fifty thousand people."[25] The comment should give pause to all the people who decry the challenges of population growth caused by immigration.

Before many people knew or visited Austin, Texas, they knew and watched *Austin City Limits*. The Austin-based PBS show is the longest-running music series in television history, a brand-defining ode to a creative city that bills itself as the "live music capital of the world," an internationally broadcast program beloved for its roots-oriented music and authenticity. In 2011, thirty-five years after the show first aired in 1976 with hometown hero Willie Nelson performing, *Austin City Limits* (*ACL*) stepped out of its homespun comfort zone and took on big new digs. The show's upscale new home is a 2,500-seat theater inside a just-built $300 million downtown tower for the W Hotel and residences—a far cry from its modest 320-seat studio on the University of Texas-Austin campus and yet another sign of change in the Texas capital. To keep it real and in touch with their heritage, the show's producers transported the well-stomped planks of the original wood stage to the new venue. But they also set their sights on an expanding universe of *ACL*-branded cafes and a partnership with the Rock and Roll Hall of Fame.

That's one picture of what growth means in Austin. And there are others—plenty of them.

ACL and Austin are starting to live large as high-end hotel properties like the W and Four Seasons reconfigure the city's skyline and its identity; this evolution has been decades in the making, even though Austinites have prided themselves on their city's relaxed, sleepy college-town feel. In 2010, in the midst of the economic downturn, Austin was still adding jobs, attracting new residents, and garnering fresh praise. *Kiplinger's* tapped Austin for the top of its 2010 list of "Best Cities of the Next Decade." With a focus on growth and growth potential, pollsters searched for an innovation mix of smart people, good ideas, and collaboration; places where governments, universities, and business communities "worked together to create economic vitality."[26] The nation's fifteenth-largest city, with a population of more than 750,000, Austin also topped the 2009 *Forbes* list of best big cities for jobs and a Portfolio.com ranking of leading cities for small-business vitality.[27] While national employment fell by half a percent between 2004 and 2009, Portfolio noted, Austin's job base grew 15.6 percent. And "no other market came close" to matching its pace in adding small businesses, aided by the strongest concentration of young people in its survey of sixty-seven metro areas. Dead last in the Portfolio vitality rankings? Detroit, which lost 298,000 jobs in the same five-year period, a drop of more than 16 percent.[28]

All these business lists talked about business-friendly tax rates, relatively low cost of living, and the stability-inducing benefits of a state capital and major research university. (Texas may be a staunchly red state, but the deeply blue Austin has the second-largest collection of state employees in the country: sixty-three thousand in 2010.) But the rankings also gave a strong nod to the more amorphous but equally significant cultural ethos that lures creative talent. In Austin, franchise businesses like Starbucks and the Hard Rock Cafe have closed down while more bohemian local operations like Jo's Coffee on South Congress and music clubs along Red River Street prosper. Call it the fun factor, what Austin has aplenty to attract not only a cutting-edge combination of music, film, gaming, and digital media makers, but also a hipster crowd of young consumers and tourists who want to be close to that action. The result is revenues exceeding $2.2 billion plus nearly fifty thousand arts-related jobs. Only San Francisco can boast more performing arts groups per capita than Austin.[29]

How did the city's leaders tap into that? One way was to recognize the value of idiosyncratic behavior and embrace a once-fringe slogan in all its freak flag–flying glory: "Keep Austin Weird." Another was to understand that even if the city is winning the growth game now, it cannot rest on its laurels and grow complacent. Listen to how Austin attorney Pike Powers described it to us: "We'll never be content. We are always looking forward to the next big thing."[30] It's easy to say, but harder to pull off when times are good. That's why Jane Jacobs's admonition about the risks of growth and the danger of relying on a dominant industry is so critical. It's also why Austin leaders dance gingerly along a high beam between big corporate players on one end and a bevy of homegrown boutique firms on the other.

Powers—known as Austin's godfather for his networking acumen and key role in the city's tech-based economic development over the last three decades—might be expected to slow down and savor his victories. But that's not his style. (Asked by a local newspaper how he unwinds, he answered that he doesn't know what the word means.) In 1983, he helped Austin beat out fifty-seven competing cities and land Microelectronics and Computer Technology Corp. (MCC), an early high-tech consortium for R&D that eventually generated more than $150 million and spun off more than a dozen companies.[31] The city already claimed manufacturing operations from IBM, Motorola, Texas Instruments, and Advanced Micro Devices. But landing MCC—the result of an aggressive campaign and close collaboration between city and state government, business leaders, and the University of Texas—significantly raised the city's technology profile. Five years later in 1988, with that team still in place, Austin did it again: SEMATECH, the consortium of semiconductor manufacturers, many of which already had a presence there, picked the Texas capital over 134 competing sites.[32] That hard work paid off: over the following decade, Austin added more than a hundred thousand tech-sector jobs, and the city's population doubled. And since 2002, Powers, determined to keep the momentum going, allied with Governor Perry to help launch two statewide technology funds totaling $500 million, providing capital for promising startups and R&D and expanding the state's competitive ability to lure business to Austin and Texas.

With its location in central Texas, Austin struggles to beat an international powerhouse like Silicon Valley, with its cluster of top universities and deep-pocketed venture capital firms. But the city has spawned an impressive entrepreneurial climate and benefited from singular success stories. University of Texas freshman Michael Dell launched his company of custom-built personal computers from his Austin dorm in 1984; several decades later, industry leader Dell Inc. was employing nearly eighty thousand people in three dozen countries, including some sixteen thousand in central Texas. Not long after Dell's emergence in the 1980s, George Kozmetsky, the visionary dean of the University of Texas business school, created the Austin Technology Incubator and its think-tank offspring IC2, supporting dozens of fledgling startups and helping define the city's collaborative identity between the university and business. As much as Powers and others in the city's economic development game understood the importance of "elephant hunting," he said "the real future was to be an economic garden where you grow your own."[33]

That meant luring young entrepreneurs and keeping university graduates from leaving town, a task made easier when students or other visitors fall in love with the city. Locals say that about one of every four UT-Austin grads ends up staying, one reason why the city boasts such an educated population. Rodney Gibbs is one of them. A gaming industry entrepreneur and Tennessee native, Gibbs left Austin for Los Angeles and the television business after pocketing a master's degree in screenwriting in 1996. "But I always pined for Austin," he told us. "Something about it is contagious."[34] So he came back, first taking freelance assignments, then launching Fizz Factor, a digital gaming company that grew to seventy-five employees and landed big projects from Hollywood film studios. After nearly eight years, he launched Ricochet Labs to build smartphone games that can be played in public places like pubs and movie theaters. He also joined the board of the Austin Film Society and other civic groups shaping the city's expanding digital media community. While the talent pool of top professionals was relatively thin compared to LA or New York, that becomes less true every day. The converging fields of music, gaming, social media, and film and TV—of technology and creativity—play to Austin's strengths. Gibbs mentioned some of the gaming world's top production talent who live in Austin. "All of these guys had the opportunity to go elsewhere," he said, "but they wanted to stay."[35]

Ironically, while the music scene defines the city's creative ethos, it remains surprisingly undeveloped, businesswise. With hundreds of music venues, the music scene has perfectly expressed the entrepreneurial, small-business ethos that permeates the town. This has rarely been a path to great riches—musicians seeking to hit it big have headed to Nashville, New York, or Los Angeles—but that has been part of what makes Austin different.

That laidback, just-for-fun sense is a part of what lured James Moody. To the New Orleans native, Austin felt familiar and good, and it also felt like an opportunity to combine his love for music and his business knowhow. "When I first came eight years ago, I was shocked by how much room for growth there was here," Moody told us as a bar band shook our floorboards from the floor below. This is Moody's club, an indoor-outdoor venue called the Mohawk. "I'm here for the same reason that a lot of creative people are interested in being here. . . . It's not because Dell is here. They're moving here because of 'Keep Austin Weird' and the lifestyle. I don't know how long that's going to last, how long Austin can hold onto it."[36]

Managing growth may sound like a quality problem if you've just arrived from Detroit or some other hard-hit urban cold spot. But that doesn't mean that Austin's leadership isn't challenged about the future. Mayor Lee Leffingwell, a seventy-year-old Austin native who was a Delta Airlines pilot for thirty-two years before being elected in 2009, said he's seen the city double its population three times in his lifetime. He was quick to praise the city's "strong and flourishing" tech sector. He ticked off for us fresh announcements like social media giant Facebook opening in Austin its first office outside Palo Alto, California, and Korean electronics maker Samsung, already a multibillion-dollar player in town, investing another $3.6 billion into a fabrication plant expansion, making it "the biggest chip fab in the Western Hemisphere." This is what confidence sounds like: "We've been doing very well," Leffingwell told us, "but it helps that it's Austin, Texas, because the city really sells itself."[37]

The affable mayor, a self-described problem solver trained as a mechanical engineer, understands that Austin's infrastructure needs improvements if the city is going to maintain its progress. With a current population of nearly eight hundred thousand, the city is estimated to nearly double over the next three decades, Leffingwell said. High on the list of problems is mass transit: Austin's I-35 freeway has the unenviable achievement of appearing four times on Forbes's top 100 worst intersections in the country; nearly every other slot was taken by roads in New York, LA, Chicago, or San Francisco.[38] Still, while that choked highway may spike road rage and hamper movement around town, it seems unlikely to slow the moves to Austin, especially if Austin's leaders land the long-discussed light rail system. For his part, Leffingwell recognizes that his job requires a high degree of communication and cooperation. "With over sixty citizen boards, we practice advanced democracy here," he said. And he's not complaining, even if all the input can be challenging: "It's better to have people who are interested in the city than not."[39]

Count club owner James Moody among that contingent. He's taken an active role on several city boards to help navigate a path that supports growth while saving space for creative expression, even when it's not financially profitable. He may not be an engineer by training, but you could call him a problem solver, too, as well as an Austinite who's optimistic about the future. "I feel my dollars are safer here than about anywhere else in the country," he said. "I just moved to the right city at the right time. Sometimes you just get lucky."[40] Luck or not, it helps to have the right pieces in place; and that includes leadership that is not afraid to recognize and polish its assets, even if it makes Austin seem weird.

While Austin is a Democratic stronghold in a predominately Republican state, this city's ethos is less defined by partisan battles than the creative drive to get things done while remaining uniquely Austin. That's a powerful brew, and just the kind of weirdness that dares to be bottled and shipped around the country.

Chapter 12

Are We Ready for Leadership That Represents the Best of Us?

We began this book by describing a nation adrift, at a moment of great urgency and grave need. We have little doubt that this is a widely shared view, whatever one's political persuasion may be. As we have described, the body politic is ailing, infected by fierce divisiveness and the cancer of money, deep distrust in government and elected officials, growing anger and frustration, a widening rift between our states and the federal government, the rising power of extremists, a lack of civic engagement, and a failure of education to ensure an informed citizenry. It's no wonder that in this intense and often intensely hostile climate, our leaders fail to cooperate with each other, fail to talk honestly to the public, and fail to seriously address the nation's pressing problems. It's no surprise that Americans suffer complacency and cynicism, even while they notice that their political leaders refuse to make hard choices, ask for sacrifice, or advocate for change by providing their own actions as examples. When our leaders fail to perform with excellence, it creates an underlying and unspoken fear that excellence itself is drifting out of reach—and that a nation wracked by seemingly insoluble problems may be incapable of finding real solutions. This fear can then deepen the resentment and the recriminations, making our cherished belief in rediscovering shared values and common purpose seem mere fantasy.

We have highlighted some individual examples of innovation and ingenuity, lest we forget that America is enhanced by and defined by the hard work, the bold imagination, the purposeful effort, and, yes, the excellence, of so many of our citizens. Yet the scale of our challenges depends on broad support, collective action, and honest and mature conversation about what's required to reawaken a great nation—even if it involves shattering false idols, even if it lays waste to the comfortable certitude of American preeminence, even if it means facing our political taboos, even if it hurts. But that can only be achieved if we expect, indeed demand, leadership that represents the best in all of us.

At the end of 2009, Democratic senator Kent Conrad of North Dakota and Republican senator Judd Gregg of New Hampshire pushed for a bipartisan congressional taskforce to address the explosion of the federal deficit and debt. Noting that the debt had ballooned beyond $12 trillion and the debt ceiling was raised eight times in the previous eight years, they acknowledged that Congress was unprepared to fix it. "Some have argued that House and Senate committees with jurisdiction over health, retirement and revenue issues should individually take up legislation to address the imbalance," they wrote in an op-ed. "But that path will never work. The inability of the regular legislative process to meaningfully act on this couldn't be clearer."[1] They could not have been more right. After their proposal garnered fifty-three votes, seven short of the sixty-vote majority needed, Gregg described the result as "yet another indication that Congress is more concerned with the next election than the next generation." Later, when asked if he would support a similar commission created by presidential executive order, Gregg said that approach "would have no force of law to bind the Congress to do anything, and there really aren't a lot of giants around here."[2]

President Obama probably did not count the number of giants, but he did authorize a bipartisan National Commission on Fiscal Responsibility and Reform, modeled on a similar eighteen-member framework and comprising half Democrats and half Republicans. The commission was charged to make recommendations and seek agreement from fourteen of the members—recommendations that then House Speaker Nancy Pelosi and Senate Majority Leader Harry Reid promised they would bring up for a vote. The stated goal was to cut the deficit by $240 billion a year beginning in 2015 and deal with entitlements for the long-term fiscal health of the country. That meant looking at how to reduce discretionary spending—areas such as education, transportation, the military, homeland security—and mandatory spending, which includes Social Security, Medicare, and Medicaid. It also meant finding a way to raise additional revenue. In the cynical climate of Washington, this was seen by some as nothing more than a strategy to provide the president cover to raise taxes or, worse, another sign that the president lacked the ability or will to make tough choices.

To lead the commission, Obama asked former Clinton chief of staff and Democrat Erskine Bowles and former Wyoming Republican senator Alan Simpson, two men who had returned to private life and were no longer absorbed in the daily power struggles of Washington. One of us, Beschloss, spoke to both men for a *Parade* magazine story that was published July 4, 2010, and he was struck by the sense that they got involved out of a genuine feeling of duty.[3] "Look," Simpson said, "If we're just going to slog around in the fact that there's no good in the world and nobody does anything out of good will or patriotism, then, what the hell—we're never going to make it anyway." Added Bowles, "This is an American problem that we've got to solve."

Neither Simpson nor Bowles sugarcoated the reality or the difficulty of finding solutions. Asked how dire the situation is, Bowles spoke passionately about his fear of inaction. His answer deserves close reading:

I haven't met a soul who doesn't think if we don't do anything we're facing the most predictable economic crisis in history. It's plain arithmetic. This debt is like cancer growing within the country. And the current path we're on is not sustainable. . . . We will be paying $1 trillion in interest cost in 2020 if we don't do something. *$1 trillion in interest cost.* I think the American people should be irate about that. Just stop for a minute: That's money we can't spend on Social Security or Medicare. That's money we can't spend on education or infrastructure or innovation to make sure America is competitive in a global economy. Half of that money will be going outside of America to foreign countries. What if the Chinese just quit buying some of our debt? What if they start to sell some of our debt? It will be a disaster—and everybody knows that. That's why we have to do something. We can't just keep rocking along on autopilot doing what we're doing today. . . .

We have to think about what we're going to do to reform Medicare, Medicaid, and Social Security. We have to look at the defense budget and the nondefense discretionary budget. All of it has to be on the table. But to get something to happen, we've all got to jump off a bridge together—and it's going to be some pretty tough medicine. None of the decisions we are going to make will be easy; they're all politically tough. That's why you have a commission to point a way, so that you have some direction and we can all go over in a bipartisan manner.[4]

Tough choices, especially in the rancorous political climate more geared for killing the opposition than serving the country. Before he agreed to participate, Simpson said he got the president's promise "to the hilt" that "everything is on the table." Despite their contrasting worldviews, both Bowles and Simpson expressed trust and admiration for each other; Simpson stressed that the bipartisan commission's members are "good people" who are listening to each other and "not sharpshooting across the way." Still, "there are plenty of other people who want to see us fail," he said, and "the tremendous forces of politics and the crush of reelection and interest groups" all conspire to block action. Bowles pointed to his success in 1997 helping Clinton achieve a balanced budget. "There wasn't a soul who believed we could get it done when we started," he said. "But we built up trust and confidence, and we ended up getting 75 percent of the Democrats and Republicans in both houses of Congress to vote for it. I think we have a chance to do that now."[5]

In fact, on December 3, they failed to get the needed fourteen votes to force congressional action. But they expressed their appreciation that a majority of eleven (including five Republican and three Democratic legislators) voted yes on a tough proposal of spending cuts and increased tax collections to reduce the deficit by nearly $4 trillion over the next decade. Crafted by Bowles and Simpson, the controversial plan's long list included overhauling individual income tax and corporate tax rates, raising the Social Security retirement age and reducing benefits for higher-income beneficiaries, and sharply cutting military spending. Illinois senator Dick Durbin gamely called the vote "a breakthrough" that sends a clear message that "people on the left have got to join with people on the right to find a solution" to the soaring national debt.[6] Idaho Republican senator Mike Crapo said he voted yes, despite reservations, because "the threat that we face is so real and so close that we do not have further time for gridlock or inaction. It's necessary that we take strong, aggressive action now."[7]

To be sure, this was encouraging rhetoric, backed up by assertions that the commission's proposals would enter the congressional agenda over the next year and make progress. Still, this assumes that US Congress members are capable of agreeing with each other on the urgency of the problem and the necessity of cooperation. And that requires leadership capable of bridging differences and transcending internecine party warfare more intent on collecting pyrrhic victories than serving the country's interest. In 2009, the obstructionist Senate had to break more filibusters than in the 1950s and 1960s combined. While this strategy has been employed by the minority party when it's out of power, does anyone believe this tactic is really good for the country?[8]

This leads us to suggest that forming separate commissions (relying on simple up-or-down majority votes) may be the only way to introduce and tackle big issues. We may have reached a point of such discord and distrust that the country can depend only on Americans released from the grip of the next election—men and women who are capable of providing leadership by speaking honestly without fear for their career or position. Such bipartisan collections combined with outside experts can give cover to elected officials reluctant to face the wrath of their party, opposition groups, or special interests that condemn stepping across ideological lines. Here's how these could work: All presidential candidates would be expected to define the five or six key issues that they believe should be the focus of such National Challenge Commissions. The selection of topics would be another way for the public to assess what the candidates really think matters most and is worth the country's attention. This may sound like a demand for more vegetables at mealtime, but if we are going to break the cycle of denial and avoidance, we believe it's worth trying. The more these commissions garner national interest and are conducted with the serious intent of addressing and solving the nation's major challenges, the more they can drive national conversation and debate; this can be especially important with subjects so thorny that no one risks touching them now. By including Congress members and linking the concrete recommendations to congressional or even national referendum-type votes, the commissions could provide a level of honesty the public craves and step closer to the democratic intentions of the Founding Fathers for an engaged and thinking citizenry.

Far too often, rather than getting the best from our national leaders, we are left with politicians who sign the Grover Norquist pledge opposing any new tax increases, whatever the country's economic circumstances. That may sound like leadership for ideologues who are determined to "starve the beast" and force a shrunken government, whatever the consequences, but it replaces strategic, creative thinking with robotic responses and the death of cooperation. Ohio senator and fiscal hawk George Voinovich, one of a minority of Republican senators who did not sign the antitax pledge, criticized his colleagues who refuse to face the country's fiscal challenges. "The fact of the matter is that we have to raise taxes and we have to cut costs," said the exasperated seventy-four-year-old senator. It's not the most popular message these days, and he voiced it the same year he announced his retirement from the Senate. He was not the only elected official tired of the political dysfunction and polarization: Fifty-four-year-old Indiana senator Evan Bayh, who was on candidate Obama's short list for vice president in 2008, shocked his colleagues by announcing his retirement in 2010. "At this time I simply believe I can best contribute to society in another way," he said, "creating jobs by helping grow a business, helping guide an institution of higher learning, or helping run a worthy charitable endeavor."[9] Personal reasons aside, when a slot in the nation's most powerful and exclusive body is no longer the best way to get things done, then it's time to question the failure of both the system and the people who are leading it.

John Gardner, the architect of Lyndon Johnson's Great Society Program, former president of the Carnegie Foundation, and founding chairman of Common Cause, authored in 1990 a powerful book about leadership. He surveyed the country's fragmentation, rising sense of disappointment, and increasing inability to react to immense threats, from terrorism and AIDS to environmental and economic disaster. Gardner worried about the disintegration of shared values, recognized the hunger for leadership, and asserted the importance of excellence. "At the time this nation was formed, our population stood at around three million," he wrote. "And we produced out of that three million people perhaps six leaders of world class—Washington, Adams, Jefferson, Franklin, Madison, and Hamilton. Today, our population stands at 245 million, so we might expect at least eighty times as many world-class leaders—480 Jeffersons, Madisons, Adamses, Washingtons, Hamiltons, and Franklins. Where are they?"

By Gardner's calculation, there should be more than six hundred of these leaders today. Where are they? And how many of that potential group were turned off by political life? That is an inestimable loss for the nation. But even if we fail to find political leaders at the level of our Founding Fathers, Gardner did not absolve citizens from responsibility and the need to hold power accountable: "Citizens must understand the possibilities and limitations of leadership. We must know how we can strengthen and support good leaders; and we must be able to see through the leaders who are exploiting us, playing on our hatred and prejudice, or taking us down dangerous paths. Understanding these things, we come to see that much of the responsibility for leaders and how they perform is in our own hands. If we are lazy, self-indulgent, and wanting to be deceived; if we willingly follow corrupt leaders; if we allow our heritage of freedom to decay; if we fail to be faithful monitors of the public process—then we shall get and deserve the worst."[10] Wise advice, always, but especially in times of crisis, and a reminder why a disengaged electorate is so dangerous.

On December 29, 1940, after the Germans occupied France and after London was pounded by bombs and engulfed in flames, the just-reelected President Roosevelt spoke to Americans with clarity and urgency about a ruthless enemy. "The Nazi masters of Germany have made it clear that they intend not only to dominate all life and thought in their own country, but also to enslave the whole of Europe, and then to use the resources of Europe to dominate the rest of the world," the president said. "If Great Britain goes down, the Axis powers will control the Continents of Europe, Asia, Africa, Austral-Asia, and the high seas. And they will be in a position to bring enormous military and naval resources against this hemisphere." He urged "courage and realism," and he emphasized the impossibility of a peaceful settlement. "There can be no appeasement with ruthlessness. There can be no reasoning with an incendiary bomb." While he stressed then that he was not committing Americans to fight on foreign soil (yet), he called for the nation's productive forces to be transformed into a "great arsenal of Democracy," an objective that transformed industrial cities such as Detroit and reconfigured the nation's goals. "I want to make it clear that it is the purpose of the nation to build now with all possible speed every machine, every arsenal, every factory that we need to manufacture our defense materiel," he said. Nearly a year would pass before Pearl Harbor was bombed and the United States officially declared war, but despite the powerful voices that resisted intervention in 1940, the president was determined to advance the nation's readiness. This is "an emergency as serious as war itself," he declared. "We must apply ourselves to our task with the same resolution, the same sense of urgency, the same spirit of patriotism and sacrifice as we would show were we at war."[11]

We can be grateful that America is not yet faced with the same imminent threat to our survival that the country endured seventy years ago. The last thing we are seeking is to romanticize a time in world history when nearly a million Americans were killed or wounded and more than 50 million people around the planet lost their lives. But it's worth recalling that the country's ability to defeat the Nazis resulted from the clarity of purpose against a well-defined enemy and from leadership that did not simply prey on fear but asked Americans to "discard the notion of 'business as usual'" and sacrifice for the defense of democracy. "Great effort requires great sacrifice," Roosevelt said. (The president also described the government's responsibility to its people: "I would ask no one to defend a democracy which in turn would not defend every one in the nation against want and privation."[12])

Will it take the same level of gravity and danger, violence and death, before the country is capable of coming together again? Will it take a clearly defined external enemy to concentrate Americans and redirect their anger away from their political opponents, who now serve as surrogate enemies? We believe that it's right to demand the best of America's leaders and citizens before the fight for the nation's survival is imminently at stake. And that entails overcoming the desire for simple solutions, even when the call to "throw out the rascals" seems so smart and powerful. The next set of rascals may look awfully familiar if the country refuses to confront the crippling failure to engage in adult conversation and govern for the good of the country rather than narrow party interests.

It's ironic that one thread of FDR's argument was that a victory by the Axis powers in Europe could lead to a "new and terrible era" in which the whole world, including the American hemisphere, would be run by threats of brute force: "To survive in such a world, we would have to convert ourselves permanently into a militaristic power on the basis of war economy." The Axis powers did not succeed, but that conversion happened anyway. It continues to define the American story, even though American leaders in recent decades have failed to address it directly.

On January 17, 1961, twenty years and nineteen days after Roosevelt's speech, President Eisenhower gave his famed "military-industrial complex" speech. In that nationally televised farewell address, following the launch of Sputnik and the intensifying Cold War, he explained that the country had moved beyond "emergency improvisation of national defense." Indeed, "we have been compelled to create a permanent armaments industry of vast proportions," he said, a defense establishment that directly engages 3.5 million people and spends each year more than the net income of all US corporations. This "immense military establishment and a large arms industry is new in the American experience. The total influence—economic, political, even spiritual—is felt in every city, every state house, every office of the federal government." Eisenhower warned against the ongoing "potential for the disastrous rise of misplaced power. . . . We must never let the weight of this combination endanger our liberties or democratic processes. We should take nothing for granted."[13]

A half century later, this wise advice has lost none of its potency, especially because the defense establishment has grown considerably more immense and the country has come to take it for granted. By 2010, defense spending was projected to hit $719 billion, nearly double its total twenty years earlier. Between 2000 and 2008 alone, military expenditures rose 63 percent. That spending is more than double the spending of China, France, the United Kingdom, and Russia combined, and it even surpasses the total of the top fifteen countries. With a fully extended imperial reach, the United States maintains more than 766 military bases in more than forty countries around the world, valued at more than $127 billion in 2005, housing more than half a million personnel and their dependents, and covering nearly eleven hundred square miles of foreign land.[14]

While Social Security, Medicare, and Medicaid are touched upon when the conversation turns to cutting the deficit, defense spending has remained essentially taboo. It will take real leadership to insert this onto the public's agenda because it requires asking anew what national security really means in a post-9/11 world, how dependent the arms industry is on US subsidies, how defense spending is used to drive trade strategy, whether the country can continue to afford this with financing borrowed from foreign sources, and if this national security policy is harming the country's economic security and ultimate survival as we know it. That same question can and should be asked in terms of the monies that the country spends on its own people for health, education, social security, and other pieces of the current social safety net, but the point is that the military should not be treated as untouchable. The country deserves an honest conversation about what it values most and at what risk.

(One concrete aid to this would be arming Americans with facts about the taxes they pay. Researchers at the Washington think tank Third Way devised a clever, easy-to-read "tax receipt" that itemizes where each dollar of any given American's tax bill actually goes. If you paid $5,400 in taxes, for example, your money paid $1,040.70 for Social Security, $625.51 for Medicare, $385.28 for Medicaid, $287.03 for interest on the national debt, $229.17 for combat operations in Iraq and Afghanistan, $192.79 for military personnel, $74.65 for veterans benefits, $63.89 for federal highways, and so forth, right down to 24 cents to fund arts and 19 cents for congressional salaries and benefits. Imagine how this information might cause some Americans to rethink their priorities.)[15]

To take seriously Eisenhower's warning about the military-industrial complex would mean looking at national defense in all its tentacles: for example, how intricately connected it has become to the nation's universities, industrial R&D, and the economies of the majority of the country's states. This should be a National Challenge, exactly because a great nation should be strong enough to consider the foundations upon which it stands. As *The Rise and Fall of Great Powers* author Paul Kennedy warned, the United States would suffer "imperial overstretch" and inexorable decline with the nation's resources heavily directed toward military purposes if we didn't change direction. He said it in 1987, and a decade later he urged Washington decision makers that they must confront the "awkward and enduring fact that the total of the United States' global interests and obligations is nowadays far too large for the country to be able to defend them all simultaneously."[16] That was six years before the Iraq and Afghanistan wars and the massive military buildup. In 2001, military analyst Andrew Bacevich noted that in American public life there was hardly "a single prominent figure who finds fault with the notion of the United States remaining the world's sole military superpower until the end of time."[17]

That may have changed as the country has suffered substantial loss of lives and treasure as well as a debilitating economic crisis. But the increasingly angry political divide and extremist, anti-intellectual climate have only intensified the emotional impulse to reject facts and cling to readymade views. That should no longer be tolerable. We have reached a moment in our history that demands the best of us. That means rejecting the antielitism that believes at its core that the country's problems can be solved without hard work, brains, or the pursuit of excellence. It requires considering the kind of leaders needed to stop the crazy dance and change the music—people who won't just tell us what they think we want to hear. This is no easy task as long as cable news fuels the extremes and political victors must be fundraisers first and thoughtful servants second. This moment also cries out for us to seek political leaders, strategic partnerships, and leadership models from outside the Washington swamp, among teachers and mayors, scientists and business leaders, talented people who are professionals first and politicians second, people who value cooperation and excellence, people who care less about reelection than making a positive difference.

"I think cities are run better because there's more professionalism," former Arizona congressman Harry Mitchell told us. He first came to Washington when he was sixty-eight, the oldest member of his freshman class, after he already had a successful career as a high school civics teacher and mayor of Tempe. "I've had my career. I'm there to do what I can to help," he said. And he admitted that being mayor was a better job, that the focus was on getting things done rather than fighting over differences and grasping for the limelight. "There is no Democrat or Republican way to pick up garbage, run parks, or run the sewer plant."[18] Mitchell is right, and even for national issues there should be an American way to do things—with excellence from the top to the bottom, in every sphere of life. "The tone of our society depends upon a pervasive and almost universal striving for good performance," John Gardner wrote two generations ago.[19]

We have drifted from this conviction, but it's not too late to regain our focus. We may have lost our expectation that the nation's leaders are committed to honesty and excellence. We may have allowed discontent and distrust to dominate the public sphere. We may think that cynicism and emotion have finally trumped sincerity and reason, but accepting that mind-set is a failing proposition that only hastens decline. The nation has faced far more challenging moments in its history and found the way to emerge stronger. America can do this again, but only if we demand the best from our leaders and our leaders inspire the best from us.

Timothy Ferris, in his book *The Science of Liberty*, argued that many of America's founding fathers were scientists who envisioned the nation as a great science experiment, where data gathering and hypothesis testing combine with the values of truth, reason, and antiauthoritarianism to shape a messy, ever-changing democratic process. "A liberal democracy in action is an endlessly changing mosaic of experiments, most of which partially or entirely fail," Ferris wrote. The operation of a free society is terribly inefficient and frustrating, he added, "inescapably fraught with flaws and mistakes."[20] Yes, it is. But when our problems feel overwhelming, our process dysfunctional, and solutions unreachable, good leadership that can help navigate a way forward could not be more urgent. Even amid the current turmoil and doubt, Americans should be empowered by the continuing struggle for answers and the fact that our future still resides in our own hands. This was the challenge that the nation's first leaders gifted us more than two centuries ago.

Winston Churchill famously said, "You can always count on Americans to do the right thing—after they've tried everything else." Well, we have tried everything else. Now we need to solve problems and make the American experiment a winning proposition again. Charting our way back to a great nation demands honesty and boldness by our leaders. It requires an intensified commitment to innovation in all areas of public life and business activity—and that means new federal and state partnerships for R&D to ensure we remain economically competitive; a mature conversation and genuine decision making on defense spending, entitlement spending, and taxation; an honest, fact-based dialogue about the size of government we want and can afford; and a renewed commitment to electing leaders who will level with us and work with each other. As President Obama promised Bowles and Simpson, everything must be on the table. We can no longer afford to drift down the same troubled path and expect a different outcome. Americans, recognizing that their survival was at stake, have faced terrible adversity before and acted with great and common purpose. We must find the strength to do it again.

Acknowledgments

We have been fortunate to connect with quite a few thoughtful people willing to share their experiences, knowledge, and insights with us. While the responsibility for this book's contents rests squarely with its authors, we could not have completed it without their input and help in a myriad of ways. This includes Leonard Fine, Thomas Bowles, Frank McCabe, Congressman Harry F. Mitchell, Congresswoman Gabrielle Giffords, Mayor Phil Gordon, Mayor Scott Smith, Mayor Lee Leffingwell, Mayor Sara Presler, Senator Fritz Hollings, Senator Alan Simpson, Erskine Bowles, Arthur Levine, Carol Peck, Tom Davison, Robert Lee, Roger Angel, Leroy Hood, Jane Poynter, Dennis Yablonsky, Tom Waseleski, Doug Heuck, Stan Fields, Mary Walshok, Warren Baker, Ira Levin, Anita Jones, Margaret Mullen, Pike Powers, James Moody, Rodney Gibbs, Adriana Cruz, Jim Butler, Leigh Morris Sloane, Matt Curtis, Fredi Lajvardi, Earl Swift, and Francesco Sisci.

Bill is especially grateful to the business and political leaders of Ireland during the period of 2001–2006 who gave him a unique opportunity to build Science Foundation Ireland (SFI), especially Chairman Brian Sweeney. Taoiseach Bertie Ahern, Tánaiste Mary Harney, and Minister of Science Noel Treacy had the courage to lead and sustain a bold investment and develop policies that have helped Ireland to remain competitive in knowledge-based industries, even now as the country addresses the financial problems arising from the property bubble and its overleveraged banks. Alastair Glass, Richard Hirsh, Fiona Renalds, Gary Crawley, and Marjorie MacFarlane were members of the team that built SFI and technology transfer capabilities, and each contributed to this effort. We are especially grateful to Erich Bloch, who not only has contributed to our thinking but also been a great mentor to Bill for many years.

Bill's work in Arizona has benefitted from the wisdom and statesmanship of Don Budinger, who, along with others in the business and philanthropic community, is committed to civility and common sense in our public discourse. He helped create Science Foundation Arizona (SFAz) to be a catalyst to a more diverse economy and spur excellence in science and math education. Each great effort begins with courage and leadership. Don, Sandra Day O'Connor, Craig Barrett, Sue Clark-Johnson, and Michael Crow are among those who provide that foundation in Arizona. And no transformation can occur in a state without a partnership built on trust with state leaders. This starts with former governor Janet Napolitano and Senate President Tim Bee and includes Speaker Kirk Adams, Bill Konopnicki, Michele Reagan, Chad Campbell, Jennifer Burns, Don Cardon, Sandra Watson, Robert Shelton and John Haeger, Tom Browning and Tom Franz, Eileen Klein, and Governor Jan Brewer. Foundations led by Jerry Bisgrove and Judy Mohraz made significant investments in SFAz, and they always have been available to assist in the development of Arizona's future. Public policy colleagues across the country have been constructive critics and advisors of our thinking over the years, including Mary Jo Waits, Lesa Mitchell, and Mark Muro. Bill Budinger has broadened Bill's thinking through the Aspen Ideas Festival and the wisdom of his experience in building a unique company with his brother. In addition, we especially want to thank Governor Bill Richardson, who was kind enough to contribute the foreword to this book and whose leadership in linking the public and private sectors has been so valuable.

We also could not have completed this manuscript without the thoughtful support of our agent, David Larabell of the David Black Agency; the early commitment and skilled guidance of Prometheus editor Linda Regan; and the reliable assistance of Monica Mendoza. Finally, there are others without whom this book could not have been written. Steven is particularly grateful for the loving and creative support of his wife and fellow writer, Kirsi-Marja Häyrinen-Beschloss, who talked him down from the ledge more than once. And he is thankful for Sara Beschloss and Katrina Beschloss, who endured their father's frequent distraction with understanding and grace beyond their years. He dedicates this book to these three special people. Bill's family members (Connie, David and Dianne, Catherine and Mike) share a commitment to learning and hard work, and each has made the world a better place because of who they are and what they do. We need to sustain the dream for Ben, Sophie, and Matthew.

NOTES

PREFACE: WHY WE'VE WRITTEN THIS BOOK

1. National Commission on Educational Excellence, "A Nation At Risk," April 1983, http://www2.ed.gov/pubs/NatAtRisk/risk.html (accessed February 3, 2010).

CHAPTER 1: ARE AMERICANS STILL CAPABLE OF BOLD ACTION AND COMMON PURPOSE?

1. Paul Dickson, *Sputnik: The Shock of the Century* (New York: Walker, 2007), 9, 117.

2. Ibid., 117; David Halberstam, *The Fifties* (New York: Fawcett Columbine, 1993), 655.

3. Martin J. Collins, *After Sputnik: 50 Years of the Space Age* (Washington, DC: Smithsonian, 2007), 44.

4. Constance McLaughlin Green and Milton Lomask, "Success and After," chap. 12 in *Vanguard: A History* (Washington, DC: NASA 1970), http://history.nasa.gov/sputnik/chap12.html (accessed October 22, 2010).

5. Dickson, *Sputnik*, 177.

6. Ibid., 226–27; Clyde Haberman, "What Sputnik Meant to a

Kid Studying Science," *New York Times*, October 5, 2007, http://www.nytimes.com/2007/10/05/nyregion/05nyc.html?_r=1&ref=todays paper&oref=slogin (accessed October 21, 2010).

7. Benjamin Fine, "14 Billions Spent in 7 Years to Educate 8,000,000 G.I.'s," *New York Times,* July 22, 1951, http://query.ny times.com/mem/archive/pdf?res=F50716F639591A7B93C0AB178CD 85F458585F9 (accessed October 22, 2010).

8. Michael J. Bennett, *When Dreams Came True: The GI Bill and the Making of Modern America* (Washington, DC: Brassey's, 2000).

9. Edith Efron, "The Two Joes Meet—Joe College, Joe Veteran," *New York Times Magazine*, June 16, 1946, 11ff.

10. Quoted in Fine, "14 Billions Spent."

11. Dickson, *Sputnik*, 215.

12. Gene Kranz, *Failure Is Not an Option* (New York: Berkeley Publishing, 2000), 201.

13. John F. Kennedy, "Special Message to the Congress on Urgent National Needs," May 25, 1961, http://www.jfklibrary.org/Historical +Resources/Archives/Reference+Desk/Speeches/JFK/003POF03 NationalNeeds05251961.htm (accessed October 22, 2010).

14. Ibid.

15. Robert Gilruth, interview by David DeVorkin and John Mauer, National Air and Space Museum, February 27, 1987, transcript at http://www.nasm.si.edu/research/dsh/TRANSCPT/GILRUTH5.HTM (accessed October 21, 2010).

16. Mary C. White, "Detailed Biographies of Apollo I Crew," NASA History Division, http://history.nasa.gov/Apollo204/zorn/grissom.htm (accessed October 18, 2010).

17. "Glenn Orbits the Earth," Glenn Research Center, NASA website, http://www.nasa.gov/centers/glenn/about/bios/mercury_mission .html (accessed October 22, 2010).

18. Jane van Nimmen, Leonard C. Bruno, and Robert L. Rosholt, *NASA Historical Data Book: 1958–1968*, vol. 1, *NASA Resources* (Washington, DC: NASA Scientific and Technical Information Office, 1976), http://history.nasa.gov/SP-4012v1.pdf.

19. John F. Kennedy, Rice University speech, September 12, 1962.

20. Jimmy Carter, "Crisis of Confidence" speech transcript, July 15, 1979, http://www.pbs.org/wgbh/amex/carter/filmmore/ps_crisis .html (accessed October 19, 2010).

21. Christopher Lasch, *The Culture of Narcissism: American Life in an Age of Diminishing Expectations* (New York: Norton, 1978).

22. Carter, "Crisis of Confidence" speech.

23. Jimmy Carter, "Proposed Energy Policy" speech transcript, April 18, 1977, http://www.pbs.org/wgbh/amex/carter/filmmore/ps_energy.html (accessed October 19, 2010).

24. Howell Raines, "Citizens Ask If Carter Is Part of the 'Crisis,'" *New York Times*, August 3, 1979, A1; Hedrick Smith et al., "Reshaping of Carter's Presidency: 16 Days of Shifts and Reappraisal," *New York Times*, July 22, 1979, A1.

25. John Herbers, "Carving Up the National Goals Leaves Very Little," *New York Times*, July 22, 1979, E1.

CHAPTER 2: IS IT TOO LATE TO RESTORE AMERICAN AMBITION?

1. Peter S. Goodman, "Despite Signs of Recovery, Chronic Joblessness Rises," *New York Times*, February 20, 2010, http://www.nytimes.com/2010/02/21/business/economy/21unemployed.html (accessed December 2, 2010).

2. Bob Willis and Anthony Feld, "Household Worth in U.S. Fell in Second Quarter," *Bloomberg Businessweek*, September 17, 2010, http://www.businessweek.com/news/2010-09-17/household-worth-in-u-s-fell-in-second-quarter.html (accessed December 2, 2010).

3. "Bankruptcy Statistics," United States Courts website, http://www.uscourts.gov/Statistics/BankruptcyStatistics.aspx (accessed November 12, 2010).

4. Paul Taylor et al., "How the Great Recession Has Changed Life in America," Pew Research Center, June 30, 2010, http://pewsocialtrends.org/2010/06/30/how-the-great-recession-has-changed-life-in-america/ (accessed December 2, 2010).

5. Neil Irwin, "Aughts Were a Lost Decade for U.S. Economy, Workers," *Washington Post*, January 2, 2010, http://www.washingtonpost.com/wp-dyn/content/article/2010/01/01/AR2010010101196.html (accessed November 12, 2010).

6. Paul Kennedy, *The Rise and Fall of the Great Powers* (New York: Vintage Books, 1989), 515.

7. Quoted in Jeremy Black, *Great Powers and the Quest for Hegemony* (New York: Routledge, 2008), 170.

8. Samuel P. Huntington, "The U.S.—Decline or Renewal?" *Foreign Affairs*, Winter 1988/89, http://www.foreignaffairs.com/articles/43988/samuel-p-huntington/the-us-decline-or-renewal (accessed January 29, 2009).

9. Barbara Tuchman, "A Nation in Decline," *New York Times Magazine*, September 20, 1987, 52ff.

10. Charles de Montesquieu, *The Spirit of the Laws* (Cambridge, MA: Cambridge University Press, 1989), 100.

11. Lucy Cockcroft, "Cult of Celebrity Is Harming Children," *Telegraph*, March 14, 2008, http://www.telegraph.co.uk/news/uknews/1581658/Cult-of-celebrity-is-harming-children.html (accessed November 28, 2010).

12. Stephane Baldi et al., "Highlights From PISA 2006: Performance of U.S. 15-Year-Old Students in Science and Mathematics Literacy in an International Context," National Center for Education Statistics, December 2007, 5–12, http://nces.ed.gov/pubsearch/pubsinfo.asp?pubid=2008016. (accessed October 19, 2010); Andrew J. Coulson, "All Americans Left Behind," Cato Institute, December 13, 2007, http://www.cato.org/pub_display.php?pub_id=8850 (accessed October 19, 2010).

13. Vivek Wadhwa et al., "Where the Engineers Are," *Issues in Science and Technology*, Spring 2007, http://www.issues.org/23.3/wadhwa.html (accessed September 10, 2010).

14. Quoted in Fred Hechinger, "A Call from the Past for Excellence," *New York Times*, July 19, 1983, http://www.nytimes.com/1983/07/19/science/about-education-a-call-from-the-past-for-excellence.html (accessed February 3, 2010).

15. National Commission on Educational Excellence, "A Nation At Risk," April 1983, http://www2.ed.gov/pubs/NatAtRisk/risk.html (accessed February 3, 2010).

16. Ibid.

CHAPTER 3: WHAT'S SO BAD ABOUT GOOD GOVERNMENT?

1. Lyndsey Layton, "Peanut Processor Knowingly Sold Tainted Products," *Washington Post*, January 28, 2009, A01.

2. Eric Schlosser, "Unsafe at Any Meal," *New York Times*, July 24, 2010, http://www.nytimes.com/2010/07/25/opinion/25schlosser.html (accessed October 15, 2010).

3. "Keep America's Food Safe: The Case for Increased Funding at FDA," Center for Science in the Public Interest, http://www.cspinet.org/foodsafety/fdafunding.html (accessed October 10, 2010).

4. Jonathan Miles, "The Rise and Fall of Rand Paul," *Details*, August 2010, http://www.details.com/culture-trends/critical-eye/201008/rand-paul-kentucky-senate-republican-campaign#ixzz15Uq7AILL (accessed November 15, 2010).

5. Milton Friedman, "Take It to the Limits: Milton Friedman on Libertarianism," Hoover Institution interview, recorded February 10, 1999, http://www.hoover.org/multimedia/uncommon-knowledge/26936 (accessed October 15, 2010).

6. Peter S. Goodman, "A Fresh Look at the Apostle of Free Markets," *New York Times*, April 13, 2008, http://www.nytimes.com/2008/04/13/weekinreview/13goodman.html (accessed March 6, 2010); Holcomb B. Noble, "Milton Friedman, Free Markets Theorist, Dies at 94," *New York Times*, November 6, 2006, http://www.nytimes.com/2006/11/16/business/17friedmancnd.html?_r=1&ref=weekinreview (accessed March 7, 2010).

7. Ronald Reagan, "First Inaugural Address," January 20, 1981.

8. William Greider, "The Education of David Stockman," *Atlantic*, December 1981, http://www.theatlantic.com/magazine/archive/1981/12/the-education-of-david-stockman/5760/ (accessed March 20, 2010); David A. Stockman, *The Triumph of Politics: Why the Reagan Revolution Failed* (New York: Avon, 1987), 357.

9. Reagan, "First Inaugural Address."

10. Stockman, *The Triumph of Politics*, 7.

11. Jerry Tempalski, "Revenue Effects of Major Tax Bills," US Department of the Treasury, September 2006, http://www.treasury.gov/resource-center/tax-policy/tax-analysis/Documents/ota81.pdf (accessed December 2, 2010).

12. Greider, "The Education of David Stockman."

13. Paul Krugman, "The Tax-Cut Con," *New York Times Magazine*, September 14, 2003, http://www.nytimes.com/2003/09/14/magazine/the-tax-cut-con.html (accessed October 15, 2010).

14. Susan Page, "Norquist's Power High, Profile Low," *USA Today*, June 1, 2001, http://www.usatoday.com/news/washington/2001-06-01-grover.htm (accessed October 5, 2010).

15. Krugman, "Tax-Cut Con."

16. Tempalski, "Revenue Effects of Major Tax Bills."

17. Bruce Bartlett, "Tax Cuts and 'Starving the Beast,'" *Forbes*, May 7, 2010, http://www.forbes.com/2010/05/06/tax-cuts-republicans-starve-the-beast-columnists-bruce-bartlett.html (accessed October 20, 2010).

18. William D. Cohan, "A Republican for Higher Taxes," *New York Times*, November 11, 2010, http://opinionator.blogs.nytimes.com/2010/11/11/a-republican-for-higher-taxes/?src=me (accessed December 4, 2010).

19. Ron Suskind, *The Price of Loyalty: George W. Bush, the White House, and the Education of Paul O'Neill* (New York: Simon & Schuster, 2004), 291.

20. Douglas G. Amy, "The Anti-Government Campaign," Government Is Good, http://www.governmentisgood.com/articles.php?aid=9 (accessed October 18, 2010).

21. Bill Clinton, "Remarks Announcing the Initiative to Streamline Government Initiative," March 3, 1993, transcript at http://govinfo.library.unt.edu/npr/library/speeches/030393.html (accessed October 15, 2010).

22. Donald F. Kettl, "Reinventing Government: A Fifth-Year Report Card," Brookings Institution, September 1998, http://www.brookings.edu/gs/cpm/government.pdf (accessed October 15, 2010).

23. Louis Goodman, in discussion with author, February 2009; Leigh Morris Sloane, in discussion with author, February 2009.

24. Krugman, "Tax-Cut Con."

25. One step in the right direction was bipartisan passage by Congress in December 2010 of a new food safety bill intended to increase FDA inspections and require food manufacturers to examine their processing systems to cut the risk of contamination. See William Neuman, "House Passes Overhaul of Food Laws," *New York Times*, December 21, 2010, http://www.nytimes.com/2010/12/22/business/22food.html

?_r=1&scp=5&sq=food%20safety%20modernization%20FDA&st =cse (accessed March 31, 2011).

CHAPTER 4: HAVE WE LOST CONTACT WITH OUR DEMOCRACY?

1. David Kestenbaum, "An American Dream: Gifts to Pay the National Debt," National Public Radio interview, June 4, 2010, http:// www.npr.org/templates/story/story.php?storyId=127412092 (accessed September 14, 2010); *Seattle Times*, "Bailing Out a Financially Strapped Uncle," March 18, 1990, http://community.seattletimes.nw source.com/archive/?date=19900318&slug=1061720 (accessed September 14, 2010).

2. Ibid.; Jody Murphy, "Public Debt Received $3 Million in Contributions in 2009," *News and Sentinel*, November 17, 2009, http:// newsandsentinel.com/page/content.detail/id/523780/Public-Debt -received—3-million-in-contributions-in-2009.html?nav=5066 (accessed September 16, 2010).

3. Jacob Goldstein, "What If Everybody Chipped in to Pay Off the National Debt?" National Public Radio podcast, June 1, 2010, http://www.npr.org/blogs/money/2010/06/the_tuesday_podcast_what _if_ev.html (accessed September 18, 2010).

4. William A. Galston and Elaine C. Kamarck, "Change You Can Believe in Needs a Government You Can Trust: A Third Way Report," Third Way, November 2008, http://content.thirdway.org/publications/ 133/Third_Way_Report_-_Trust_in_Government.pdf.

5. Curtis Gans, "2010 Primary Voter Data Research," Center for the Study of the American Electorate, American University's School of Public Affairs, http://www.american.edu/media/upload/2010_Primary TurnoutData_webversion_.pdf (accessed September 20, 2010).

6. Ibid.

7. Curtis Gans, "Table for One, Please: America's Disintegrating Democracy," *Washington Monthly*, 2007, http://www.washington monthly.com/books/2000/0007.gans.html (accessed September 21, 2010).

8. Rafael López Pintor, Maria Gratschew, and Kate Sullivan, *Voter Turnout Rates from a Comparative Perspective* (Stockholm, Sweden: International Institute for Democracy and Electoral Assis-

tance), 84, http://www.idea.int/publications/vt/upload/Voter%20turn out.pdf.

9. Robert D. Putnam, *Bowling Alone: The Collapse and Revival of American Community* (New York: Simon & Schuster, 2000), 33–35.

10. Ibid., 342.

11. Ibid., 337.

12. Ibid., 341.

13. Gregory Korte, "'Tea Party' Rallies Put Focus on November Races," *USA Today*, September 12, 2010, http://www.usatoday.com/news/nation/2010-09-12-tea-party-rallies_N.htm?csp=usat.me (accessed September 17, 2010).

14. Michael Scherer, "Can the Tea Party Cross the Delaware?" *Time*, September 9, 2010, http://www.time.com/time/politics/article/0,8599,2016993,00.html (accessed October 2, 2010).

15. Putnam, *Bowling Alone*, 341.

16. Center for Responsive Politics, "The Money behind the Elections," Open Secrets, http://www.opensecrets.org/bigpicture/index.php (accessed October 2, 2010).

17. Pew Research Center, "The People and Their Government: Distrust, Discontent, Anger, and Partisan Rancor," Pew Research Center news release, April 18, 2010, 50, http://people-press.org/http://people-press.org/files/legacy-pdf/606.pdf.

18. Pew Research, "People and Their Government," 5.

19. Ibid., 3.

20. Intercollegiate Studies Institute, "The Coming Crisis in Citizenship," American Civic Literacy Program report, 2006, http://www.americancivicliteracy.org/2006/summary.html (accessed March 31, 2011). Also, Intercollegiate Studies Institute, "Failing Our Students, Failing America," American Civic Literacy Program report, 2007, http://www.americancivicliteracy.org/2007/summary_summary.html (accessed March 31, 2011).

21. Intercollegiate Studies Institute, "Our Fading Heritage: Americans Fail a Basic Test on Their History and Institutions," American Civic Literacy Program report, 2008, http://www.americancivicliteracy.org/2008/summary_summary.html (accessed March 31, 2011).

22. Intercollegiate Studies Institute, "The Shaping of the American Mind: The Diverging Influences of the College Degree and Civic Learn-

ing on American Beliefs," American Civic Literacy Program report, December 2009, 22.

23. Putnam, *Bowling Alone*, 269.

24. "US Federal Individual Income Tax Rates History, 1913–2010," Tax Foundation, June 15, 2010, http://www.taxfoundation.org/publications/show/151.html (accessed October 2, 2010).

25. Putnam, *Bowling Alone*, 258.

26. Steven A. Bank, Kirk J. Stark, and Joseph J. Thorndike, *War and Taxes* (Washington, DC: Urban Institute Press, 2008), xii.

27. "U.S. Federal Individual Income Tax," Tax Foundation.

28. Ron Suskind, "Faith, Certainty, and the Presidency of George W. Bush," *New York Times Magazine*, October 17, 2004, http://www.nytimes.com/2004/10/17/magazine/17BUSH.html?_r=1&scp=1&sq=empire%20suskind&st=cse (accessed October 18, 2010).

29. As Benjamin Franklin pithily remarked to his fellow delegates of the Continental Congress, "We must all hang together, or most assuredly we shall all hang separately."

30. Thomas L. Friedman, "Palin's Kind of Patriotism," *New York Times*, October 7, 2008, http://www.nytimes.com/2008/10/08/opinion/08friedman.html?_r=1&em (accessed October 2, 2010).

31. Michael Kinsley, "The Least We Can Do," *Atlantic*, October 2010, http://www.theatlantic.com/magazine/archive/2010/10/the-least-we-can-do/8228/ (accessed October 20, 2010).

32. Andrew J. Bacevich, "Americans Should Be Asked to Sacrifice for the War on Terrorism. But Sacrifice What?" *New Republic*, August 4, 2010, http://www.tnr.com/blog/foreign-policy/76771/americans-should-be-asked-sacrifice-the-war-terrorism-sacrifice-what (accessed October 18, 2010).

CHAPTER 5: CAN AMERICA PROSPER IN THE TWENTY-FIRST CENTURY WITHOUT CLASSROOM EXCELLENCE?

1. Tom Davison, in discussion with author, March 2009.

2. Ibid.

3. "America's Best High Schools: Arizona," *Bloomberg Business-*

week, http://images.businessweek.com/ss/09/01/0115_best_schools/4.htm (accessed October 18, 2010).

4. "America's Best High Schools: The List," *Newsweek*, http://www.newsweek.com/feature/2010/americas-best-high-schools/list.html (accessed October 18, 2010).

5. Arthur Levine, "Educating School Teachers," Education Schools Project, September 2006, http://www.edschools.org/pdf/Educating_Teachers_Report.pdf (accessed October 18, 2010).

6. Claudia Wallis, "How to Make Great Teachers," *Time*, February 13, 2008, http://www.time.com/time/nation/article/0,8599,1713174,00.html (accessed October 16, 2010).

7. Robert Lee, in discussion with author, April 2009.

8. Levine, "Educating School Teachers," 11.

9. Arthur Levine, in discussion with author, April 2009.

10 Sara Corbett, "Games Theory," *New York Times Magazine*, September 19, 2010, 56–57.

11. Sam Dillon, "Teach for America Sees Surge in Popularity," *New York Times*, May 14, 2008, http://www.nytimes.com/2008/05/14/education/14teach.html (accessed October 15, 2010).

12. Zeyu Xu, Jane Hannaway, and Colin Taylor, "Making a Difference? The Effect of Teach for America on Student Performance in High School," Urban Institute, http://www.urban.org/publications/901157.html (accessed October 15, 2010).

13. Lucia Graves, "The Evolution of Teach for America," *U.S. News and World Report*, October 17, 2008, http://www.usnews.com/articles/education/k-12/2008/10/17/the-evolution-of-teach-for-america.html?PageNr=2 (accessed October 16, 2010).

14. Carol Peck, in discussion with author, June 2009.

15. Jay Mathews, "Ivy League Aspirations," *Newsweek*, January 17, 2009, http://www.newsweek.com/2009/01/16/ivy-league-aspirations.html (accessed October 16, 2010).

16. Ibid.

17. Ibid.

18. Mike Feinberg and David Levin, "What 'Yes, We Can' Should Mean for Our Schools," *Washington Post*, January 9, 2009, A17.

19. Levine, "Educating School Teachers," 107.

20. Leonard Fine, in discussion with authors, August 2009.

CHAPTER 6: DON'T WE WANT THE BEST AND BRIGHTEST TO COME AND STAY?

1. "History of Harbin," China Travel, http://www.justchina .org/china/harbin/harbin-history.asp (accessed September 18, 2010); *Encyclopedia Britannica Online*, s.v. "Harbin (China): History," accessed September 18, 2010, http://www.britannica.com/EBchecked/ topic/254877/Harbin/256258/History; and "Jews in Harbin," *Beijing Review*, August 5, 2008, http://www.bjreview.com.cn/special/jews_in _harbin/txt/2008-08/05/content_138583.htm (accessed September 18, 2010).

2. "Profile of HIT," Harbin Institute of Technology website, http://en.hit.edu.cn/about/profile.htm (accessed September 19, 2010).

3. "Key Figures," Harbin Engineering University website, http:// english.hrbeu.edu.cn/showarticle.php?articleid=51 (accessed October 22, 2010).

4. "Students of Shanghai Jiaotong University Crowned World Champions of the IBM-Sponsored 'Battle of the Brains,'" IBM press release, Harbin, China, February 5, 2010, http://www-03.ibm.com/ press/us/en/pressrelease/29351.wss#release#release (accessed October 22, 2010).

5. Steve Hamm, "A Red Flag in the Brain Game," *Bloomberg Businessweek*, May 1, 2006, http://www.businessweek.com/magazine/ content/06_18/b3982053.htm (September 10, 2010).

6. "Students of Shanghai Jiaotong," IBM press release; Christine McFadden, "CS Team Places 14th at World Finals," *Stanford Daily*, February 10, 2010, http://www.stanforddaily.com/2010/02/10/cs-team -places-fourteenth-at-world-finals/ (accessed October 22, 2010).

7. Quoted in Hamm, "Red Flag in the Brain Game," *Businessweek*.

8. Joan Burrelli, "Foreign Science and Engineering Students in the United States," National Science Foundation website, July 2010, http:// www.nsf.gov/statistics/infbrief/nsf10324/ (accessed October 22, 2010).

9. Philip M. Boffey, "Foreign Students: A Boon or a Threat?" *New York Times*, September 2, 1984, http://www.nytimes.com/1984/ 09/02/weekinreview/foreign-students-a-boon-or-a-threat.html (accessed October 22, 2010).

10. Vivek Wadhwa, "The Reverse Brain Drain," *Bloomberg Businessweek*, August 22, 2007, http://www.businessweek.com/smallbiz/content/aug2007/sb20070821_920025.htm (accessed September 18, 2010).

11. Vivek Wadhwa, "Foreign-Born Entrepreneurs: An Underestimated American Resource," in *Kauffman Thoughtbook 2009* (Kansas City, MO: Ewing Marion Kauffman Foundation, 2009), 180.

12. Wadhwa, "Foreign-Born Entrepreneurs," 181.

13. Stuart Anderson, "Regaining America's Competitive Advantage: Making Our Immigration System Work," US Chamber of Commerce report, August 12, 2010, 1, http://www.uschamber.com/sites/default/files/reports/100811_skilledvisastudy_full.pdf.

14. *Hearing Commemorating the Fiftieth Anniversary of the House Committee on Science and Technology*, 110th Cong. (March 12, 2008), (statement of Bill Gates, CEO of Microsoft).

15. Tim Harper, "U.S. losing global fight for talent," *Toronto Star*, April 1, 2008, http://www.thestar.com/News/World/article/407789 (accessed October 22, 2010).

16. Giovanni Peri, "The Effects of Immigrants on U.S. Employment and Productivity," Federal Reserve Bank of San Francisco Economic Letter, August 30, 2010, http://www.frbsf.org/publications/economics/letter/2010/el2010-26.html (accessed December 2, 2010).

17. Center for an Urban Future, "A World of Opportunity," February 2007, 3–4, http://www.NYCfuture.org/images_pdfs/pdfs/IE-final.pdf.

18. Benito Almanza, in discussion with authors, August 2010.

19. Peter Schrag, *Not Fit for Our Society: Immigration and Nativism in America* (Berkeley, CA: University of California Press, 2010), 4.

20. Roger Daniels, *Coming to America: A History of Immigration and Ethnicity in American Life* (New York: HarperCollins, 2002), 265–266.

21. Schrag, *Not Fit for Our Society*, 5.

22. Daniels, *Coming to America*, 272.

23. Schrag, *Not Fit for Our Society*, 49, quoting Josiah Strong, *Our Country: Its Present Crisis and Possible Future* (New York: Baker and Taylor, 1885), 165ff.

24. Daniels, *Coming to America*, 283.

25. "Who Was Shut Out?: Immigration Quotas, 1925–1927," History Matters, http://historymatters.gmu.edu/d/5078/ (accessed October 22, 2010). Also, US Census Bureau data, "Foreign Born Population: 1850 to 1930," http://www.census.gov/population/www/documentation/twps0029/tab02.html (accessed October 22, 2010).

26. Daniels, *Coming to America*, 283–4.

27. Seth Hoy, "Proposed 'Start-Up Visa Act' Would Help Create American Jobs," Immigration Impact, http://immigrationimpact.com/2010/03/03/proposed-%E2%80%9Cstart-up-visa-act%E2%80%9D-would-help-create-american-jobs/ (accessed October 20, 2010).

28. Andrew Walker, "Operation Paperclip: Dark Side of the Moon," BBC News, November 21, 2005, http://news.bbc.co.uk/go/pr/fr/-/2/hi/uk_news/magazine/4443934.stm (accessed October 20, 2010).

29. Ibid.; "Ex-Nazi Tries to Renew Citizenship," *New York Times*, July 21, 1991, http://select.nytimes.com/gst/abstract.html?res=F2061EFA3F590C728EDDAE0894D9494D81&scp=27&sq=nazi%20scientist%20von%20braun&st=cse (accessed October 22, 2010).

30. Christine Gibson, "The Nazi Scientists of America," *American Heritage*, November 16, 2005, http://www.americanheritage.com/articles/web/20051116-nazi-operation-overcast-harry-truman-henry-morgenthau-allies-japan-ussr-scientists-missile-sputnik-apollo-immigration.shtml (accessed September 18, 2010); Linda Hunt, *Secret Agenda: The United States Government, Nazi Scientists, and Project Paperclip, 1945 to 1990* (New York: St. Martin's Press, 1991).

31. Joshua Davis, "La Vida Robot," *Wired*, April 2005, http://www.wired.com/wired/archive/13.04/robot.html (accessed October 22, 2010).

32. This happened again when the act was attached as an amendment to a defense authorization bill. See Maggie Jones, "Coming Out Illegal," *New York Times Magazine*, October 21, 2010, http://www.nytimes.com/2010/10/24/magazine/24DreamTeam-t.html (accessed October 24, 2010); and Jeanne Batalova and Margie McHugh, "DREAM vs. Reality: An Analysis of Potential DREAM Act Beneficiaries," Migration Policy Institute study, July 2010, 1–2, http://www.migrationpolicy.org/pubs/DREAM-Insight-July2010.pdf.

33. Richard Ruelas, "ASU Grad Who Deported Self Gains Legal Residency," *Arizona Republic*, August 30, 2010, http://www.azcentral

.com/community/tempe/articles/2010/08/30/20100830asu-grad-self
-deported-returns-arizona-legal-citizen.html (accessed October 21, 2010).

34. Richard Ruelas, "For Carl Hayden Robotics Team, Beating Immigration Is Tougher than Beating the Competition," *Arizona Republic*, July 31, 2008, http://www.azcentral.com/arizonarepublic/arizonaliving/articles/2008/07/31/20080731robotkids0731.html (accessed October 22, 2010).

35. Hamm, "Red Flag in the Brain Game," *Businessweek*.

CHAPTER 7: WHAT CAN AMERICA LEARN FROM IRELAND?

1. Jason Walsh, "Ireland Bailout: Young Irish Flee 'Celtic Tiger' for a Better Life," *Christian Science Monitor*, November 21, 2010, http://www.csmonitor.com/World/Europe/2010/1121/Ireland-bailout-Young-Irish-flee-Celtic-Tiger-for-a-better-life (accessed December 2, 2010).

2. David Gardner and John Murray Brown, "Ireland: The Long Hangover," *Financial Times*, October 3, 2010, http://www.ft.com/cms/s/0/d7bcff58-cf1c-11df-9be2-00144feab49a.html#axzz175iZkbqs (accessed November 29, 2010).

3. David Gardner, "How Bankers Brought Ireland to Its Knees," *Financial Times*, May 15, 2010, http://www.ft.com/cms/s/2/67ae51e2-5e35-11df-8153-00144feab49a,dwp_uuid=f39ffd26-4bb2-11da-997b-0000779e2340.html#axzz175k7vBki (accessed November 27, 2010).

4. Ibid.

5. Ed Power, "The Irish Generation That Got Squeezed Out," *Guardian*, http://www.guardian.co.uk/commentisfree/2010/oct/04/irish-generation-squeezed (accessed December 2, 2010).

6. Neil Shah, "Ireland Outlines Austerity Measures," *Wall Street Journal*, November 25, 2010, http://online.wsj.com/article/SB100014 24052748703572404575634452116491286.html (accessed November 27, 2010).

7. Jeffrey Sachs, interview by Erik Schatzker, *Inside Track*, Bloomberg TV, November 15, 2010.

8. "Saving the Euro: Ireland's Woes Are Largely of Its Own Making but German Bungling Has Made Matters Worse," *Economist*, November 18, 2010.

9. Gardner, "How Bankers Brought Ireland to Its Knees."

10. Sean Dorgan, "How Ireland Became the Celtic Tiger," Heritage Foundation, June 23, 2006, http://www.heritage.org/Research/Reports/2006/06/How-Ireland-Became-the-Celtic-Tiger (accessed October 17, 2010); William C. Harris, "Secrets of the Celtic Tiger: Act Two," *Issues in Science and Technology*, Summer 2005, http://www.issues.org/21.4/p_harris.html.

11. "The Luck of the Irish," *Economist*, October 14, 2004.

12. http://www.economist.com/node/3261071?story_id=3261071 (accessed March 11, 2009).

13. Frank Barry, "Convergence Is Not Automatic: Lessons for Ireland from Central and Eastern Europe," *World Economy* 23, no. 10 (November 2000): 1379–94, http://www.tcd.ie/business/staff/fbarry/papers/papers/WldEc2.pdf (accessed October 18, 2010).

14. "The UK Economist Who Coined Term 'Celtic Tiger,'" FinFacts Ireland, http://www.finfacts.ie/irecon.htm (accessed October 19, 2010).

15. "The Luck of the Irish," *Economist*.

16. Rob Norton and Mark Borden, "The Luck of the Irish," *Fortune*, October 25, 1999, http://money.cnn.com/magazines/fortune/fortune_archive/1999/10/25/267793/index.htm (accessed October 19, 2010).

17. Dorgan, "How Ireland Became the Celtic Tiger."

18. Ibid.; and "Economic Development, 1958," Novelguide, http://www.novelguide.com/a/discover/eich_01/eich_01_00115.html (accessed October 20, 2010).

19. Dorgan, "How Ireland Became the Celtic Tiger."

20. Marshall Loeb, "Pied Piper for Industry," *Time*, December 18, 1978, http://www.time.com/time/magazine/article/0,9171,916543,00.html (accessed October 20, 2010).

21. Ibid.

22. "Celebrating 20 Years in Ireland," Intel website, http://www.intel.com/corporate/europe/emea/irl/intel/spotlight/20years.htm (accessed October 15, 2010); Frank McCabe, in discussion with authors, June 2009.

23. Norton and Borden, "The Luck of the Irish."

24. Diarmaid Ferriter, "12 Defining Moments in Irish History," *Sunday Business Post*, December 24, 2006, http://archives.tcm.ie/businesspost/2006/12/24/story19759.asp (accessed October 18, 2010).

25. Dorgan, "How Ireland Became the Celtic Tiger."

26. Harris, "Secrets of the Celtic Tiger."

27. Ibid.; and Dorgan, "How Ireland Became the Celtic Tiger."

28. Frank McCabe, in discussion with authors, June 2009.

29. *Transforming Ireland: A Better Quality of Life for All*, Ireland National Development Plan 2007–2013, 15, http://www.ndp.ie/documents/ndp2007-2013/NDP-2007-2013-English.pdf.

CHAPTER 8: DO WE STILL CARE ABOUT JOBS AND MAKING THINGS?

1. Thomas L. Friedman, *The World Is Flat: A Brief History of the Twenty-First Century* (New York: Picador, 2007), 278ff.

2. Fareed Zakaria, "How Long Will America Lead the World?" *Newsweek*, June 12, 2006, http://www.msnbc.msn.com/id/13123358/site/newsweek (accessed August 18, 2010).

3. Andy Grove, "How America Can Create Jobs," *Bloomberg Businessweek*, July 1, 2010, http://www.businessweek.com/magazine/content/10_28/b4186048358596.htm (accessed August 18, 2010).

4. Ernest F. Hollings, "They're All Against Jobs," *Huffington Post*, December 18, 2009, http://www.huffingtonpost.com/sen-ernest-frederick-hollings/theyre-all-against-jobs_b_397405.html (accessed September 2, 2010).

5. Ernest "Fritz" Hollings, in discussion with author, March 2010.

6. Clyde Prestowitz, *The Betrayal of American Prosperity* (New York: Free Press, 2010), 269–70.

7. Conor Dougherty and Sara Murray, "Lost Decade for Family Income," *Wall Street Journal*, September 17, 2010, http://online.wsj.com/article/SB10001424052748703440604575495670714069694.html (accessed October 21, 2010); "The Lost Decade for the Economy, *Washington Post*, January 1, 2010, http://www.washingtonpost.com/wp-dyn/content/graphic/2010/01/01/GR2010010101478.html (accessed October 18, 2010).

8. Elliot Schwartz et al., "The Industrial Policy Debate," Congressional Budget Office report, December 1983, http://www.cho.gov/doc.cfm?index=5320&type=0.

9. US Census Bureau, Foreign Trade Division data; US International Trade in Goods and Services data, US Department of Commerce Bureau of Economic Analysis, February 10, 2010, http://www.bea.gov/newsreleases/international/trade/2010/trad1209.htm.

10. "Industrial Metamorphosis," *Economist*, September 29, 2005, http://www.economist.com/node/4462685?story_id=4462685 (accessed September 18, 2010).

11. Jeff Green, "Most U.S. Factory Jobs Lost in Slump May Stay Empty in Recovery," *Bloomberg Businessweek*, April 28, 2010, http://www.businessweek.com/news/2010-04-28/most-u-s-factory-jobs-lost-in-slump-may-stay-empty-in-recovery.html (accessed October 22, 2010).

12. Robert Kuttner, *The Squandering of America* (New York: Knopf, 2007), 21; Bob Herbert, "The Recovery's Long Odds," *New York Times*, September 13, 2010, http://www.nytimes.com/2010/09/14/opinion/14herbert.html (accessed September 2, 2010).

13. Alexander Hamilton, *Report on Manufactures*, Communication to the House of Representatives, December 5, 1791, 33.

14. Prestowitz, *Betrayal of American Prosperity*, 56.

15. Steven C. Beschloss, "Economic Trends across the Decades," *Entrepreneur*, December 12, 2008, http://www.entrepreneur.com/money/howtoguide/article199174.html

16. Prestowitz, *Betrayal of American Prosperity*, 72.

17. John G. Craig Jr., "You've Come a Long Way, City," *Pittsburgh Quarterly*, Fall 2009, 92–93.

18. Barry Bluestone and Bennett Harrison, *The Deindustrialization of America: Plant Closings, Community Abandonment and the Dismantling of Basic Industry* (New York: Basic Books, 1982), 6.

19. Ibid., 15.

20. Ibid., 6.

21. "The Reindustrialization of America," *Bloomberg Businessweek*, June 30, 1980, 56.

22. Otis L. Graham Jr., *Losing Time: The Industrial Policy Debate* (Cambridge, MA: Harvard University Press, 1992), 173–175.

23. Sam Walton, Wal-Mart press release, March 13, 1985; "Buy American Campaign Gains Momentum," *Discount Store News*,

December 9, 1985, http://findarticles.com/p/articles/mi_m3092/is _v24/ai_4055903/ (accessed September 18, 2010).

24. Caroline E. Mayer, "Wal-Mart Flies the Flag in Import Battle," *Washington Post*, April 21, 1985, E1.

25. "Trade in Goods (Imports, Exports, and Trade Balance) with China," US Census Bureau, Foreign Trade Division data, http://www .census.gov/foreign-trade/balance/c5700.html#2010 (accessed September 18, 2010).

26. Hedrick Smith, "Is Wal-Mart Good for America?" *PBS Frontline* transcript, November 14, 2004.

27. Ibid.

28. Charles Fishman, "The Wal-Mart You Didn't Know," *Fast Company*, December 1, 2003, http://www.fastcompany.com/magazine/ 77/walmart.html (accessed October 18, 2010).

29. US Census Bureau, Foreign Trade Division data; US International Trade in Goods and Services data, US Department of Commerce Bureau of Economic Analysis, February 10, 2010.

30. US-China Economic and Security Review Commission, *2009 Report to Congress* (Washington, DC: US Government Printing Office, 2009); and Bloomberg News, "China Denies Japan Rare-Earth Ban amid Diplomatic Row," *Washington Post*, September 23, 2010.

31. Ralph E. Gomory, "Testimony to the Committee on Science and Technology of the U.S. House of Representatives," June 12, 2007, http://democrats.science.house.gov/Media/File/Commdocs/hearings/ 2007/full/12jun/gomory_testimony.pdf (accessed August 18, 2010).

32. Annalyn Censky, "GE: 7,000 tax returns, $0 U.S. tax bill," CNNMoney.com, April 16, 2010, http://money.cnn.com/2010/04/16/ news/companies/ge_7000_tax_returns/ (accessed September 18, 2010).

33. Alan S. Blinder, "Free Trade's Great but Offshoring Rattles Me," *Washington Post*, May 6, 2007, http://www.washingtonpost .com/wp-dyn/content/article/2007/05/04/AR2007050402555.html (accessed October 18, 2010).

34. Ernest F. Hollings and Kirk Victor, *Making Government Work* (Columbia, SC: University of South Carolina Press, 2008), 260.

35. Ibid., 259–60.

36. Ibid., 215ff.

37. Hollings, in discussion with author, March 2010.

CHAPTER 9: HAVE WE LOST OUR EDGE FOR INNOVATION?

1. Roger Angel, "Solar Energy as a Major Replacement for Fossil Fuel," video of MIT lecture, filmed October 9, 2007, http://mitworld .mit.edu/video/523/ (accessed September 24, 2010).

2. Roger Angel, in discussion with authors, April 2010.

3. Ibid.

4. Adrian Slywotzky, "Where Have You Gone, Bell Labs? How Basic Research Can Repair the Broken U.S. Business Model," *Bloomberg Businessweek*, August 27, 2009, http://www.businessweek.com/ print/magazine/content/09_36/b4145036681619.htm (accessed September 24, 2010); and Richard Van Atta, "Fifty Years of Innovation and Discovery," in *50 Years of Bridging the Gap* (Tampa, FL: Faircourt, 2008), http://www.darpa.mil/Docs/Intro_-q_Van_Atta_200807 180920581.pdf (accessed October 22, 2010).

5. "Innovation and Growth: Rationale for an Innovation Strategy," Organisation for Economic Co-operation and Development report, 2007, 6, http://www.oecd.org/dataoecd/2/31/39374789.pdf.

6. Stephen Ezell, "America and the World: We're No. 40!" *Democracy Journal*, Fall 2009, 13–14.

7. Ibid.

8. Stephen Ezell, "Benchmarking Foreign Innovation: The United States Needs to Learn from Other Industrialized Democracies," *Science Progress*, January 12, 2009, http://www.scienceprogress.org/2009/01/ benchmarking-foreign-innovation/ (accessed October 22, 2010).

9. Martin Grueber and Tim Studt, "Emerging Economies Drive Global R&D Growth," *R&D Magazine*, December 22, 2009, http:// www.rdmag.com/Featured-Articles/2009/12/Policy-And-Industry -Global-Funding-Report-Emerging-Economies-Drive-Global-R-D -Growth/ (accessed October 22, 2010).

10. Titus Galama and James Hosek, *U.S. Competitiveness in Science and Technology* (Santa Monica, CA: RAND, 2008), 67.

11. Between 1942 and 1951, the number of students earning college degrees each year more than doubled. See Michael J. Bennett, *When Dreams Came True: The GI Bill and the Making of Modern America* (Washington, DC: Brassey's, 2000), 242.

12. Priya Ganapti, "Bell Labs Kills Fundamental Physics Research," *Wired*, August 27, 2008, http://www.wired.com/gadgetlab/2008/08/bell-labs-kills/#ixzz0nXWP6fM8 (accessed October 24, 2010); and Slywotzky, "Where Have You Gone, Bell Labs?"

13. Slywotzky, "Where Have You Gone, Bell Labs?"

14. Jeong Kim, "Where's Bell Labs? Its President Responds," *Bloomberg Businessweek*, September 10, 2009, http://www.businessweek.com/bwdaily/dnflash/content/sep2009/db20090910_891521.htm (accessed October 24, 2010).

15. Fred Block and Matthew R. Keller, "Where Do Innovations Come From? Transformations in the U.S. National Innovation System, 1970–2006," Information Technology and Innovation Foundation report, July 2008, http://www.itif.org/files/Where_do_innovations_come_from.pdf (accessed October 22, 2010).

16. National Research Council, *Rising above the Gathering Storm Two Years Later: Accelerating Progress toward a Brighter Economic Future* (Washington, DC: National Academies Press, 2009), 14.

17. Ibid., 3.

18. Ibid.; "Biography," Washington State University website, http://www.wsu.edu/augustine/biography.html (accessed October 24, 2010).

19. Adrian Woolridge, "A Special Report on Innovation in Emerging Markets: The World Turned Upside Down," *Economist*, April 15, 2010, http://www.economist.com/node/15879369?story_id=15879369 (accessed October 24, 2010).

20. Cong Cao, Richard P. Suttmeier, and Denis Fred Simon, "China's 15-year Science and Technology Plan," *Physics Today*, December 2006, 38–40.

21. National Economic Council, "A Strategy for American Innovation: Driving towards Sustainable Growth and Quality Jobs," Presidential whitepaper, September 2009, http://www.whitehouse.gov/assets/documents/SEPT_20_Innovation_Whitepaper_FINAL.pdf (accessed September 22, 2010).

22. Chuck Lawton, "Making Science Cool: Educate to Innovate," *Wired*, November 24, 2009, http://www.wired.com/geekdad/2009/11/making-science-cool-educate-to-innovate/ (accessed October 24, 2010).

23. "Science Innovation Legislation Receives Bipartisan Support,

but Does Not Garner the Two-Thirds Majority Required," US House Committee on Science and Technology press release (Washington, DC, May 19, 2010), http://science.house.gov/press/PRArticle.aspx?News ID=2842 (accessed October 24, 2010).

24. "NSF Selects 11 Science Centers as Boon to US Competitiveness," *Physics Today*, January 1989, 57–58.

25. Ronald Reagan, "Address before a Joint Session of Congress on the State of the Union," January 27, 1987.

26. Leroy Hood, in discussion with author, April 2010.

CHAPTER 10: WILL OUR STATES BE PART OF THE SOLUTION?

1. Steven C. Beschloss, "The South's Broken Promise: A Seven-Part Series," *Virginian Pilot and Ledger-Star* reprint, July 14, 1987, 12–13.

2. James C. McKinley, "Texas Governor's Secession Talk Stirs Furor," *New York Times*, April 17, 2009, http://www.nytimes.com/2009/04/18/us/politics/18texas.html (accessed July 18, 2010).

3. "Gov. Perry Backs Resolution Affirming Texas' Sovereignty Under 10th Amendment: HCR 50 Reiterates Texas' Rights Over Powers Not Otherwise Granted to Federal Government," Office of the Governor press release (Austin, TX, April 9, 2009), http://governor.state.tx.us/news/press-release/12227/ (accessed July 10, 2010).

4. William Yardley, "Bids to Push States' Rights Falter in Face of Stimulus," *New York Times*, May 8, 2009, http://www.nytimes.com/2009/05/08/us/politics/08sovereignty.html (accessed July 15, 2010).

5. While the sale-leaseback arrangement generated more than $735 million for the state, it carried $400 million in interest costs over thirty years. See Mary Jo Pitzl, "State Is Selling More Buildings to Ease Budget," *Arizona Republic*, June 2, 2010, http://www.azcentral.com/12news/news/articles/2010/06/02/20100602buildingsale0602.html #ixzz0r9GID9QN (accessed December 3, 2010).

6. Interview with Greta Van Susteren, *On the Record*, Fox News, July 29, 2010.

7. Ted Robbins, "The Man behind Arizona's Toughest Immigrant

Laws," National Public Radio, March 12, 2008, http://www.npr.org/templates/story/story.php?storyId=88125098 (accessed July 12, 2010).

8. Ginger Rough, "Brewer: Most Illegal Immigrants Smuggling Drugs," *Arizona Republic*, June 25, 2010, http://www.azcentral.com/news/articles/2010/06/25/20100625arizona-governor-says-most-illegal-immigrants-smuggle-drugs.html (accessed July 12, 2010).

9. US Census Foreign Trade Database noted by Bill Hart, C. J. Eisenbarth Hager, and Joseph Garcia, "Global Arizona 100: A New Century, A World Stage," Morrison Institute for Public Policy report, November 2010, 10, http://morrisoninstitute.asu.edu/publications-reports/2010-global-arizona-100-a-new-century-a-world-stage/view.

10. Robbins, "The Man Behind Arizona's Toughest Immigrant Laws."

11. Ross C. DeVol et al., *Manufacturing 2.0: A More Prosperous California* (Santa Monica, CA: Milken Institute, June 2009), 57.

12. This was part of the international research led by the Greater Phoenix Leadership, a group of strategic-minded business leaders, to identify the best model for Arizona to create a roadmap to diversify its economy and produce high-paying jobs for future generations.

13. "Stardust Charitable Fund Gives $25 million to SFAz," Flinn Foundation, October 4, 2007, http://www.flinn.org/news/587 (accessed July 16, 2010).

14. Mary Jo Waits et al., "Innovation America: Investing in Innovation," National Governors Association report, July 2007, 17, http://www.nga.org/Files/pdf/07007InnovationInvest.pdf.

15. Battelle Institute, "Battelle Technology Partnership Practice, Metrics and Key Outcome Related to SFAz Grant Programs," February 9, 2010, 2–3. Several months later, SFAz was singled out as one of twenty incubators "supercharging" new businesses nationwide. See Nitasha Tiku and April Joyner, "Incubation Nation: Where Great Ideas Are Born," *Inc.*, May 2010, http://www.inc.com/magazine/20100501/the-best-business-incubators.html (accessed December 5, 2010).

16. Waits, "Investing in Innovation," 47.

17. Matthew Benson, "Brewer in 1994: Secretary of State Is Unfit to Govern," *Arizona Republic*, November 30, 2008, http://www.azcentral.com/news/articles/2008/11/30/20081130brewer1130.html (accessed July 14, 2010).

18. "Rep.'s Sam Crump & Steve Montenegro at AZ Capitol Tea

Party," YouTube video, 3:51, filmed April 15, 2009, posted by "aztelegraph," April 18, 2009, http://www.youtube.com/watch?v=fSghdUw NsMo.

19. Jim Nintzel, "Experiment Goes Awry," *Tucson Weekly*, February 11, 2009, http://www.tucsonweekly.com/tucson/the-skinny/Content?oid=1149064 (accessed July 15, 2010).

20. Ken Altucker, "The Struggle to Save Arizona's Science Push," *Arizona Republic*, October 3, 2009, http://www.azcentral.com/news/articles/2009/10/02/20091002biz-foundation1003.html#ixzz0sInZH eXA (accessed July 16, 2010).

21. Michelle Price, "Arizona Lawmaker Russell Pearce Takes Aim at Automatic Citizenship," *Christian Science Monitor*, June 15, 2010, http://www.csmonitor.com/From-the-news-wires/2010/0615/Arizona-lawmaker-Russell-Pearce-takes-aim-at-automatic-citizenship (accessed October 10, 2010).

22. Jon Stewart, *The Daily Show*, April 26, 2010.

23. Stephen Colbert, *The Colbert Report*, April 21, 2010.

24. "Lawmakers, Bury the 'Birther Bill,'" *Arizona Republic*, April 21, 2010, http://www.azcentral.com/arizonarepublic/opinions/articles/2010/04/21/20100421wed2-21.html (accessed July 16, 2010).

25. Cathy Luebke, "ECOtality Still Expects Local Growth," *Phoenix Business Journal*, June 30, 2010, http://bizjournals.com/phoenix/stories/2010/06/28/daily30.html (accessed October 18, 2010).

26. William Brandeis, US Supreme Court dissenting opinion in *New State Ice Co. v. Liebmann*, decided March 21, 1932, http://ase law.lp.findlaw.com/cgi-bin/getcase.pl?court=us&vol=285&invol=262 (accessed October 19, 2010).

27. Peggy Noonan, "A Cold Man's Warm Words," *Wall Street Journal*, July 2, 2010, http://online.wsj.com/article/SB1000142405274 87035717045753414032345452 96.html (accessed July 16, 2010).

28. "Election 2010 Primary Results," *New York Times*, August 24, 2010, http://elections.nytimes.com/2010/results/primaries/arizona (accessed October 19, 2010).

CHAPTER 11: CAN OUR CITIES SHOW THE WAY FORWARD?

1. Daniel Okrent, "Detroit: The Death—and Possible Life—of a Great American City," *Time*, September 24, 2009, http://www.time .com/time/printout/0,8816,1925796,00.html (accessed October 19, 2010); and Richard Freeman, "Death of Detroit: Harbinger of Collapse of Deindustrialized America," *Executive Intelligence Review* 31, no. 16 (April 23, 2004), http://www.larouchepub.com/other/2004/ 3116detroit_dies.html (accessed October 22, 2010).

2. Susan Saulny, "Razing the City to Save the City," *New York Times*, June 20, 2010, http://www.nytimes.com/2010/06/21/us/21 detroit.html (accessed October 22, 2010).

3. Citizens Research Council of Michigan, "The Fiscal Condition of the City of Detroit," April 2010, v, http://www.CRCmich.org/ Publicat/2010s/2010/rpt361.html.

4. Alex P. Kellogg, "Detroit Shrinks Itself, Historic Homes and All," *Wall Street Journal*, May 17, 2010, http://online.wsj.com/article/ SB10001424052748703950804575242433435338728.html (accessed September 4, 2010).

5. Franklin Delano Roosevelt, "The Great Arsenal of Democracy," (speech), December 29, 1940, transcript at http://www.american rhetoric.com/speeches/fdrarsenalofdemocracy.html (accessed October 4, 2010).

6. "Battle of Detroit," *Time*, March 23, 1942, http://www.time .com/time/magazine/article/0,9171,802251,00.html (accessed September 18, 2010).

7. "Michigan: Decline in Detroit," *Time*, October 27, 1961, http://www.time.com/time/magazine/article/0,9171,873465,00.html (accessed September 18, 2010).

8. Joshua Zeitz, "Why Did America Explode in Riots in 1967?" *American Heritage*, July 23, 2007, http://www.americanheritage.com/ articles/web/20070723-detroit-riots-1967-housing-african-american .shtml (accessed October 21, 2010).

9. Coleman Young and Lonnie Wheeler, *Hard Stuff: The Autobiography of Mayor Coleman Young* (New York: Viking, 1994), xvii.

10. Citizens Research Council, " Fiscal Condition," 6.

11. Jane Jacobs, *The Economy of Cities* (New York: Vintage Books, 1969), 124–25.

12. Howard Fineman, "What Pittsburgh (Don't Laugh) Can Teach Obama," *Newsweek*, June 6, 2009, http://www.newsweek.com/2009/06/05/what-pittsburgh-don-t-laugh-can-teach-obama.html (accessed October 20, 2010).

13. James Parton, *Triumphs of Enterprise, Ingenuity, and Public Spirit* (Hartford, CT: A. S. Hale, 1871), 186.

14. Melvin G. Holli, *The American Mayor: The Best and The Worst Big-City Leaders* (University Park, PA: Pennsylvania State University Press, 1999), 100–04.

15. Ibid., 106.

16. "How People Respond to Life in Pittsburgh," *Life*, January 13, 1958.

17. Dennis Yablonsky, in discussion with author, August 2010.

18. Ibid.

19. Harold D. Miller, "Regional Insights: It's Still Steel City, but Pittsburgh Has Changed," *Pittsburgh Post-Gazette*, September 6, 2009, http://www.post-gazette.com/pg/09249/995692-28.stm (accessed September 8, 2010).

20. Jared L. Cohon, Mark Nordenburg, and Jeffrey Romoff, "Transforming Pittsburgh," Carnegie Mellon University video, 46:37, filmed September 21, 2009, posted September 23, 2009, http://www.youtube.com/user/CarnegieMellonU#p/search/0/l1pCGCAlks8.

21. Richard S. Caliguiri et al., "Strategy 21: Pittsburgh/Allegheny Economic Development Strategy to Begin the 21st Century," June 1985.

22. Sally Kalson, "Pittsburgh Named Most Livable City Again," *Pittsburgh Post-Gazette*, May 4, 2010, http://www.post-gazette.com/pg/10124/1055313-53.stm#ixzz0xATRDbxZ (accessed October 21, 2010).

23. Christopher Briem, "Educational Attainment in the Pittsburgh Regional Workforce," *Pittsburgh Quarterly*, March 2010, 1.

24. Sabina Deitrick and Christopher Briem, "Pittsburgh's New Workers Have Left Behind the Region's Industrial Psyche," *Pittsburgh Post-Gazette*, May 2, 2010, http://www.post-gazette.com/pg/10122/1054559-109.stm (accessed September 12, 2010).

25. Tom Waseleski, in discussion with author, August 2010.

26. Bob Frick, "Best Cities 2010: Austin, Texas," *Kiplinger's Personal Finance*, July 2010, http://www.kiplinger.com/magazine/archives/best-cities-2010-austin-texas.html.

27. Joel Kotkin, "Austin's Secrets for Economic Success," *Forbes*, May 11, 2009, http://www.newgeography.com/content/00794-austins-secrets-for-economic-success (accessed October 18, 2010).

28. G. Scott Thomas, "Don't Mess With Texas Small Biz," Portfolio.com, January 18, 2010, http://www.portfolio.com/business-news/2010/01/18/austin-tops-small-business-vitality-survey/ (accessed October 20, 2010).

29. "The Economic Impact of the Cultural Sector in Austin," City of Austin report, January 2006, http://www.ci.austin.tx.us/redevelopment/downloads/txp_2005.pdf.

30. Pike Powers, in discussion with author, August 2010.

31. Stacey Higginbotham, "Final Bell Ringing for MCC," *Austin Business Journal*, November 3, 2004, http://www.bizjournals.com/austin/stories/2004/11/01/story3.html (accessed October 20, 2010).

32. David V. Gibson and Everett M. Rogers, *R&D Collaboration on Trial: The Microelectronics and Computer Technology Corporation* (Cambridge, MA: Harvard Business Press, 1994), 484–85.

33. Pike Powers, in discussion with author, August 2010.

34. Rodney Gibbs, in discussion with author, August 2010.

35. Ibid.

36. James Moody, in discussion with author, August 2010.

37. Lee Leffingwell, in discussion with author, August 2010.

38. Jon Bruner, "America's Worst Intersections," *Forbes*, February 25, 2009, http://www.forbes.com/2009/02/24/traffic-intersections-worst-lifestyle-autos_intersections_full-list.html (accessed September 14, 2010).

39. Lee Leffingwell, in discussion with author, August 2010.

40. James Moody, in discussion with author, August 2010.

CHAPTER 12: ARE WE READY FOR LEADERSHIP THAT REPRESENTS THE BEST OF US?

1. Kent Conrad and Judd Gregg, "A Bipartisan Solution to the Nation's Fiscal Crisis," *Hill*, December 17, 2009, http://thehill.com/opinion/op-ed/72849-a-bipartisan-solution-to-the-nations-fiscal-crisis (accessed October 11, 2010).

2. Jackie Calmes, "President Plans Own Panel on the Debt," *New York Times*, January 27, 2010, http://www.nytimes.com/2010/01/27/us/politics/27budget.html?_r=1 (accessed September 29, 2010).

3. Steven C. Beschloss, "Can These Men Fix the Deficit?" *Parade*, July 4, 2010, 8.

4. Erskine Bowles, in discussion with author, June 2, 2010.

5. Ibid.

6. Brady Dennis and Lori Montgomery, "Deficit Plan Wins 11 of 18 Votes," *Washington Post*, December 3, 2010, http://www.washingtonpost.com/wp-dyn/content/article/2010/12/02/AR2010120205913.html?sid=ST2010120206074 (accessed December 4, 2010).

7. Ibid.

8. "What Happens When Congress Fails to Do Its Job?" *Newsweek*, March 27, 2010, http://www.newsweek.com/2010/03/26/what-happens-when-congress-fails-to-do-its-job.html.

9. Mary Beth Schneider, "Evan Bayh Will Not Seek Reelection," *Indianapolis Star*, February 15, 2010, 1; and George Voinovich, transcript of comments at Third Way Conference on May 27, 2010, http://www.thirdway.org/events/25/transcript (accessed October 2, 2010).

10. John Gardner, *On Leadership* (New York: Free Press, 1990), xviii.

11. Franklin Delano Roosevelt, "The Great Arsenal of Democracy," (speech), December 29, 1940, transcript at http://www.americanrhetoric.com/speeches/fdrarsenalofdemocracy.html (accessed October 4, 2010).

12. Ibid.

13. Dwight D. Eisenhower, "Farewell Address," January 17, 1961, transcript at American Rhetoric: Top 100 Speeches, http://www.americanrhetoric.com/speeches/dwightdeisenhowerfarewell.html.

14. "Recent Trends in Military Expenditure," Stockholm Interna-

tional Peace Research Institute, http://www.sipri.org/research/armaments/milex/resultoutput/trends (accessed October 22, 2010); and Fareed Zakaria, *The Post-American World* (New York: Norton, 2008), 238.

15. David Kendall and Jim Kessler, "A Taxpayer Receipt," Third Way report, September 2010, 3, http://content.thirdway.org/publications/335/Third_Way_Idea_Brief_-_A_Taxpayer_Receipt.pdf.

16. Paul Kennedy, *The Rise and Fall of Great Powers* (New York: Vintage Books, 1989), 515.

17. Andrew Bacevich, quoted in Chalmers Johnson, *The Sorrows of Empire* (New York: Metropolitan Books, 2004), 67.

18. Harry Mitchell, in discussion with authors, May 2010.

19. John Gardner, quoted in "Selected Writing and Excerpts," PBS website, http://www.pbs.org/johngardner/sections/writings.html (accessed October 5, 2010).

20. Timothy Ferris, *The Science of Liberty: Democracy, Reason, and the Laws of Nature* (New York: Harper, 2010), 13–14.

Bibliography

Bank, Steven A., Kirk J. Stark, and Joseph J. Thorndike. *War and Taxes*. Washington, DC: Urban Institute Press, 2008.

Bennett, Michael J. *When Dreams Came True: The GI Bill and the Making of Modern America*. Washington, DC: Brassey's, 1996.

Bluestone, Barry, and Bennett Harrison. *The Deindustrialization of America: Plant Closings, Community Abandonment, and the Dismantling of Basic Industry*. New York: Basic Books, 1982.

Bush, Vannevar. *Science, the Endless Frontier: A Report to the President on a Program for Postwar Scientific Research*. Washington, DC: National Science Foundation, 1945.

Collins, Martin J. *After Sputnik: 50 Years of the Space Age*. Washington, DC: Smithsonian/Collins, 2007.

Daniels, Roger. *Coming to America: A History of Immigration and Ethnicity in American Life*, 2nd ed. New York: HarperCollins, 2002.

Dickson, Paul. *Sputnik: The Shock of the Century*. New York: Walker, 2007.

Ferris, Timothy. *The Science of Liberty: Democracy, Reason, and the Laws of Nature*. New York: Harper, 2010.

Florida, Richard. *The Flight of the Creative Class: The New Global Competition for Talent*. New York: Collins, 2007.

Friedman, George. *The Next 100 Years: A Forecast for the 21st Century*. New York: Anchor Books, 2010.

Friedman, Milton. *Capitalism and Freedom*. Chicago: University of Chicago Press, 1962.

Friedman, Thomas L. *The World Is Flat: A Brief History of the Twenty-First Century*, 3rd ed. New York: Picador, 2007.

Gomory, Ralph E., and William J. Baumol. *Global Trade and Conflicting National Interests*. Cambridge, MA: MIT Press, 2001.

Graham, Otis L., Jr. *Losing Time: The Industrial Policy Debate*. Cambridge, MA: Harvard University Press, 1992.

Halberstam, David. *The Fifties*. New York: Fawcett Columbine, 1993.

Hollings, Ernest F. "Fritz," and Kirk Victor. *Making Government Work*. Columbia: University of South Carolina Press, 2008.

Hunt, Linda. *Secret Agenda: The United States Government, Nazi Scientists, and Project Paperclip, 1945 to 1990*. New York: St. Martin's Press, 1991.

Jacobs, Jane. *The Economy of Cities*. New York: Vintage Books, 1970.

Johnson, Chalmers. *The Sorrows of Empire: Militarism, Secrecy, and the End of the Republic*. New York: Metropolitan Books, 2004.

Kennedy, Paul. *The Rise and Fall of the Great Powers: Economic Change and Military Conflict from 1500 to 2000*. New York: Vintage Books, 1989.

Khanna, Parag. *The Second World: Empires and Influence in the New Global Order*. New York: Random House, 2008.

Kuttner, Robert. *The Squandering of America: How the Failure of Our Politics Undermines Our Prosperity*. New York: Alfred A. Knopf, 2007.

Lasch, Christopher. *The Culture of Narcissism: American Life in an Age of Diminishing Expectations*. New York: Norton, 1978.

de Montesquieu, Charles. *The Spirit of the Laws*. Cambridge, MA: Cambridge University Press, 1989.

Norquist, Grover. *Leave Us Alone: Getting the Government's Hands Off Our Money, Our Guns, Our Lives*. New York: William Morrow, 2008.

Parton, James. *Triumphs of Enterprise, Ingenuity and Public Spirit*. Hartford, CT: A. S. Hale, 1871.

Pinsky, Drew, and S. Mark Young. *The Mirror Effect: How Celebrity Narcissism Is Seducing America*. New York: HarperCollins, 2009.

Postman, Neil. *Amusing Ourselves to Death: Public Discourse in the Age of Show Business*. New York: Penguin Books, 2006.

Prestowitz, Clyde. *The Betrayal of American Society: Free Market Delusions, America's Decline, and How We Must Compete in the Post-Dollar Era.* New York: Free Press, 2010.

Putnam, Robert D. *Bowling Alone: The Collapse and Revival of American Community.* New York: Simon & Schuster, 2000.

Schrag, Peter. *Not Fit for Our Society: Immigration and Nativism in America.* Berkeley, CA: University of California Press, 2010.

Steingart, Gabor. *The War for Wealth: The True Story of Globalization, or Why the Flat World Is Broken.* New York: McGraw-Hill, 2008.

Stockman, David A. *The Triumph of Politics: Why the Reagan Revolution Failed.* New York: Avon, 1987.

Suskind, Ron. *The Price of Loyalty: George W. Bush, the White House, and the Education of Paul O'Neill.* New York: Simon & Schuster, 2004.

Young, Coleman, and Lonnie Wheeler. *Hard Stuff: The Autobiography of Mayor Coleman Young.* New York: Viking, 1994.

Zakaria, Fareed. *The Post-American World.* New York: Norton, 2008.

Index